New Voices in Iranian Archaeology

New Voices in Iranian Archaeology

edited by

Karim Alizadeh and Megan Cifarelli

OXBOW | books
Oxford & Philadelphia

Published in the United Kingdom in 2025 by
OXBOW BOOKS
81 St Clements, Oxford OX4 1AW

and in the United States by
OXBOW BOOKS
1950 Lawrence Road, Havertown, PA 19083

Paperback Edition: ISBN 979-8-88857-145-3
Digital Edition: ISBN 979-8-88857-146-0

A CIP record for this book is available from the British Library

Library of Congress Control Number: 2024946394

Printed in the United Kingdom by CMP Digital Print Solutions
Typeset in India by DiTech Publishing Services

For a complete list of Oxbow titles, please contact:

UNITED KINGDOM
Oxbow Books
Telephone (0)1226 734350
Email: oxbow@oxbowbooks.com
www.oxbowbooks.com

UNITED STATES OF AMERICA
Oxbow Books
Telephone (610) 853-9131, Fax (610) 853-9146
Email: queries@casemateacademic.com
www.casemateacademic.com/oxbow

Oxbow Books is part of the Casemate Group

Front cover: Kiyasar Gorge, Eastern Caspian Sea Corridor (Photograph by Elham Ghasidian)
Back cover: General view of the Farsan plain and its valleys, from the northeast from the western flanks of Jahānbin Mount (Photograph by Alireza Khosrowzadeh)

Contents

List of contributors

Mehdi Abedini Araghi (Fig. 0.1A) is the founder and head of the Centre for Espahbad Khorshid Historical Cave and Related Research in Mazandaran, Iran. He earned his MA from Azad University of Tehran. His research interest is the Bronze and Iron Age era, and ethnography and linguistics in Mazandaran, and he has published extensively. He is currently the deputy director of the Iranian Cultural Heritage, Handicrafts and Tourism Organization in Mazandaran, Iran.

Ahmadali Asadi (Fig. 0.1B) was born in 1981 in Iran, earned a BA and MA from Tehran University, and received his PhD in archaeology from Tarbiat-e Modarres University in Tehran. He was a member of the Persepolis Archaeology Department (2003–2012) and served as its director. He is currently a faculty member in the Archaeology Department of Shiraz University of Arts. He has done several excavations in southwestern Iran, mostly Achaemenid and Sasanian sites in the Fars and Hormozgan provinces. He has directed the Persepolis Channels excavations from 2012 up to present. His interests are settlement patterns during historical periods in Iran and ancient hydraulic structures. He has published more than 50 Persian and English articles in various journals.

Liu Binbin (Fig. 0.1C) graduated from the School of History, Nanjing University, China in 2018 with a master's degree in archaeology. From 2015 to 2018, he participated in archaeological survey and excavation in Iran. He completed his master's thesis on painted pottery from the Neolithic to Bronze Age of northeastern Iran. Liu started working for Suzhou Museum in 2021, where his research interests transferred to curation and comparison on ancient materials between East and West, as well as interpretation and display of excavated materials in a museum context.

Mehrdad Parsaei Borazjani (Fig. 0.1D) is the director of the Siraf Cultural Heritage Office. He earned his master's degree from the University of Mazandaran and possesses a wealth of experience in archaeological excavations, particularly within the Bushehr province.

Nasrollah Ebrahimi (Fig. 0.1E) is the deputy at the Bushehr branch of the Iranian Cultural Heritage, Handicrafts and Tourism Organization. He earned his PhD from the University of Tehran and has extensive experience in archaeological excavations, particularly focusing on various sites, including the Achaemenid palatial sites in Borazjan.

Homa Fathi (Fig. 0.1F) is an archaeozoology technician who works in the Archaeozoology section of the Bioarchaeology Laboratory of the University of Tehran. She directs the study and curation of the faunal remains of Tepe Naderi from 2019.

Sharareh Ghasemi (Fig. 0.1G) received a master's degree in Horticulture from the Corvinus University of Budapest (Hungary) in 2009. She continued her education in Prehistory at Islamic Azad University of Marvadasht, Iran, in 2013, where she carried out her research on the 'Agricultural process in Fars region from the Neolithic to the Bronze Age.' During 2017–2020, she worked as a doctoral researcher in plant genetics in Spain. Her research interests included genetic processes in archaeobotany and domestication of plants, and she has taken part in excavations in Iran and Portugal. In addition to many articles, in 2019 she published a book entitled *Genetic Resources and Agricultural Evolution*.

Elham Ghasidian (Fig. 0.1H) earned her PhD in the Palaeolithic Archaeology from the Eberhard Karls University of Tübingen, Germany (2010) and completed a post-doctoral fellowship at the Leverhulme Centre for Human Evolutionary Studies, University of Cambridge, UK. She is a senior researcher at the Neanderthal Museum in Mettmann, Germany. Her main research interests revolve around human evolution and hominin cultural diversity, focusing on the development of ecological and cultural behavior in the Iranian Plateau and neighboring areas during the late Pleistocene. She participated in more than 30 archaeological expeditions as team member and head. Since 2018, she has served as the supervisor of the research project 'Southern Caspian Corridor: a biogeographical hominin dispersal route' in the Neanderthal Museum.

Hossein Habibi (Fig. 0.1I) is an archaeologist of the Late Antique period. He is currently an associate professor at the Department of Archaeology at the University of Jiroft and was formerly a Postdoctoral Research Fellow at the Institute for Advanced Studies at the University of Edinburgh. His research interests fall into three main areas – the archaeological landscapes of Sasanian territories, the material culture of the Sasanian period, and political ideologies in the Late Antique world. His first monograph, *Socioeconomic Transformation in the Sasanian Empire: Late Antique Central Zagros*, was published in 2022. He has also published several articles in peer-reviewed academic journals and attended international conferences related to Sasanian Studies and Late Antique archaeology.

Saman H. Guran (Fig. 0.1J) earned his PhD in Palaeolithic Archaeology from the Eberhard Karls University of Tübingen, Germany (2010) and completed a post-doctoral fellowship at the Leverhulme Centre for Human Evolutionary Studies, University of Cambridge, UK. He is a senior researcher at the Neanderthal Museum in Mettmann, Germany. His main research is on human evolution and investigating the patterns of cultural variation across the Middle East, especially the Iranian Plateau during the Upper Pleistocene. He has participated in more than 40 archaeological expeditions as a team member and head. Since 2016, he has been supervising a research project on the Middle to Upper Palaeolithic transition in the Zagros Mountains at the University of Cambridge and the Neanderthal Museum.

Jaleh Kamalizad (Fig. 0.1K) received her PhD degree in Islamic archaeology from the University of Tehran (2016) and was recently appointed as assistant professor at Shahid Chamran University in Khuzestan, Iran. As an Islamic archaeologist, her focus is on society and subsistence in Isfahan during the medieval and post-medieval period. Her current research interests stem from her desire to understand the effect of Zayandeh-rud river water management on the settlement patterns and agriculturally based economy of Isfahan. In 2021, she directed the first season of archaeological survey along the river basin in a long-term project entitled 'Isfahan Hydraulic Heritage' with emphasis on landscape archaeology.

Alireza Khosrowzadeh (Fig. 0.1L) holds a PhD in historical archaeology and currently is an associate professor at the Department of Archaeology at Shahrekord University. His research has been focused on the archaeology of the Parthian and Sasanian periods in Iran. He has conducted several archaeological excavations across the country, including systematic surveys on Qeshm Island and Bardsir County in southern and southeastern Iran, and the highlands of Ardal and Farsan in Chaharmahal va Bakhtiyari Province, alongside two seasons of excavation at Tappe Bardnakoon in Farsan. He has also published two books and several articles about different aspects of archaeology and history of the mentioned eras.

Marjan Mashkour (Fig. 0.1M) is an archaeozoologist and bioarchaeologist specializing in southwest Asian mammalian and bird remains. Her work is concentrated on the Iranian Plateau and adjacent regions. Through a diachronic approach to the subsistence economies, she is interested in a better characterization of the sedentary and non-sedentary societies in the past. She leads several projects for the characterization of herding strategies using biogeochemistry and isotopic analyses, as well as morphometric analyses, while collaborating with geneticists. In 2011 she cofounded the Laboratory of

Bioarchaeology at the University of Tehran. She is currently the co-director of the Archaeozoology and Archaeobotany Research Group (AASPE) at the CNRS and the Natural History Museum of Paris.

Hossein Moradi (Fig. 0.1N) was born in 1978 and from 1999 he has overseen excavations in Shahr-i Sokhta. Since 2009, he has been assistant director of Iranian archaeological expedition in the Residential Areas of Shahr-i Sokhta. He also conducted several archaeological surveys in the Baluchistan region in 2006–2011. He received a PhD in archaeology in 2016 from the University of Tehran. Currently, he is excavating at the Eastern Residential Area of Shahr-i Sokhta by focusing on the Proto Elamite period. Some of his recent publications are *The Ancient Art of Baluchestan: Petroglyphs of Saravan, The Archaeology of Baluchestan, Social Complexities in the Ancient Middle East* (translated articles by some Iranian scholars in Persian), the translation of *Excavations at Bampur, a Third Millennium Settlement in Persian Baluchistan* by Beatrice De Cardi and *Kalut*, a Persian novel about the Shahr-i Sokhta.

Hosein Ramzanpour (Fig. 0.1O) earned his PhD from Azad University of Tehran, Iran (2020). He is currently the director of Gohar Tape Research Centre in Behshahr, Mazandaran, Iran. His research is focused on the hominin evolution and social behavior during the Pleistocene, particularly in the eastern part of the Southern Caspian Corridor of the Iranian Plateau. He has participated in more than 30 archaeological expeditions as a team member and leader in the Iranian Plateau. He is currently the director of excavations in Shoupari Cave in the eastern Alborz Mountains.

Seyed Mansur Seyed Sajjadi (Fig. 0.1P) was born in 1949 in Karaj, Iran. He received his PhD in Iranian Studies, majoring in archaeology in 1989 from the Istituto Universitario Orientale, Naples, Italy. He participated in various archaeological expeditions in Iran and other countries. He has been directing different archaeological expeditions at Tepe Taleb Khan, Tepe Bampur, Dahane-ye Qolaman and since 1997, Shahr-i Sokhta. He is the author of numerous articles and more than 30 volumes of books in the fields of Iranology and archaeology on Iran, including: *The First Cities of the Iranian Plateau, The Archaeological History of Indian Subcontinent; Archaeology of Central Asia, Shahr-i Sokhta. Archaeology and Art of the Delta of Hyrmand River*, and *The Iranian World and its Neighbors in Prehistory*.

Ahmad Bavand Savadkoohi (Fig. 0.1Q) is a PhD candidate at the Azad University of Tehran whose dissertation work focuses on the Pahlavi documents of Sasanid Period from Savadkouh Region. His more than 25 years of research on the Savadkouh Region culture and history resulted in the publication of 10 books and 20 papers. He is the founder of the Center for Culture and History of Savadkouh, Mazandaran, dedicated to recognizing and protecting the cultural heritage of Savadkouh. He has discovered more than 20 caves with historic and prehistoric finds in the Savadkouh Region.

Zohreh Shirazi (Fig. 0.1R) received her PhD in environmental archaeology from the University of Paris 1, Panthéon-Sorbonne, in 2012. Her main area of specialization is archaeobotany. She has worked on archaeobotanical collections in Iran coming from different chronological contexts ranging from the Palaeolithic to the Islamic periods. She has participated in archaeological fieldwork in southeastern Iran including Shahr-i Sokhta, Tepe Sadegh, Tepe Taleb Khan, Tepe Yalda, Konar Sandal, and Tepe Gav Koshi. Shirazi is the author of several scientific peer-reviewed articles and is currently the founding director of the archaeobotanical laboratory of the Southeastern Regional Museum of Iran at Zahedan and World Heritage Base of Shahr-i Sokhta.

Shui Tao (Fig. 0.1S) was born in 1960, graduated from Peking University in 1982, and earned a PhD from Peking University in 1994. He served as a visiting scholar at the University of Pennsylvania in 1996–1997. He is now a professor of archaeology in Nanjing University. He primarily studies the Bronze Age cultures of China and Central Asia and has published a book of *Papers on the Bronze Age Archaeology of Northwest China* (2001), and other articles. In the past decade he has done field works in Russia (2014, 2016), Iran (2015, 2016), and Pakistan (2017, 2018, 2019).

Margareta Tengberg (Fig. 0.1T) explores the relationship between human societies and the plant world in the Ancient East, with a predilection for the Iranian plateau sensu lato and for the periods from the Neolithic to the Bronze Age. She has a dual training in oriental archaeology and archaeobotany. Her work focuses on the origin and diffusion of agriculture, the organization of agrosystems, the beginnings of the cultivation of fruit species, the exploitation of wood, and the impact of human activities on the vegetation cover of the past. Appointed professor at the Muséum national d'Histoire naturelle in 2013, she is also fully involved in teaching (co-responsible for the master's program 'Quaternary, Prehistory, Bioarchaeology'), supervising students and doctoral students, and managing collections (curator of the wood collection of the Natural History Museum).

Ali A. Vahdati (Fig. 0.1U) is Associate Researcher and Field Archaeologist at the Iranian Ministry of Cultural Heritage, Tourism, and Handicrafts, North Khorasan Province, Bojnord. His research interests comprise Bronze and Iron Age archaeology of northern and northeastern Iran, and Central Asia. Since 2007 he has been involved in several field projects in Iranian Khorasan, Sistan, and Afghanistan, and has been co-director of several international expeditions including the joint expeditions at Tepe Naderi and Tepe Chalow in northern Khorasan, Iran. He has published several books and over 50 papers in various journals and international conferences.

Zohreh Zehbari (Fig. 0.1V) is an Iranian archaeologist currently serving as a post-doctoral researcher at Philipps-Universität Marburg. She earned her PhD from the University of Tehran in 2019 and has conducted extensive research on ceramics and art across various historical periods, with a particular focus on the Achaemenid and Sasanian eras.

Liangren Zhang (Fig. 0.1W) is a professor in the School of History, Nanjing University, China. He earned his doctoral degree from University of California, Los Angeles, in 2007. His research interests include Bronze Age archaeology of northwestern China, Russia, and Iran, as well as ancient ceramics of China. He has been co-directing the joint expeditions at Tepe Naderi in Northern Khorasan, Iran, and Soviet Road settlement in Altai Krai, Russia. He has published, apart from over 50 articles, the monograph *Ancient Metallurgy and Society* (2012), and two volumes of *Archaeology and Conservation along the Silk Road* (I, 2018; II, 2022).

Editors

Karim Alizadeh (Fig. 0.1X) is Assistant Professor in the Department of Anthropology at the University of Tennessee-Knoxville, USA. He is an anthropological archaeologist and holds a PhD in anthropology from Harvard University. He has conducted several field projects in Iranian Azerbaijan and his research focuses on the rise of complex societies and empires in Southwest Asia through the lens of landscape archaeology. His research interests include social inequality and complexity; material culture and craft production; archaeology of empires; abandonment and collapse; borders and borderland dynamics; heritage and nationalism; archaeology of Iran and the Caucasus.

Megan Cifarelli (Fig. 0.1Y) is Professor Emerita at Manhattanville University in New York. She is an art historian who holds a PhD in art history and archaeology from Columbia University. Her scholarly interests include the visual culture of western Asia in the 1st millennium BCE, in particular that of Assyria and northwestern Iran. She has published extensively on the material culture of Tepe Hasanlu, near Lake Urmia in the Eastern Azerbaijan province of Iran, and has edited several volumes on dress, jewelry, and gender in western Asia.

Fig. 0.1

Introduction: The history of archaeology in Iran[1]

Karim Alizadeh and Megan Cifarelli

The present-day nation of Iran is culturally complex, geographically diverse, and archaeologically rich. It is currently the 17th largest nation (by area) in the world today, covering a territory of 1,648,000 km^2 (636,000 square miles). It shares borders with Iraq in the west, Turkey, Armenia, and Azerbaijan in the northwest, Turkmenistan in the northeast, and Afghanistan and Pakistan in the east. The Caspian Sea forms part of the northern border, and the southern border is formed by the Persian Gulf and the Gulf of Oman. The Zagros Mountains, running south from the northwest corner of Iran, are one of the country's most important topographical features. A second mountain range, the Alborz, separates the Caspian littoral from the Central Plateau of Iran, an enormous, arid expanse that includes massive salt deserts. At the east, mountain ranges in Khorasan and the foothills of the Hindu Kush mountains separate Iran from southeast Asia. In many parts of Iran, deep gorges and well-watered valleys are separated by long ridges of mountains and foothills, forming corridors for movement of people, animals, goods, and ideas.

These geographic features have had an impact on the ways settlements and sites have developed in Iran. Unlike the ancient landscapes of Egypt or Mesopotamia, Iran has no major rivers or river valleys, and many of its smaller rivers are dry for much of the year, particularly in the Central Plateau. It will be no surprise that so many of the papers included in this issue discuss the archaeology of water management, detailing innovative strategies for providing water to settlements large and small. While agriculture characterized the economy of southwestern Iran from the 8th millennium BCE onward, with agricultural settlements increasing in size, a range of pastoralist strategies continued to be economically important at higher elevations as late as the 20th century.

Early investigations

Engagement with and reverence for the past has been a thread running through Iranian culture since antiquity. Millennia before European and American archaeologists began to break ground on excavations in the lands that would be called Iran, Ancient Iranian rulers and residents admired, interacted with, inscribed, and imitated the ruined monuments of their ancestors that dotted the landscape, particularly in the archaeologically rich southwestern province of Fars, home to the visible remains of rock reliefs and destroyed capitals of the Achaemenid Persian empire. In the late 16th to early 17th centuries CE, European visitors looking for trade opportunities were welcomed in the court of the Safavid ruler Shah Abbas (Mousavi 2013), many of whom passed through the province of Fars and described the Achaemenid ruins at Naqsh-e Rustam, Persepolis, and Pasargadae. By the 18th century, engravings of ancient Iranian monuments and copies of their cuneiform inscriptions were circulating in European universities, including copies of the trilingual (Old Persian, Elamite, and Babylonian) Behistun Inscription, found with a rock relief in Kermanshah Province. This cuneiform inscription from the Achaemenid period played a critical role in the 19th-century European decipherment of the cuneiform writing system that was in use throughout ancient Western Asia from the 4th millennium BCE through the 1st century CE, opening the door to the modern study of Western Asian history.

In the 19th century, French and British diplomatic missions to Iran were staffed by aristocrats and adventurers steeped in classical era travelogues and history writing, such as Herodotus, including histories of earlier encounters between travelers and this ancient landscape. This background made it possible for visitors to Fars like James Morier (1780–1849) to recognize that the structure at Persepolis known locally as the 'Tomb of the Mother of Solomon' could be the tomb of Cyrus II as described by Strabo (Mousavi 2013). Correctly identifying Persepolis as a political, economic, and cultural center of the Achaemenid Persian Empire (550–330 BCE), Morier and a colleague dug for sculptures there in 1810–12. Scottish artist and diplomat Sir Robert Ker Porter produced highly detailed, measured drawings of monuments at Persepolis and other sites (Porter 1821). An extensive illustrated account of the monuments at Persepolis was created by French artist and diplomat Eugène Flandin and architect Paul Coste, who visited the region between 1839 and 1841 (Coste and Flandin 1843–54). These accounts, and particularly the illustrations, drew the eyes of the world to the site and its incredible material culture. European interest in Western Asian antiquity was further fueled by the founding in the late 18th century of national, encyclopedic museums, like the Louvre Museum and the British Museum, whose collections were augmented by travelers who bought, were given, or removed works of art and architectural fragments and carried them back to Europe.

The second phase of archaeology in Iran was dominated by French archaeologists. By 1894, France had secured exclusive rights to excavate in Persia and soon created Délégation en Perse under the direction of French traveler and geologist Jacques de Morgan. The first major French excavation in Iran was the southwestern Iranian site of Susa (Biblical Shushan) in the low-lying plains of Khuzestan, a region enmeshed with southern Mesopotamia. Susa had been briefly excavated between 1849 and 1851 by the British archaeologist William Loftus (Curtis 1993).[2] Decades later, the French engineer Marcel-Auguste Dieulafoy was given royal permission to excavate the site of Susa, where he described the site in detail, and excavated deposits of decorated glazed bricks, and attempted to work out the plan of architecture. His efforts, however, were severely hampered by the inability to detect the mud-brick walls that formed the structure of the buildings at Susa. Morgan followed Dieulafoy at Susa, digging the 'Grand Tranchée,' an exploratory trench across the middle of the mound that served as the primary axis of excavations, and which yielded some of the most renowned archaeological discoveries of that century, now enshrined in the Louvre. These include Mesopotamian monuments taken in military campaigns, like the Stele of Hammurabi, the Stele of Naram Sin, and a collection of Babylonian kudurrus, or decorated boundary stones. In addition, the excavations at Susa also shed light on a people known previously from only a few mentions in biblical and classical texts: the Elamites. Finds at Susa included important monuments of Elamite production, like the massive bronze statue of Queen Napir-Asu. Much of the history of the Elamite civilization, from its earliest stages in the 5th millennium BCE to its annexation into the Achaemenid Persian Empire, could be traced at Susa, where the French continued to excavate until 1979 (Mousavi 2013). Finds from the Susa excavations were divided between Iran and France through the division of artifacts, or partage, and can now be found in the Louvre Museum and in the pages of history and art history survey textbooks. Remarkably, it was not until 2015 that Susa was declared a UNESCO World Heritage site, one of 26 in Iran (Chevalier 2018).

The rise of the Pahlavi dynasty in the 1920s ushered in the third phase in Iranian archaeology. Like oil, archaeology had been a battleground between Iran and colonial powers, but the story of archaeology in Iran is also the story of the process of modernization of the country and the nation-building project of the new monarchy and its attempts to secure a place for the country in the growing network of modern nation-states. In the early 20th century, an interest in Iran's cultural heritage entered the national conversation, leading to the creation of a national antiquities service, the first antiquities museum in Tehran, and in 1923 the Society for National Heritage for preserving antiquities and handicrafts was founded. In 1927 the French archaeological monopoly was eliminated, and new antiquities laws encouraged international teams to open new excavations in Iran. A new antiquities museum (the Iran Bastan Museum) was founded and placed under the direction of French archaeologist André Godard (Grigor 2018).

The period between 1927 and the Islamic Revolution in 1979 was thus a time of productive collaboration between Iranian and outside archaeologists. Excavations officially opened at Persepolis in 1931 under the direction of the German archaeologist Ernst Herzfeld on behalf of the University of Chicago's ISAC (formerly the Oriental Institute). The structures uncovered in this excavation are now well known, and included the monumental Terrace and its buildings, the massive, elaborately decorated staircases of the Apadana and the Tripylon, a sophisticated system of canals under the terrace, extensive fortifications, and masses of texts (Herzfeld 1941). Herzfeld was stripped of his post in Germany – because he had Jewish grandparents – and forced into exile in the United States. The University of Chicago then appointed Erich Schmidt, a pioneer of the use of aerial photography in archaeological investigations, to lead the excavations at Persepolis and its surroundings from 1935–39. Their work documenting sites and monuments in Fars from the Achaemenid period (6th–4th centuries BCE) through the early Islamic period was published in three massive volumes (Schmidt 1953; 1957; 1970).

In the early 20th century, the academic discipline of archaeology was still in its infancy, its focus beginning the slow shift from the extraction of artifacts for museum collections to gathering information about ancient peoples and places. A new generation of excavators was interested in a broader range of sites, beyond the visible vestiges of great empires in the landscape, including the excavation of prehistoric site sequences, inspired by the intensive work on the development of early villages and cities of the low-lying plains and tells of Southern Iraq. Among them was Roman Ghirshman, a Ukrainian refugee educated in Paris.[3] Ghirshman excavated numerous sites in Iran, including the important prehistoric site of Tepe Sialk east of the Zagros Mountains near Kashan, whose lowest strata represent the earliest occupation in the Iranian plateau dated to 6000 BCE. Early periods at Sialk saw technical and cultural innovation, with naturalistically painted ceramics and metallurgy, including evidence for silver working. Among other sites, Ghirshman excavated and published several volumes on the Elamite site of Chogha Zanbil in the Khuzestan province, the 3rd-century BCE Sasanian capital of Bishapur in Fars, and Parthian and Sasanian levels at Susa (Martinez-Sève 2001). Ghirshman's book titled *Iran: From the Earliest Times to the Islamic conquest* (1954) and later his two volumes titled *Perse: Proto-Iraniens, Mèdes, Achéménides* (1963) and *Iran: Parthes et Sassanides* (1962) became essential literature underlying the formation of national history before the 1979 revolution and remained primary sources for textbooks for the students of archaeology even during the Islamic Republic.

Iranian archaeologists

Before the founding of academic archaeology programs many Iranian excavators of this era – like their North American and European counterparts – were from affluent families, and were educated as poets, scientists, geologists, lawyers, architects, or artists. Among the earliest graduates of the University of Tehran's archaeology program, Fereidoon Tavallali (1919–85), a noted modernist poet, excavated important sites in the region of Fars, including Susa, Pasargadae, and Tal-i Malyan (Mousavi 2013). Ali Hakemi earned an MA in archaeology from the University of Tehran in 1940, after which he earned an architecture degree and joined the architecture faculty at the University of Tehran. He had a long and storied career at the Iran Bastan Museum, and excavated sites across Iran, most notably the important site of Hasanlu in northwestern Iran, and the Bronze Age site of Shahdad at the eastern edge of the Kerman mountains and the expansive Lut desert, a site where the Early Bronze Age Jiroft culture flourished and mediated contact between east and west (Lamberg Karlovsky 1997).

Perhaps the best-known Iranian archaeologist, Ezatollah Negahban is sometimes called the father of modern archaeology in Iran. Educated in Tehran and then the

University of Chicago, he served on the faculty of the Department of Archaeology at the University of Tehran, as technical director of the Iranian archaeological service, and advisor of the Iranian Ministry of Culture. Throughout his career he championed a scientific approach to the discipline and integrated mandatory field work into the archaeology programs at the University of Tehran. One of his most significant excavations was the remarkably rich late 2nd–early 1st millennium BCE burials at the site of Marlik, near the Caspian Sea (Negahban 1996).

Negahban's excavations at Haft Tepe in Khuzestan mark an important milestone in the history of Iranian archaeology. The French archaeologists working nearby at Susa had noted the archaeological potential of a group of mounds referred to collectively as Haft Tepe as early as 1908, but when it was threatened by agricultural development in the 1950s it became the first major site in the region excavated by an Iranian mission (Negahban 1977; Carter 1999). The site and the museum Negahban founded there became a training ground for a generation of Iranian archaeologists through 1979.

Despite the growth of archaeological training in Iran, many excavations in Iran during the early to mid-20th century were led by foreign archaeologists. World War II, however, had put an end to many major archaeological missions in Iran, with the notable exception of Ghirshman's delegation in Susa. Ali Hakemi with M. Rad briefly excavated the site of Hasanlu in 1947 under a commercial license. Their findings, added to those of the earlier explorations of the site by Sir Aurel Stein in 1937, brought Hasanlu and its environs to the attention of American archaeologist Robert H. Dyson Jr, of the University of Pennsylvania, who directed a joint expedition to the site from 1956–77 (Stein and Andrews 1940; Hakemi and Rad 1950). Dozens of archaeologists were trained at Hasanlu and then moved to other sites in Iran and elsewhere, and the expedition is credited with ushering in an intellectual and scholarly explosion in Iran during the 1960s and 1970s. When the excavations at Hasanlu began, as was typical for the time, the artifacts excavated were divided among the participating institutions – the University Museum in Philadelphia, the Metropolitan Museum in New York, and the Iran Bastam Museum in Tehran. In 1972, after the creation of the Iranian Center for Archaeological Research (ICAR) under the direction of Firouz Bagherzadeh, partage ended, and archaeological finds were no longer permitted to be removed from Iran.

Throughout the early to mid-20th century, major European and North American museums collected and exhibited hundreds of works of art from ancient Iran, some obtained in partage, others through sponsored excavations, and unfortunately many more through illicit excavations and the antiquities market. It was not uncommon for western archaeologists working in the region to collect antiquities for sale to institutions at home. Materials thus obtained and exhibited in museums outside of Iran ranged from small, portable items like gems, seals, or jewelry, to monumental relief sculptures, glazed tile compositions, and massive architectural fragments.

The increased awareness of and appreciation for ancient Iranian art increased its value on international antiquities markets, with mixed consequences for

Iranian archaeology. In some cases, as for Tepe Sialk, looted objects ultimately led archeologists to a site that could be scientifically excavated and published, and which proved to be important. In other instances, as assiduously documented by the late Oscar White Muscarella, spectacular chance finds at sites like Ziwiye and in regions like Luristan created demand for more of the same, leading unscrupulous dealers and the archaeologists who supported them, to deliberately attach these 'findspots' to market antiquities – and likely forgeries – to enhance their value. In effect these false attributions contributed to what Muscarella called 'the forgery of a provenience' (1977). To further complicate matters, the government of Iran had at times issued licenses for 'commercial excavations' to landowners and others, with the understanding that finds would be divided between the excavators/speculators to be brought to the market and the government (Eisvand *et al.* 2018). To this day, it can be difficult at times to determine which artifacts in various museum collections were obtained through scientific excavations and which were not, as earlier publications did not carefully distinguish them.

Bagherzadeh's newly created ICAR established scientific laboratories for the study and restoration of excavated artifacts now no longer permitted to be removed from Iran. In 1977 Bagherzadeh was elected the first President of the World Committee of Cultural and Natural Heritage (UNESCO), and three Iranian monuments were inscribed in the World Heritage List: Chogha Zanbil, Persepolis, and Naqsh-e Jahan Square. By 1979, however, the Islamic Revolution nearly halted archaeological work, and international collaborations were curtailed. Archaeology continued to languish through the 1980s, in part due to the war between Iran and Iraq (Mousavi 2013).

Post-revolutionary archaeology in Iran

This volume highlights the important ways in which archaeology in Iran has not only recovered from this hiatus but has evolved, expanded, and incorporated new voices. When projects resumed in the 1990s, they were sporadic, small-scale, and directed predominantly by male archaeologists. While male students were trained in the field, after the Islamic Revolution female students were mostly secluded in labs and museums sorting, classifying, or illustrating archaeological materials. It was not until 1996 that the late Dr Hassan Tala'i, a professor in the Department of Archaeology at the University of Tehran, took female students to the field school so that they could gain field training (although separately from their male peers). A generation later, this volume features the work of many female archaeologists.

In the early 2000s, Dr Massoud Azarnoush re-established ICAR, opening the doors for international collaborative projects after a 20-year hiatus (Abdi and Curtis 2010). When the government proposed massive construction projects, particularly dams that would flood both known and potential archaeological sites, ICAR directed international projects toward rescue archaeology at hundreds of sites. In addition, the Chinese government's Belt and Road Initiative (BRI), a project to connect China and

Iran through Central Asia, has led to numerous collaborative archaeological projects with Chinese and Iranian archaeologists working together to explore connections between their regions (Chan *et al.* 2023). In Iran, archaeology continues to be primarily a state-based enterprise, is funded by the government, and generally follows a cultural-historical approach that is, in part, in service of national history.

Our goal in presenting this special issue is to highlight the work being done in Iran by Iranian archaeologists. Archaeology is flourishing in Iran, home to 26 designated UN World Heritage sites, a third of which are archaeological sites. Unfortunately, many of the hundreds of archaeological projects are relatively unknown outside of Iran. Aside from the few joint international projects, often published bilingually in Persian and other languages, many projects remain unpublished, and others are published in Persian in journals difficult to access outside of Iran.

This volume shares an incredible range of archaeological projects, digging into thousands of years of human history in Iran. This volume features the work of 26 archaeologists, women and men at various points in their careers, from graduate students to senior scholars. The sites they report on range from the earliest chapters of human history in the Paleolithic era (**Ghasidian *et al.***, Chapter 1) to the bustling medieval city of Isfahan (**Kamalizad, Chapter** 7) and cover all major archaeological areas of Iran. **Ghasidian *et al.*** (Chapter 1) discuss the significance of the Caspian littoral in northern Iran as both a corridor and home to the Middle Pleistocene hominins. From the eastern reaches of Iran, near the border with Pakistan and Afghanistan, Chapter 2 by **Sajjadi and Moradi** investigates the 3rd millennium BCE foundational levels of the UN World Heritage Site of Shahr-i Sokhta, concluding that its material culture is far less entangled with that of Mesopotamia than had been believed. Further north in eastern Iran, Chapter 3 by **Vahdati *et al.*** details the results of a project at Tepe Naderi, a large mound on an important route from central Iran to Central Asia. Originally settled in the late 4th millennium BCE, the material culture at the site illustrates its shifting regional alliances and networks of interaction, a fitting result for a project led jointly by Iranian and Chinese archaeologists. In the province of Bushehr in southwestern Iran, **Zehbari *et al.*** (Chapter 5) explore the archaeological evidence for a corridor – incorporating their work at the site of Dehqāed – that was strategically important to the Achaemenid, Sasanian, and Seleucid/Parthian empires for connecting the Persian Gulf and the interior of southwestern Iran.

The remaining chapters feature excavations related to water management in ancient and medieval Iran. **Asadi *et al.*** (Chapter 4) examine archaeobotanical samples found in the network of channels cut into the bedrock of the Terrace at Persepolis in southwestern Iran, an enormous man-made platform underlying the imperial city. These samples likely date to the late Achaemenid Period, allowing the authors to compare archaeobotanical data to contemporary written sources about food rations and storage at the site itself.

The Zāyandeh-Rōd river, one of the longest in Iran, connects the last two chapters. The first, by **Khosrowzadeh and Habibi** (Chapter 6), look at the region watered by its highland basin in the Chaharmahal and Bakhtyari Province in the Central Zagros Mountains in western Iran. Their research indicates that there was an increase in agricultural settlements during the late Seleucid-Parthian period (3rd century BCE–3rd century CE) with the rise of the Elymaea, an independent kingdom that controlled trade routes between Babylonia and the Iranian Plateau. The final chapter (Chapter 7) follows the course of the same river into the medieval city of Isfahan during the Safavid dynasty (1502–1722), where **Jaleh Kamalizad** has started a long-term project on the relationship between water management strategies and the prosperity of the city of Isfahan. Her survey demonstrates how, in a semi-arid climate, Isfahan created innovative hydraulic structures and systems to distribute water to city districts and hinterlands, providing it with the resilience to flourish even in times of political and military upheaval.

Individually, each of these papers offers an innovative case study demonstrating the archaeological and scientific sophistication of these new voices in Iranian archaeology, and each chapter is accompanied by an editor's introduction providing context for the research presented. As a collection, with papers that range from the Paleolithic era to the late Islamic period, across the entirety of the vast nation of Iran, this chorus of papers demonstrate the enduring commitment of Iranian archaeologists to their nation's diverse and complex past.

Notes

1 This project began as a conversation several years ago between colleagues about the challenges faced by young archaeologists in Iran. In the years that separate this publication and its conception, global events like the Coronavirus Pandemic and geopolitical unrest throughout the world have regrettably delayed our efforts. We are grateful to the authors for trusting us with their research and are delighted to see their hard work in print. We are also beyond appreciative of Julie Gardiner of Oxbow Books for her consistent and tireless support for archaeology in Iran.

2 Loftus followed the same excavation strategy used at Nimrud and Khorsabad – he opened trenches to look for large stone relief sculptures such as those found at Persepolis or Assyrian sites. When they were not found at Susa, the British ended their efforts (see Curtis 1993).

3 Ghirshman was the quintessential figure of an early 20th-century archaeologist. His biography in the *Encyclopedia Iranica* (Martinez-Sève 2001) states 'Ghirshman came from an affluent family in Kharkov [Ukraine] and was enlisted in 1914 into the Russian army. In 1917, he joined the counter-revolutionary camp, and after the Communist victory took refuge in Istanbul, where he earned a living as a violinist. He then joined a kibbutz in Palestine, near the ancient city of Caesarea, a location which instilled in him a passion for history. Subsequently he began an intensive course of studies in Paris, which enabled him to keep company with the great authorities of Near East epigraphy and archeology.'

Bibliography

Abdi, K. and Curtis, J. (2010) Obituaries: Masoud Azarnoush 1945–2008. *Iran* 48, v–x.

Carter, E. (1999) Kabnak (Haft Tappeh) and Al Untash-Napirisha (Chogha Zanbil), Elamite Cities of the Late Bronze Age. In A. Alizadeh, Y. Majidzadeh, S.M. Shahmirzadi (eds) *The Iranian World: Essays on Iranian Art and Archaeology Presented to Ezat O. Negahban*, 114–130. Tehran, Iran University Press.

Chan, V., Hui, Y.-F., Hui, D., and Vafadari, K. (2023) *Heritage Conservation and China's Belt and Road Initiative*. Oxford, Routledge.

Chevalier, N. (2018) France and Elam. In J. Álvarez-Mon, G.P. Basello, Y. Wicks (eds) *The Elamite World*, 41–62. London, Routledge.

Coste, P. and Flandin, E. (1843–54) *Voyage en Perse, entrepris par ordre de M. le Ministre des Affaires Etrangères, d'après les instructions dressées par l'Institut (6 vols.)*. Paris, Gide et J. Baudry.

Curtis, J. (1993) William Kennett Loftus and his Excavations at Susa. *Iranica Antiqua* 28 (1993), 1–55.

Eisvand, S.F., Hariri, N., and Zadeh, A.J. (2018) Subsistence Digging in Iran's Archeology and the Cultural Heritage. *Archaeologies* 14, 527–552.

Ghirshman, R. (1954) *Iran from the Earliest Times to the Islamic Conquest*. Harmondsworth, Penguin.

Ghirshman, R. (1962) *Iran: Parthes et Sassanides*. Paris, Gallimard.

Ghirshman, R. (1963) *Perse: Proto-Iraniens, Mèdes, Acheéménides*. Paris, Gallimard.

Grigor, T. (2018) 'They Have Not Changed in 2,500 Years': Art, Archaeology, and Modernity in Iran. In B. Effros and G. Lai (eds) *Unmasking Ideology in Imperial and Colonial Archaeology: Vocabulary, Symbols, and Legacy*, 121–146. Los Angeles, Cotsen Institute of Archaeology Press.

Hakemi, A. and Rad, M. (1950) Sharḥ va Natīje-ye Kāvoshhā-ye 'elmi-ye Ḥasanlū, Soldūz (The Description and Results of the Scientific Excavations of Hasanlu, Solduz). *Gozareshha-ye Bāstān-Shenasī* 1329 1, 1–103.

Herzfeld, E. (1941) *Iran in the Ancient East*. London, Oxford University Press.

Lamberg-Karlovsky, C.C. (1997) Ali Hakemi. *Paléorient* 23, 128.

Martinez-Sève, L. (2001) Roman Ghirshman. *Encyclopaedia Iranica* X (6), 583–586.

Mousavi, A. (2013) The History of Archaeological Research in Iran: A Brief Survey. In D.T. Potts (ed.) *The Oxford Handbook of Ancient Iran*, 3–16. Oxford, Oxford University Press.

Muscarella, O.W. (1977) 'Ziwiye' and Ziwiye: The Forgery of a Provenience. *Journal of Field Archaeology* 4, 197–219.

Negahban, E.O. (1977) *A Guide to the Haft Tepe Excavation and Museum*. Tehran, Ministry of Culture and Arts.

Negahban, E.O. (1996) *Marlik: The Complete Excavation Report*. Philadelphia, University of Pennsylvania Museum of Archaeology and Anthropology.

Porter, R.K. (1821) *Travels in Georgia, Persia, Armenia, Ancient Babylonia, Etc. during the Years 1817, 1818, 1819, and 1820*. London, Longman, Hurst, Rees, Orme, and Brown.

Schmidt, E.F. (1953) *Persepolis I. Structures, Reliefs, Inscriptions.*, Oriental Institute Publications. Chicago, University of Chicago Press.

Schmidt, E.F. (1957) *Persepolis II. Contents of the Treasury and Other Discoveries*. Chicago, University of Chicago Press.

Schmidt, E.F. (1970) *Persepolis III: Royal Tombs and Other Monuments*. Chicago, University of Chicago Press.

Stein, A. and Andrews, F. (1940) *Old Routes of Western Iran*. London, Macmillan and Co.

Chapter 1 Prologue

The earliest hominins in Iran

The following chapter by Elham Ghasidian and her colleagues deals with two fascinating issues in the study of human origins: 1) the dispersals and 2) coexistence of hominins. The spread of genus *Homo* throughout most of Africa and Eurasia continued during the middle and late Pleistocene periods. Scholars have studied a complex pattern of migration within Africa and Eurasia, particularly human dispersal 'Out of Africa' (Smith and Karriger 2023). Moving into a variety of environments led to the increase of differentiation among human populations. These differentiations are reflected both in the morphology and cultural materials of hominins. In this chapter, Ghasidian and colleagues argue that the Southern Caspian Corridor is one of the important environments through which various hominins, particularly Neanderthals and early modern humans, may have migrated; where they encountered and even coexisted with each other.

There are an abundance of fossil and material culture remains of Neanderthals, and we know more about them compared to earlier hominins. Neanderthals lived in a vast portion of Eurasia from ~150 ky through ~30. Their fossil and material remains are found from Spain, France, and Germany in Western Europe to the Near East, Uzbekistan in Central Asia, and Siberia (Higham *et al.* 2014). During glacial periods, Neanderthals appeared to move south and east into southwest Asia, including the Caucasus. At the same time that Neanderthals were living in Europe and western Asia, hominin evolutionary developments were also taking place in other parts of the world, most significantly the evolution of anatomically modern *Homo sapiens* in Africa. Modern humans evolved in East Africa and spread throughout the continent first and ultimately into Eurasia. The earliest evidence of modern humans outside of Africa comes from a few cave sites such as Skhul and Qafzeh in the Levant of southwestern Asia sometime between 80,000 to 100,000 years ago, in fact from the same region as the Amud and Kebara Neanderthals in Israel. The overlap in dates between Neanderthals and early modern humans indicates that the two groups coexisted at least several thousand years. Although it is not clear what kinds of interactions modern humans and Neanderthals had, the data suggest that they lived in the same area at about the same time (Smith and Karriger 2023).

Earlier morphological analyses of Neanderthals and early modern humans in Western Asia suggested that the earliest modern *Homo sapiens* had clear Neanderthal features indicating interbreeding between Neanderthals and early modern people

(Thackeray *et al.* 2005). In a breakthrough study led by Swedish geneticist Svante Paabo, scholars applied a new technology to the analysis of three female Neanderthal bones from Vindija Cave in Croatia, which allowed them to sequence more of the genome. The results are breathtaking and demonstrate that modern Eurasians and Neanderthals share between 1% and 4% of their nuclear DNA, an indication of a significant admixture (Fu *et al.* 2015). Later geneticists extracted DNA from three early modern human fossils: one in central Siberia at a site near Denisova Cave, a second from a site in western Russia, and a third from a site in Romania. The genetic evidence strongly suggests that modern humans migrated from Africa and interbred with other hominin species beyond Neanderthals.

There is no doubt that migration corridors have played a significant role in these encounters, interbreeding, and similarities in material cultures. In addition to known areas where hominins migrated through and encountered others, in the Levant and Eastern Europe, Ghasidian and her colleagues set forth another corridor for potential migration and encounter, hypothesizing that the Southern Caspian Corridor could have played an important role in the migration of hominins from the Caucasus to Central Asia, and promoted encounters with other hominins. To them, the Southern Caspian Corridor's 'mild climate, dense vegetation, rich water resources, marine and terrestrial food resources even during glacial periods,' makes it potentially an ideal bio-geographical corridor, and the large number of cave sites and rock shelters attests to hominin presence.

To test the hypothesis, they have focused on material remains from cave sites in the Southern Caspian Corridor and their techno-typological aspects. To this end, they have applied two different types of analyses: attribute analysis and *chaîne opératoire*. After analysis of similarities and differences attributes in various assemblages, the goal is to understand to what extent the similarities are the results of cultural transmission between hominin groups. To achieve this, Ghasidian and her colleagues first review lithic assemblages. Then, they conducted their own surveys to find Paleolithic sites in the Southern Caspian Corridor. The results from surveys and the analysis of material assemblages indicate that lithic industries had some unique characteristics, deviating from the known lithic assemblages such as Zagros Mousterian and Aurignacian, Baradostian, and Rostamian, complicating our understanding of possible cultural transmission in the Palaeolithic period.

Bibliography

Fu, Q., Hajdinjak, M., Moldovan, O.T., Constantin, S., Mallick, S., Skoglund, P., *et al.* (2015) An Early Modern Human from Romania with a Recent Neanderthal Ancestor. *Nature* 524 (7564), 216–219.

Higham, T., Douka, K., Wood, R., Ramsey, C.B., Basell, L., *et al.* (2014) The Timing and Spatiotemporal Patterning of Neanderthal Disappearance. *Nature* 512 (7514), 306–309.

Smith, F.H. and Karriger, W.M. (2023). Panmixis in Middle and Late Pleistocene Human Subspecies: The Genetic/Genomic Revolution in Paleoanthropology. In C.S. Larsen (ed.) *A Companion to Biological Anthropology (2nd Edition)*, 440–457. Malden, Blackwell.

Thackeray, F., Maureille, B., Vandermeersch, B., *et al.* (2005) Morphometric Comparisons Between Neanderthals and 'Anatomically Modern' Homo sapiens from Europe and the Near East. *Annals of the Transvaal Museum* 42, 47–51.

Chapter 1

The Southern Caspian Corridor: A hominin biogeographical expansion route

Elham Ghasidian, Hosein Ramzanpour, Ahmad Bavand Savadkouhi, Mehdi Abedini Araghi, and Saman H. Guran

Abstract

The narrow area of the Southern Caspian Sea Corridor is bounded by the northern slopes of high and rugged east-west oriented Alborz Mountain ranges that separate the interior lowland deserts of the Iranian Plateau in the south from the Caspian Sea in the north. In its easternmost part, the Alborz Mountains join the Kopet Dagh-Khorasan Mountains, while from the northwest and west it connects to the Lesser Caucasus and Zagros Mountains respectively. In its remarkable setting, the Southern Caspian Sea Corridor is partly covered by the Caspian Hyrcanian mixed forest. This forest covers around 55,000 km^2. Despite being narrow, the wide elevational gradient range, *diverse topography, and strong environmental heterogeneity provided floral and faunal diversity in this area. Phylogeographical studies of floral and faunal species show the persistence of several species during glacial periods in this area, identifying it as a* refugium of Hyrcania. *Following C. McBurney's idea that any movement from the west might be expected to pass this area en route to Central Asia, the Palaeolithic investigation in this area has been renewed since 2018 to track late Pleistocene hominins. This contribution presents a new look on the human/environment interactions and their developments during the late Pleistocene. We hypothesize that the Southern Caspian Corridor acted in a dual role as a biogeographical corridor of expansion and habitat, and also witnessed a series of human evolutionary events that occurred during the late Pleistocene.*

Introduction

Despite the considerable evidence from Africa and Europe, a growing body of research in western Asia has revealed it as the 'cradle of mankind' (Bae *et al.* 2017, 6) and confirms its potential to answer questions regarding the origins of modern humans,

Neanderthal colonization and their replacement by *Homo sapiens*, and the dawn of the Upper Palaeolithic revolution (Boyle *et al.* 2010).

During the last few decades, great progress has been made in several domains, particularly palaeogenetics, which have revealed the complex ancestry of early Eurasians. This progress – including the identification of a *ghost lineage*[1] of Eurasians in the Middle East – is providing important new biogeographical hypotheses (Malaspinas *et al.* 2016).

Recent molecular and morphological research on Neanderthal remains document that this species appeared in Europe at least 400 thousand years ago (ka) (Stringer and Hublin 1999; Harvati 2010) and ca. 150 ka in western Asia (Grün and Stringer 2000). During this period, until ca. 30 ka, they colonized a vast territory that covered the entire European continent, the Levant and extended towards the Central Asia and Siberia (Krause *et al.* 2007; Kolobova *et al.* 2020).

The location of the Iranian Plateau (Fig. 1.1) puts it at the center of major changes in the story of human evolution as it is a land of crossroads between the west and the east. In addition, the Iranian Plateau includes diverse geographical and climatic zones. As a result, we expect high diversity among the late Pleistocene hunter-gatherer populations in this vast area (Ghasidian 2019; Ghasidian *et al.* 2019). Despite the

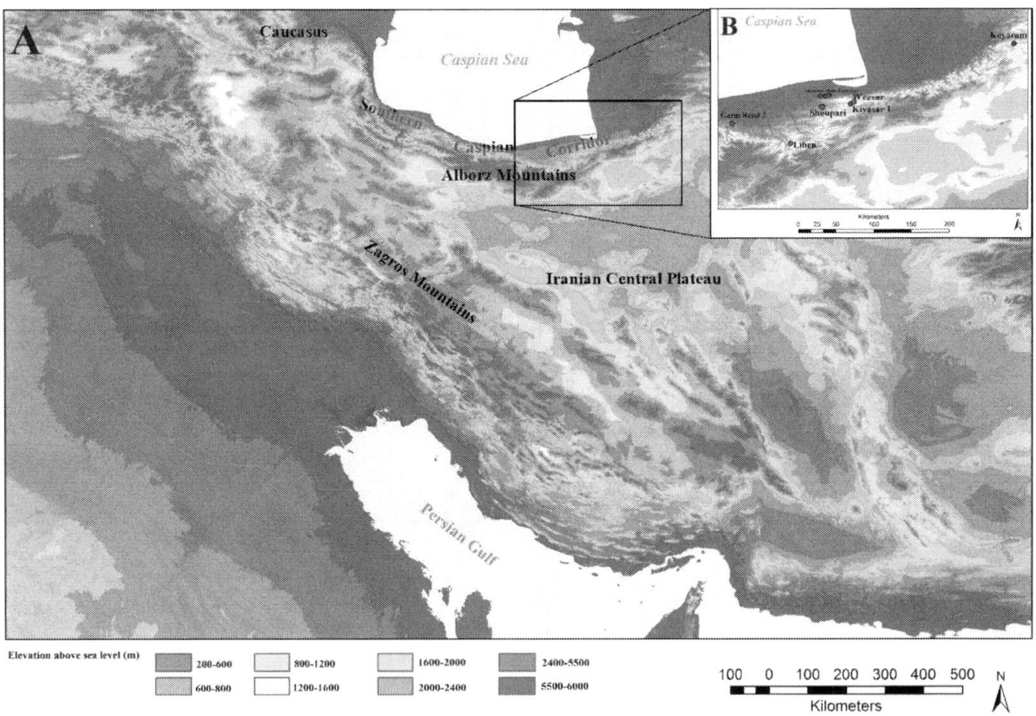

Fig. 1.1: A: Iranian Plateau and three geographical macrozones: Zagros Mountains, Iranian Central Plateau, Alborz Mountains, note the location of the Southern Caspian Sea Corridor. B: Some of the important Palaeolithic and post-Palaeolithic sites from Eastern and central of Southern Caspian Sea Corridor mentioned in the text. All photos and drawings by the authors unless otherwise specified.

ground-breaking potential of this region, only sporadic investigations have been conducted on the Palaeolithic population dynamics in the Iranian Plateau (e.g. Vahdati Nasab *et al.* 2013; Heydari-Guran and Ghasidian 2017; 2020).

In this chapter we put the spotlight on the southern Caspian area as having more evidence for Palaeolithic population dynamics than has been known previously. Various characteristics lend credence to this suggestion, including its geographical position and climatic conditions. Regarding the geographical distribution of the Neanderthals in western Eurasia, the warm MIS[2] 5e played an important role in the eastern extension of Neanderthals. Perhaps, in this period, Neanderthals were able to occupy territories between the Ural Mountains and the Caspian depression, and eventually part of Central Asia (Hublin 1998). In addition, during later periods, due to the mild climatic conditions between high mountains and the Caspian Sea, the southern Caspian area acted as a glacial *refugium* – an area where fauna and flora could survive and from which they could recolonize – during the cold episodes of MIS 5 and MIS 4 (Dennell 2017). Therefore, the region could serve as an important expansion route for the late Pleistocene populations as well as a place of settlement.

Evidence from the western Iranian Plateau at the Zagros Mountain region show that during MIS 5 and 4, the region was fully occupied by Neanderthals (Solecki 1963; Heydari-Guran and Ghasidian 2020; Heydari-Guran *et al.* 2021). The most significant supporting data comes from the Zagros sites. Among them, only two sites – Shanidar Cave in the Northern Zagros and the Bawa Yawan Rock Shelter in the West-Central Zagros – yielded evidence for Middle Palaeolithic artifacts in association with Neanderthal remains between ca. 50 and 100 ka (Solecki 1963, 189; Heydari-Guran *et al.* 2021). The associated Middle Palaeolithic lithic industry is called the Zagros Mousterian, which is typologically dominated by tool types with intensive Mousterian retouch including convergent scrapers and Mousterian points (Solecki 1963; Dibble 1984; Heydari-Guran *et al.* 2021). Generally, the use of the Levallois technique[3] is well known to the Middle Palaeolithic knappers of the Zagros, but not as extensively used as has been observed in the Levant (Dibble and Holdaway 1993). Mousterian industry is known in the Zagros region, and yet is the only known Middle Palaeolithic industry throughout the Iranian Plateau sites (Biglari *et al.* 2009; Vahdati Nasab and Hashemi 2016). However, recent research in Kermanshah and the Central Iranian Plateau documents other Middle Palaeolithic industry than Mousterian and could potentially indicate the admixture between the Neanderthals and *Homo sapiens* (Heydari-Guran and Ghasidian 2021). This issue contributes to the notion that other hominin species (i.e. *Homo sapiens*) were responsible for this different Middle Palaeolithic industry.

The phylogeny of the Neanderthals documents splitting among the Neanderthal groups around 150 ka, and it has been hypothesized that a population turnover is likely to have occurred in the Caucasus (Hajdinjak *et al.* 2018). But what about the other parts of the Iranian Plateau, especially the southern Caspian area which is in the geo-ecologically continuum of the Caucasus? How can the available data explain the model of colonization of the Iranian Plateau with late Pleistocene hominins, including Neanderthals and *Homo sapiens*?

Despite the common assumption that the Iranian Plateau is a single geographical unit, this plateau consists of at least three large-scale and separated geographical macrozones which stand in contrast to each other (Fig. 1.1). These regions include a) Zagros highlands located at the west and stretching towards the south of the Iranian Plateau; b) the Central Plateau of Iran consisting of deserts and playas, and c) the Alborz Mountains. The region located north of the Alborz Mountains is geoecologically different than the rest of the Iranian Plateau and we refer to it as the Southern Caspian Corridor (SCC). This is a ca. 800 km long and narrow region between the Caspian Sea and the high mountains of Alborz, with a change in elevation from 27 m below sea level at the shore to ca. 5700 m above sea level at the pinnacle, a factor that limited the interactions between this region and the inner parts of the Plateau. The SCC stretches from the Caucasus Mountains in the west to the Turkmenistan plains towards Central Asia to the east.

The narrow SCC region provides the closest and fastest route connecting Europe and Caucasus to Central Asia and Siberia (Ghasidian *et al.* 2023), and is presented as one of the most important corridors of hominin expansion during late Pleistocene ('route B': Vahdati Nasab *et al.* 2013). While the northern Caspian Sea was affected by sea level fluctuations, the southern coast remained relatively less disturbed by regression and transgression of the sea during glacial and interglacial cycles (Yanina *et al.* 2018; Krijgsman *et al.* 2019). Given its geographical location as part of the large biome of Eastern Mediterranean–Black Sea–Caspian-Corridor (Marinova *et al.* 2018), this region might have been highly populated in the warm and moist episodes of MIS 5 (Hublin 1998; Vlaminck *et al.* 2018), and serving as a refugium during MIS 4 and 3 – the same era as the Ust'-Ishim man in western Siberia (Fu *et al.* 2014) – acting as population source during glacial events.

Despite the availability of resources to support life in the region, few Palaeolithic sites have been discovered in the area. The most important sites are the following: in the west of the SCC the Darband Rashi Cave (Biglari and Jahani 2011) and the Ganjpar open air site (Biglari *et al.* 2006) dated to the Lower Palaeolithic, and Malehan Cave (Vahdati Nasab 2009) probably related to the Upper Palaeolithic; at the central part of the SCC is the Garm Roud 2 river terrace site dated to the Upper Palaeolithic (Berillon *et al.* 2009); and at the east of the SCC are the Hotu and Kamarband (Belt) caves (Coon 1951), Komishan (Mahforouzi 2003; Vahdati Nasab *et al.* 2020) and Eltape caves (McBurney 1968), which all revealed post-Palaeolithic periods, and the open air sites of Komishani and Khanehsar (Ramzanpour 2020) probably to the Middle Palaeolithic and the Middle Palaeolithic cave site of Keyaram. Aside from some post-Palaeolithic sites (Komishan, Eltape, and Hotu caves), the only absolute date from a Palaeolithic site was obtained from Garm Roud 2 and revealed an age of 33878 ± 3300 cal. BP (Berillon *et al.* 2007).

The physio-geographic conditions of the SCC suggest the following hypotheses:

1. The SCC was inhabited by different hominin groups during late Pleistocene. This area has been attractive for hominin species even during glacial periods when it acted as a refugium. Therefore, Middle and Upper Palaeolithic occupation are

likely to be found in this area. The expansion and dispersals of hominins (including Neanderthals) occurred via the SCC towards the east (Central Asia and Siberia).
2. The exceptional environmental conditions present in the SCC suggest that this area could hypothetically have dual roles as bio-geographical corridor for expansion and habitat that witnessed a series of human evolutionary events in the late Pleistocene, and a place of admixture of different hominins.

To test these hypotheses, the following questions must first be answered:

1. What are the characteristics of the technology and typology of Palaeolithic artifacts from the SCC sites?
2. Do the lithic assemblages from the SCC, the Zagros Palaeolithic sites, and the interior of the Iranian Plateau have common cultural characteristics that indicate cultural exchange? Or do they indicate cultural diversity?
3. What can we understand from the evidence for hominin behavior, ecology, and adaptation in the SCC and what is the role of this area in the dispersal of different hominin groups (especially Neanderthals and *Homo sapiens*)?

To answer these questions, the SCC research project started in 2018 by reviewing lithic assemblages from previous excavations in Keyaram Cave. Targeted surveys had been conducted in order to find Palaeolithic sites in this area (Ghasidian 2018). To understand the relationship between the Palaeolithic sites in the SCC and other Palaeolithic sites in Iran, we undertook techno-typological studies applying attribute analysis (Tostevin 2012) and the *chaîne opératoire*[4] (Inizan *et al.* 1999) methods. Using these methods, it is possible to see the similarities and differences of the lithic collections and understand the cultural transmission or isolation of hominin groups in different parts of the Iranian Plateau.

New Palaeolithic research in the SCC

In the early 1960s, Charles McBurney began research in the southern region of the Caspian Sea with the notion that any movement from the west would be expected to pass through this region en route to Central Asia (McBurney 1964). The Upper Jurassic limestone areas of this region feature caves, some of which appear to preserve substantial depths of deposits (Coon 1957). This region also provided rich, stone raw materials, such as chert and flint nodules embedded in limestone deposits (Heydari [Guran] 2004). McBurney's discovery of the key Middle Palaeolithic site of Keyaram Cave in the eastern area of the SCC (Plate 1.1) confirmed the importance of the SCC. Before starting our survey in the area, one of the authors (EG) reviewed the assemblage from McBurney's 1963 excavation in Keyaram Cave to gain insight into the material culture of the region.

Keyaram Cave

In 1963, McBurney investigated several caves and rock shelters in the SCC, of which only the Keyaram Cave yielded Palaeolithic finds. The cave is located at 793 m above sea level on the northern slopes of the Alborz Mountains, in the easternmost stretch of the SCC. A river flows close by the cave, and its periodic flooding may explain the disturbed nature of the sediments (McBurney 1964). McBurney's excavation revealed intermingled Iron Age and Middle Palaeolithic layers. Despite the disturbance and admixture of these two layers, using techno-typological analysis of the lithics, McBurney documented evidence for Mousterian stone tool industry, limited in using Levallois technology, with tools of medium size. In this respect, it is reminiscent of the Zagros Mousterian industry from Bisetun Cave in the West-Central Zagros, and so McBurney called it Mousterian type B (McBurney 1964). Moreover, he documented that the Keyaram assemblage is similar to the Mousterian assemblage from the Teshik Tash Cave in Uzbekistan (McBurney 1964). In addition, the recovery of a hippopotamus bone from the Keyaram assemblage indicates that, at least during the warm and humid phases of the MIS 5, the region was covered with dense forest, as it is today (McBurney 1964; Smith 1986).

All lithics from Keyaram held by the University of Cambridge were reviewed. The lithic artifacts are divided into two groups: Those found *in situ* in undisturbed layers, and the disturbed Layer 3. Unfortunately, the bulk of the artifacts was obtained from the disturbed layer. Regardless of this issue and the lack of absolute chronology, the techno-typological analysis of the lithics shows the extensive use of Levallois technology. However, no Levallois blade or Levallois core was recovered. Out of a total of nine cores, four pieces are centripetal (Fig. 1.2a). The presence of a Kombewa core obtained from an *in-situ* layer is interesting and could be related to the Kombewa flakes coming from the disturbed layer (Fig. 1.2b). Except for one platform blade core, four remaining are platform flake cores.

The Keyaram tool assemblage is interesting, having elements from both the Middle and Upper Palaeolithic periods. The undisturbed, *in-situ* Middle Palaeolithic layer yielded retouched blades, along with side and *déjeté* scrapers, retouched Levallois flakes, and truncated facetted tools (Fig. 1.2b). The presence of point tools with impact point, which were probably caused by hitting, indicates their use as hunting tools (Fig. 1.2b). Although there are no bladelet cores, the presence of several points made on bladelet blanks evidence Upper Palaeolithic traits in the assemblage.

A Levallois core recovered from the disturbed layer has parallel negative scars on one surface (Fig. 1.2a). The presence of Levallois technology and parallel reduction on one core raises an important hypothesis; that the knappers of this element were aware of both Middle and Upper Palaeolithic knapping techniques for obtaining bladelets and flakes from a single core or resuming a bladelet core and reducing it with Levallois technique.

More than half of the assemblage is made of light brown chert. One of its important sources is located in Behshahr Region around 190 km west of Keyaram (Heydari [Guran] 2004). This issue raises the possibility of long-distance communication between different parts of the SCC for the exchange and transfer of raw materials.

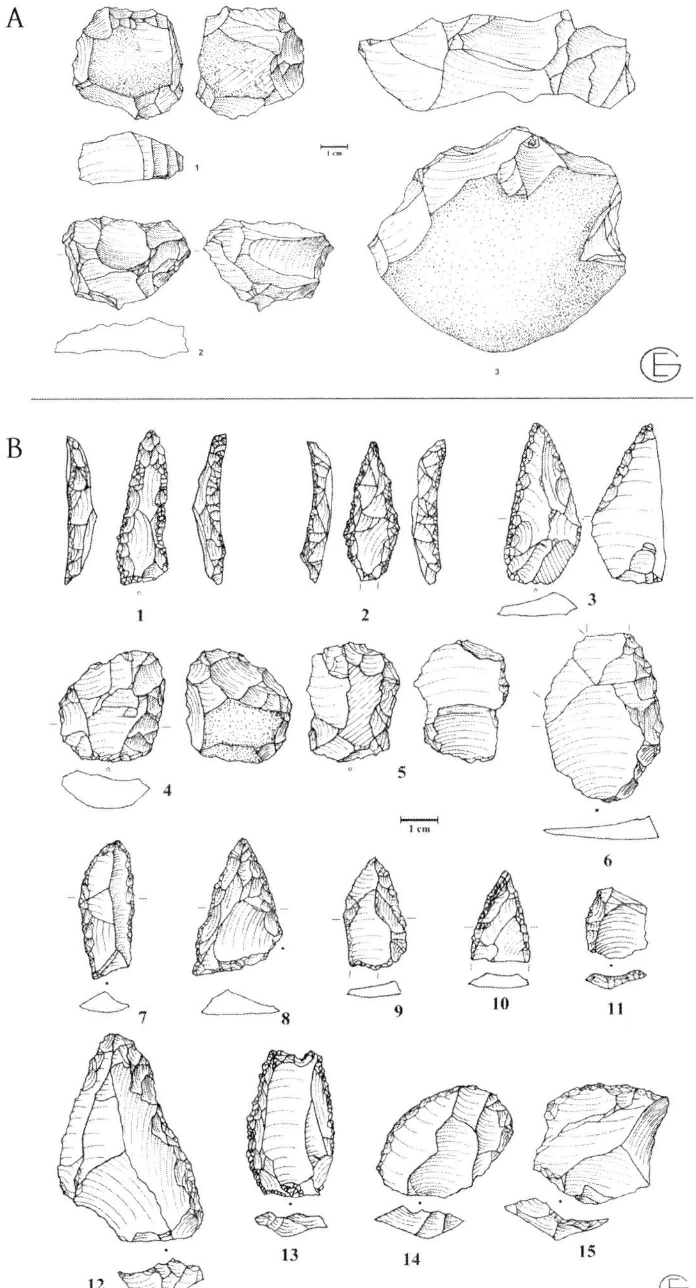

Fig. 1.2: Keyaram lithics. A: 1. Centripetal core with parallel negative on side, 2. Levallois core, 3. Large scraper/irregular core. B: 1 and 2. Pointed scrapers, 3. Convergent scraper with ventral retouched edge, 4 and 5. Truncated facetted, 6 and 11. Kombewa retouched flakes, 8–10. Pointed flakes, 12. Convergent scraper, 13–15. Retouched Levallois flakes.

Although the Levallois technology was used in this collection, we hesitate to label the Keyaram collection Mousterian, as the Mousterian-type retouches and the tools like those proposed for the Zagros Mousterian sites (Dibble 1984; Dibble and Holdaway 1993) are absent. Instead, Upper Palaeolithic elements were observed among the tool types. The presence of two Middle and Upper Palaeolithic technological traits pushes forward the idea of the Initial Upper Palaeolithic for the Keyaram assemblage. However, stratified data along with absolute dating is essential for confirming this idea and/or Middle–Upper Palaeolithic transition.

Survey in Eastern Alborz Mountains

Our survey area in the Eastern Alborz is around 80 km far from the Caspian Sea and elevated between ca. 200 and 2000 m asl. These areas are far from the effects of sea level fluctuations and as a result, we expected well-preserved Palaeolithic deposits.

Carlton Coon, in his book *Seven Caves* (1957), describes his visit to the southern shores of the Caspian Sea, mentioning several caves and rock shelters in the east of Mazandaran, especially the Hezarjarib Region. His investigations resulted in the discovery of Hotu and Kamarband caves, whose contents date to later phases of Palaeolithic, which he named Mesolithic. Following his lead, our team started with a systematic survey in the Yanesar region of Hezarjarib, which could potentially reveal Palaeolithic occupation.

Our survey area in Hezarjarib is geographically far from the shore of the Caspian Sea and includes the northern slopes of the Alborz Mountains. We chose this location because, according to the studies conducted on the sea level fluctuations during the late Pleistocene and Holocene, the lower plains between the mountains and the sea were likely affected by the rise and fall of sea level (Kehl *et al.* 2021) as was observed at the bottom of the Mesolithic layer in Hotu Cave (Coon 1951). Here the study of loess-palaeosol sequences in northern Iran revealed that during the middle and late Pleistocene this region witnessed significant changes from a dry and cold to a humid and warm climate in Northern Iran (Kehl *et al.* 2021). Geographically, this relatively high-elevation area encompassed several natural corridors from the inner parts of the Iranian Plateau and could possibly act as part of the dispersal route towards east. Since the region is rich in high quality and abundant stone raw material resources (Heydari [Guran] 2004), we expected to find open air Palaeolithic localities as well. Surface surveys are difficult in this setting due to the dense vegetation of the slopes, which obscures possible lithic artifacts. As we moved from the northern slopes of Alborz Mountains towards south to higher elevations and away from the Caspian Sea, more arid conditions yield less vegetation, improving visibility.

In the first survey season, we identified 14 Palaeolithic and post-Palaeolithic sites. Our survey in the eastern parts of the corridor showed that the Palaeolithic sites are mostly located in the main valleys of the southern Alborz overlooking the intermountain plains. Some areas yielded a large number of lithic artifacts scattered on a large plain (see section on Wezwar). Despite these discoveries, large parts of the studied area remain unknown and await further survey. Among the investigated sites, the Kiyasar 1 rock shelter, the Wezwar open-air site, and Shoupari Cave are the most promising sites in the eastern SCC.

Kiyasar rock shelter 1 (Fig. 1.1)

Kiyasar 1 is located in the Kiyasar path of Hezarjarib at 36.574825°N, 53.912391° E and is 1050 m above sea level (Plate 1.1, Fig. 1.3). The Kiyasar path is a gorge with an approximate length of 600 m and an average width of 70 m. It is a strategic corridor for the movements of large animals such as cattle and horses. It is one of the several north–south directed paths connecting the inner parts of the Iranian Central Plateau to the SCC. The permanent Kiyasar River passes through this gorge (Ghasidian *et al.* 2020).

An illegal excavation at this rock shelter uncovered several lithic artifacts scattered on the sediments accumulated around the looters' pit. A few lithics have been recovered from the exposed profile. The first 30 cm of the profile consist of Holocene followed by 45 cm of Pleistocene deposits (Ghasidian *et al.* 2020). In total, Kiyasar 1 yielded 253 lithic artifacts and numerous bone fragments.

The lithic assemblage is composed of flakes, tools, and a number of cores. The bladelet cores have single platform with their reduction surface on the narrow side, while the flake cores have the wide side as reduction surface (Fig. 1.4). Despite the

Fig. 1.3: A: Kiyasar 1 Rock shelter. B: A lithic exposed from looter's pit in Kiyasar 1.

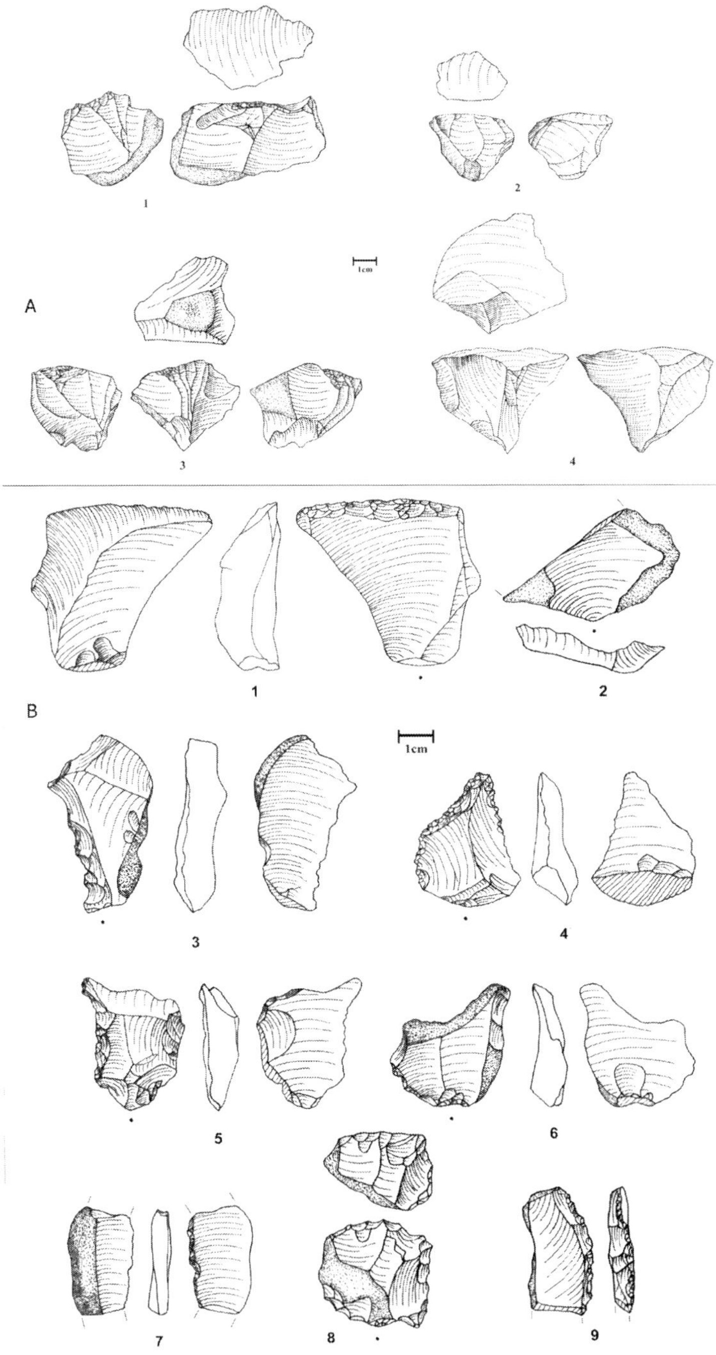

Fig. 1.4: Kiyasar 1 lithics. A: 1-3. Platform bladelet core, 4. Platform flake core. B: 1. Backed knife, 2. Flat flake with prepared platform, 3. Denticulate, 4. Perforator, 5 and 6. Retouched flakes, 7. Retouched blade, 8. Carinated scraper, 9. Side scraper.

presence of bladelet cores, no blades or bladelets are in the collection. The tools found include 98 items and mainly consist of notched and denticulate tools, single scrapers, a borer, and a carinated scraper (Fig. 1.4B: 8).

A comparison of tools from Kiyasar 1 with those found in Palaeolithic sites in the Zagros (Dibble and Holdaway 1993; Olszewski and Dibble 1994; Ghasidian 2014; Heydari-Guran *et al.* 2021) shows the strong local characteristics of the Kiyasar 1 assemblage. In the absence of typical scrapers of the Zagros Middle Palaeolithic, a Keilmesser – a later stone knife created by flaking off shards of stone to create sharpened edges, typically on both sides of the tool – in the assemblage is interesting. Semi-abrupt retouched bladelets, carinated end scrapers and burins – all common Zagros Upper Palaeolithic tool types – are absent in Kiyasar 1. Most tools are flakes with scattered retouching. The geographical conditions of the northern slopes of the Alborz probably demanded specific hunting and gathering strategies that are reflected in the lithic industry. Kiyasar 1 lithics are also different from those found at Garm Roud 2, where knappers seems to have concentrated on the production of bladelets and small number of tools (about 4% of the whole collection) (Abolfathi *et al.* 2015), whereas at Kiyasar 1 the assemblage is flake oriented and more than 38% of the entire collection consists of tools.

In general, the techno-typological characteristics of Kiyasar 1 lithics align with both Middle and Upper Palaeolithic dates. Despite the flake-based nature of the collection, the presence of two platform cores for bladelet production point to the Upper Palaeolithic. And while the flakes are not diagnostic, two flakes with centripetal negative scars and scrapers similar to the lithics recovered from Keyaram Cave indicate manufacture in the Middle Palaeolithic period. Due to these elements, we conclude that the site was probably used during the Middle and Upper Palaeolithic (Ghasidian *et al.* 2020); a point which awaits confirmation by systematic excavation.

Wezwar open-air site (Plate 1.1)

Wezwar (36°36′19.64″N, 53°52′14.31″E) is a vast area of ca. 11 ha in the Yanehsar region of Hezarjarib in the eastern SCC (Fig. 1.5). The locality overlooks the Kiyasar 1 rock shelter and is located ca. 6 km (as the crow flies) to its northeast. Here we found chunks of light brown chert abundantly evident on the surface (Plate 1.2a), as well as scattered lithic artifacts, and in some places, concentrations of lithics indicating workshops (Plate 1.2b). The main concentration was found on a plateau near where a labyrinth of shelters has been formed. No lithic artifacts have been found in these shelters. In our short survey into the Wezwar locality, we focused on collecting a selection of lithic artifacts mainly from two areas of concentration, as the whole locality is covered by numerous lithics.

A techno-typological study of the lithics documents the high frequency of Levallois technique in this assemblage (Fig. 1.6a and b). Preferential and recurrent Levallois cores are abundant, and typical Levalloisian elements – including parallel Levallois flake and blade cores, Levallois points, flakes, and blades, and retouched

Fig. 1.5: Wezwar locality.

tools on the Levallois blanks – are present in Wezwar. Retouched tools are scarce, and several unretouched Levallois points have been collected from the concentration areas. The retouched tools are different from Zagros Mousterian. They lack heavily retouched edges. Tools like scrapers on Levallois flake, specifically convergent scrapers which are abundant among Zagros Mousterian assemblages, are totally absent from Wezwar. The high frequency of the use of the Levallois technique and the infrequent appearance of retouched tools at Wezwar are reminiscent of several Middle Palaeolithic sites from the Levant, like Kebara Cave (Meignen 2019). Frequent use of the Levallois technique has been reported from the sites in the interior of the Iranian Plateau as well. In Holabad and Qal'eh Gushe around Kashan (Heydari-Guran and Ghasidian 2021), the Middle Palaeolithic assemblages contain abundant Levallois pieces with few retouched tools, but no Mousterian-like tools. However, the Middle Palaeolithic assemblages in Mirak and the sites nearby in the Semnan district have been assigned to the Mousterian techno-complex (Vahdati Nasab *et al.* 2019). The Zagros Mousterian is found in association with Neanderthal physical remains in Shanidar and in Bawa Yawan Rock shelter (Solecki 1963; Heydari-Guran *et al.* 2021). However, it has been argued that the knappers of the Middle Palaeolithic period found in the Iranian Central Plateau could be *Homo sapiens* coming from the south (Heydari-Guran and Ghasidian 2021). Both Kiyasar 1 and Wezwar are located at

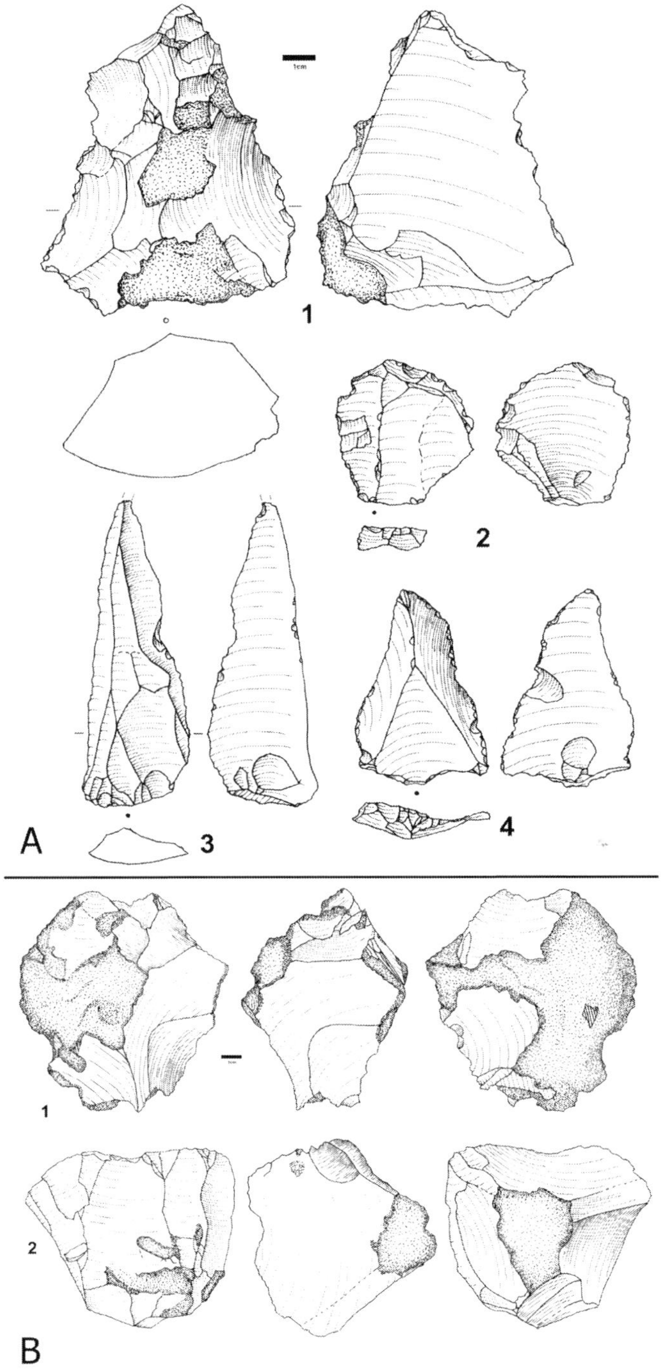

Fig. 1.6: Lithic artifacts from Wezwar. A: 1. Levallois flake, 2. Retouched flake, 3 and 4. Levallois points. B: 1. Levallois flake core, 2. Levallois flake and blade core.

the strategic Kiyasar path (Galougah-Damghan road), which connected the interior of the Iranian Central Plateau and the SCC. The presence of these assemblages favors the hypothesis of the importance of north–south passes through the Alborz for the expansion of the Late Pleistocene hominins (i.e. *Homo sapiens*) across the Iranian Plateau towards north and east.

Shoupari Cave (Plate 1.3)

Approximately 45 km west of the Kiyasar 1 Rock Shelter is Shoupari Cave (36°36′38.1″N, 53°24′47.6″E), in the Rostamkola district of the eastern SCC. Access to the cave is complicated by its small entrance and the density of the Hyrcanian Forest. A large river called the Nekaroud flows nearby, ca. 500 m down the slopes of the escarpment where Shoupari is formed. Shoupari is a large karstic cave ca. 78 m deep with a small entrance (3 m wide and 1.5 m high) that makes the cave very dark (Plate 1.3). Looters' pits are evident in several areas of the cave. Neolithic and more recent historical pottery sherds were scattered among the contents of the pits. The first season of excavation in 2022 has been carried out close to the entrance and consisted of cleaning and widening one of these pits (Ramzanpour 2022). In this pit, the surface Layers 1 and Neolithic Layer 2 are 120 cm deep, and in parts disturbed. From the depth of ca. 120 cm, the ground appeared undisturbed. Layer 3 contains *in-situ* Palaeolithic material culture, mainly lithic artifacts. Palaeolithic materials continue in Layers 4 and 5. The excavation stopped at Layer 5 at the depth of 277 cm and did not reach the bedrock yet.

Nearly all lithic artifacts found at Shoupari were made of grey chert nodules formed in the limestone bed from the cave wall. A small number of lithics were made of high-quality light brown or grey chert sourced in the Behshahr outcrop (Heydari [Guran] 2004). Most of the lithic artifacts were found in Layers 3 and 5, while Layer 4 was nearly empty of lithics and yielded few faunal remains. This indicated two separate occupational episodes.

Lithic techno-typological analysis documents Levallois flakes and cores (Fig. 1.7a and b). Retouched tools are very few, and mostly include retouched flakes, as well as a truncated facetted and an end scraper.

The Shoupari assemblage is entirely flake oriented with a small number of parallel shaped blanks including blades. Nearly 60% of the flakes are core preparation and decortication flakes indicating on-site tool making from the available raw material in the cave. These flakes mostly removed the cortex for reaching the high-quality chert nodules embedded in the limestone stuck to the cave wall. This is very surprising given the dark cave interior and the need for adequate light for knapping. Alternatively, the cave may have been a dumping area.

The presence of Levallois, centripetal, and platform cores together in the same assemblage is interesting. This issue, along with some of the tools (truncated faceted and end scraper), suggest the presence of both Middle and Upper Palaeolithic technologies. In general, the Shoupari lithic assemblage are different and at odds

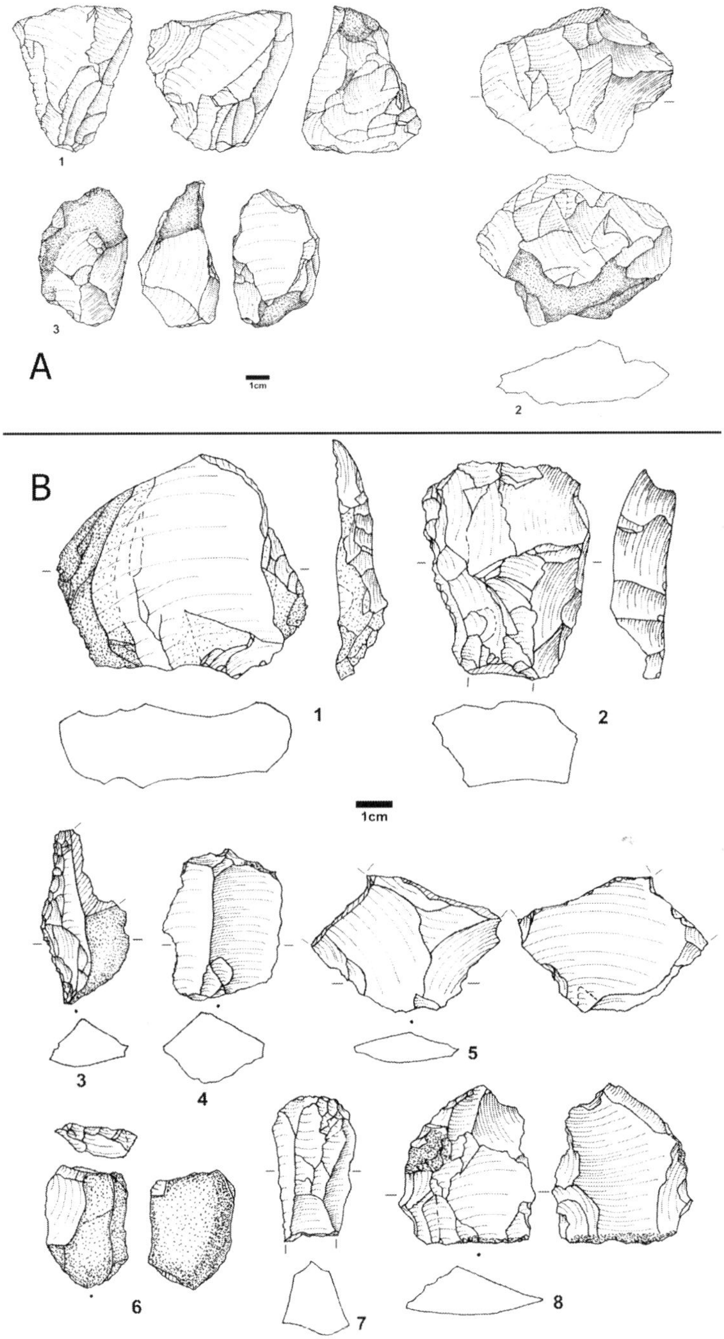

Fig. 1.7: Lithic artifacts from Shoupari Cave. A: 1. Platform core with parallel negatives, 2. Levallois core, 3. Levallois preferential core. B: 1. Levallois flake, 2. Core tablet, 3. Retouched elongated flake, 4. Truncated blade, 5. Levallois flake, 6 and 7. End scrapers, 8. Truncated facetted.

with what is known from other parts of the Iranian Plateau, including the Zagros region and the Iranian Central Plateau, in terms of the period they represent. The collection cannot be attributed to a specific Palaeolithic period. Shoupari bears no affinities to any collection in the SCC including Keyaram, Kiyasar 1, or Wezwar. This might be partially due to the specific raw material. In all, Shoupari lithics are unique and important, and may open a new chapter in the Palaeolithic studies of Iran. Meanwhile, we are studying the absolute dates of samples from this cave, which will be critical.

Survey in the Central Alborz Mountains

Recently, we have begun to survey the Central Alborz region, particularly the Telar River basin drainage system. So far, only one cave site in Savadkouh Region yielded Palaeolithic data.

Liben Cave (Plate 1.4, 1.5)

Liben Cave (36°07′41.5″N, 53°10′01.5″E) is located in the Telar River basin drainage system in the northern foothills of the Central Alborz Mountains. The cave is located 950 m above sea level in the heart of Caspian Hyrcanian mixed forests in the Savadkouh Region. The Kaselian River and a permanent spring flows ca. 100 m down the slopes from Liben. It seems that the stone raw materials had been obtained from this river, as we observed some silicified river stones in the Kaselian River. This karstic cave is around 127 m deep, with the entrance of 6 m towards the northeast, formed along a vertical fault in Alvat Mountain (Plates 1.4 and 1.5). Unfortunately, looters' excavations damaged a large part of the cave close to the entrance and uncovered a historical structure of two chambers ca. 4 × 4 m and 3 m deep (Plate 1.5b). This structure had already damaged Palaeolithic sediments in the historical period. Islamic pottery sherds are scattered around it.

In the entrance and near the dripline was a large looters' pit with Pleistocene sediments piled close by. In these sediments, numerous pieces of lithics and fauna are found. Preliminary study of the fauna documents the remains of cave bear (*Ursus deningeri kudarensis*) (Plate 1.6), Hyrcanian red deer, wild boar, and *Capra* species.

The Liben Cave lithic assemblage is flake oriented with some flakes with centripetal negative scars (Fig. 1.8). Tools are mostly retouched flakes. Triangle points with abrupt truncated base are also among the tools. Preliminary techno-typological study of the lithics documents an industry with strong local characteristics that differentiate it from what is known elsewhere of the Iranian Palaeolithic. Liben shares few similarities with SCC Palaeolithic sites including Keyaram (Middle Palaeolithic) (McBurney 1964), Garm Roud 2 (Upper Palaeolithic) (Berillon *et al.* 2007), and Kiyasar 1 (Middle–Upper Palaeolithic) (Ghasidian *et al.* 2020). Based on the presence of centripetal flakes and laminar products, Liben is a promising site in reconstructing Middle Palaeolithic to the Late Palaeolithic sequence. Due to the absence of any other known Palaeolithic site in the Telar Basin, the absolute dating

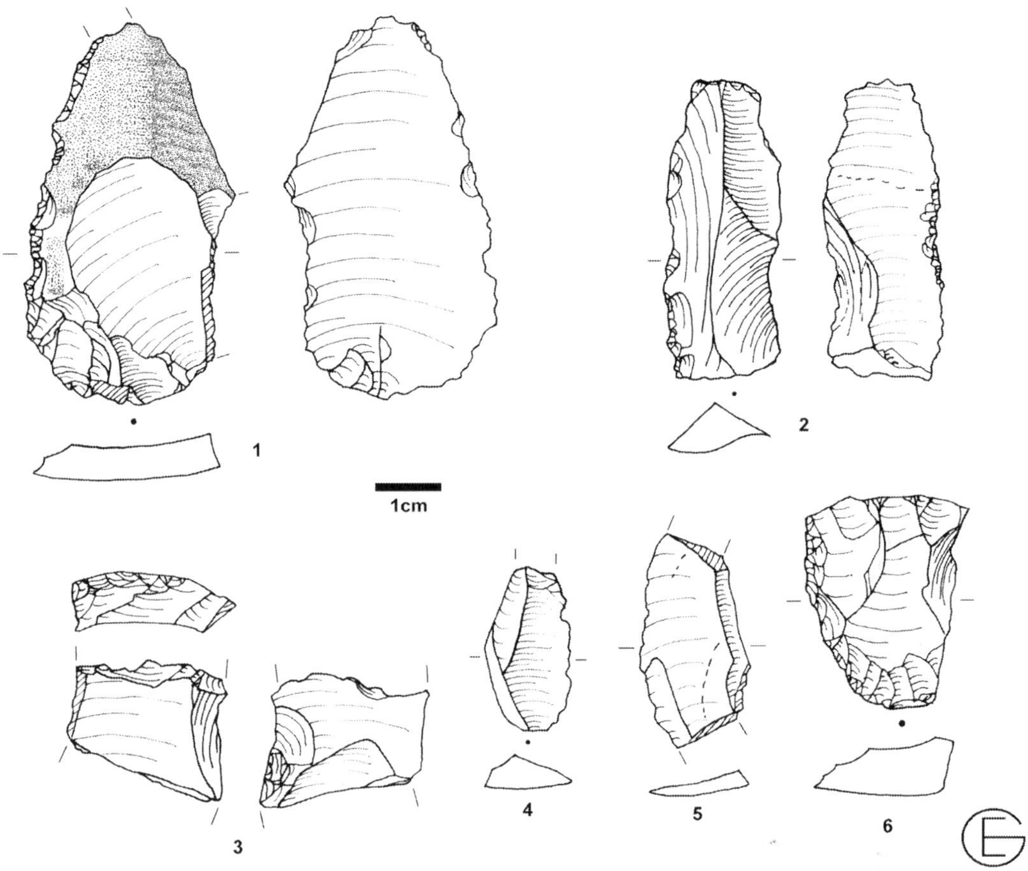

Fig. 1.8: Liben lithic artifacts. 1. Retouched flake, 2. Retouched Levallois blade, 3. End scraper, 4. Blade, 5. Elongated flake, 6. Retouched core preparation flake.

of the Palaeolithic layers of Liben and stratified data are needed to reconstruct settlement pattern and cultural traits. A combination of these data will form the foundation for identifying the Palaeolithic period in Telar Basin as one of the most important north–south corridors connecting Central Iranian Plateau to the SCC and the lands beyond including Central Asia.

Discussion and conclusion

The expansion of hominin groups is highly dependent on the geographical distribution of resources and the corridors connecting these resources (Heydari-Guran 2014). Climatic conditions have an impact on these corridors for hominin migrations and dispersals (Hublin 1998; Dennell 2017). As Neanderthals moved from Europe towards the east, probably one of the first areas that Neanderthals encountered was the Caucasus and the Alborz Mountain regions.

The unique location of the bio-geographical corridor of the SCC gave the region its mild climate, dense vegetation, rich water resources, marine and terrestrial food resources even during glacial periods, along with a large number of caves and rock shelters. These factors make this region attractive for different hominin groups (Ghasidian *et al.* 2023). The High Alborz Mountains, located south of this area, are hard to cross and effectively separates the interior of the Iranian Plateau from the north. However, several north–south corridors, such as the Telar Valley and the Kiyasar Path, may have acted as dispersal corridors allowing the newcomers (i.e. *Homo sapiens*) to arrive from the south.

Despite the fluctuations of the Caspian Sea level, which takes many parts of the coastal flat areas out of our Palaeolithic research, this area is still considered as one of the most important areas in the study of hominin population dynamics during the Pleistocene. During the glacial periods (e.g. MIS 4) the regression of the Caspian Sea (Yanina 2014; Krijgsman *et al.* 2019), exposed vast areas and provided opportunities for larger settlements and a corridor of expansion for hominins. Undoubtedly, unlike the interior of the Iranian Plateau, the abundant water resources of permanent rivers and the rich terrestrial and aquatic food resources were available throughout the year in the SCC. This area, with numerous caves and rock shelters that were far above sea level fluctuations, served as a refugium for hominin groups during the glacial periods (Dennell 2017). This issue is important regarding possible connections between hominin species that entered from the west and east of this passage and probably admixed with each other. The SCC could serve as a meeting point for different hominin species; Neanderthals from west, *Homo sapiens* from south, and other species (perhaps Denisovans) from east.

The goal of the SCC research project is to gain an understanding of the complex nature and dynamics of hominin groups during the Pleistocene in this part of Eurasia and is in the initial stage. The data obtained so far show the complexity of settlement patterns and dynamics of hominins in this area. This research tries to present a model for Pleistocene population dynamics with an eye toward relationships between different hominin groups from the Caucasus at the crossroads of Europe and Asia through the SCC, with dual role of expansion corridor and settlement, towards Central Asia.

To discover this connection, the first stage of the research was to study lithics from Keyaram Cave, although we decided not to renew the excavation at this site due to its disturbed nature and lack of intact sediments for Palaeolithic sequence reconstruction. We then conducted systematic surveys mostly in the eastern and central parts of the Alborz Mountains around 200 km west of Keyaram, where according to the observations by Coon (1957) there were numerous caves and rock shelters. Techno-typological analysis of the lithics and comparison to the Palaeolithic sites from the Iranian Central Plateau and the Zagros is necessary to understand possible cultural exchange, and to track hominin migration routes. While McBurney pointed out the similarities of Keyaram lithics with the Zagros Mousterian and called it Mousterian Type B (McBurney 1964), our review of the Keyaram lithics and the collections obtained from our survey shows that the SCC lithics cannot be directly linked to known Palaeolithic assemblages including Zagros Mousterian for Middle Palaeolithic, Zagros Aurignacian, Baradostian, LaK or Rostamian (Solecki 1963; Dibble 1984; Olszewski and Dibble 1994; Ghasidian 2014; 2019) for the Upper Palaeolithic period.

Our investigations carried out in the SCC showed that this area has great potential for the reconstruction of hominin ecological and settlement patterns during the Pleistocene. The location and geography of the SCC facilitate its important role in hominin dispersals from the Caucasus to Central Asia and Siberia. However, conducting research in this area is challenging. Steep northern slopes of Alborz Mountains, the high rate of sedimentation in these areas, and dense vegetation made access to the caves and rock shelters difficult. The unique characteristics of the lithics in this area adds to the complicated picture of the SCC Palaeolithic. We are just beginning to define the taxonomy of Palaeolithic artifacts of the SCC. More stratified data associated with absolute dating is essential for describing techno-complexes and their chronology in this under-explored area of the Iranian Plateau.

Acknowledgments

This chapter is dedicated to the memory of Masoumeh Moradian, our young and active colleague and friend in Mazandaran. We are grateful to the Iranian Cultural Heritage, Handicraft and Tourism Organization in Mazandaran. Many thanks go to the Museum of Archaeology and Anthropology of the University of Cambridge for access to the Keyaram lithic assemblage. Many people have assisted us in our fieldwork; Ali Abedi, Faramarz Azizi, Hadi Amirkhanlou, Shapour Ebrahimnejad, Zahra Gorzin, Pouya Gholami, Nemat Hariri, Akbar Imani, Ramzan Isapour, Neda Jalali, Solaleh Nopour, Hadi Norouzaghaei, Sareh Peyman, Nasrin Rahnama, Kiyan Tavakoli, and the Sanjabi Esasi and Zahedi Galougahi families. This research is funded by German Research Foundation (DFG) grant no. 414357211 to Elham Ghasidian.

Notes

1 *Ghost lineage* is the ancestral population of all non-Africans that admixed with Neanderthals that has left no fossil evidence but genomic evidence (Malaspinas *et al.* 2016)

2 Marine isotope stages (MIS) or oxygen isotope stages are alternating cold and warm climate episodes. The database uses core drillings from different parts of the world to reconstruct past climate and is used widely in archaeology.

3 Levallois is a well-known technique from the Middle Paleolithic Period. It involves centripetal preparation of a stone by striking flakes off the edges to shape a turtle shell like core, which is flat on the bottom and humped on the top. In this stage the knapper can apply a controlled force to get an ideal form of a flat and thin flake. This flake could be used as is or retouched to be a tool (see Brantingham and Kuhn 2001).

4 *Chaîne opératoire* methodology is the step-by-step study of the lithics from raw material acquisition to tool use and discard. In this method, the plan for shaping out the raw material and later use is in the mind of the knapper, and is regarded as an important element (see Inizan *et al.* 1999).

Bibliography

Abolfathi, M., Vahdati Nasab, H., Fazeli Nashli, H., Khaneghah, A.A., Berillon, G. and Chevrier, B. (2015) Techno-typological analysis of lithic assemblages of upper paleolithic open air site of Garm Rud 2, Baliran, Amol, Mazandaran. *Quaternary Journal of Iran (Iranqua)*, 1 (1), 15–27.

Bae, C.J., Douka, K., and Petraglia, P. (2017) On the Origin of Modern Humans: Asian Perspectives. *Science* 358 (6368), eaai9067.

Berillon, G., Khaneghah, A.A., Antoine, P., Bahain, J.J., Chevrier, B., Zeitoun, V., Aminzadeh, N., Beheshti, M., Chanzanagh, H.E. and Nochadi, S. (2007) Discovery of new open-air Paleolithic localities in Central Alborz, Northern Iran. *Journal of Human Evolution*, 52 (4), 380–387.

Berillon, G., Khaneghah, A.A., Chevrier, B., Auguste, P., Zeitoun, V., Beheshti, M., Nochadi, S., Ebadollahi Chanzanagh, H., Ramirez Rozzi, F., Bahain, J-J., Antoine, P. and Vercoutere, C. (2009) Late Pleistocene Prehistory in Central Alborz: Preliminary results of the French and Iranian Palaeoanthropological Programme 2006 on the Excavation of Garm Roud 2 (Amol, Mazandaran). In M. Otte, F. Biglari and J. Jaubert, eds. *Iran Paleolithic/ Le Paléolithique d'Iran*. BAR International series: 101–108.

Biglari, F. and Jahani, V. (2011) The Pleistocene Human Settlement in Gilan, Southwest Caspian Sea: Recent Research. *Eurasian Prehistory* 8 (1–2), 3–28.

Biglari, F., Heydari-Guran, S., and Shidrang, S. (2006) Ganj Par: The First Evidence for Lower Paleolithic Occupation in the Southern Caspian Basin, Iran. *Antiquity* 78 (302), 160–168.

Biglari, F., Javeri, M., Mashkour, M., Yazdi, M., Shidrang, S., Tenberg, M., Taheri, K., and Darvish, J. (2009) Test Excavations at the Middle Paleolithic Sites of Qaleh Bozi, Southwest of Central Iran, A Preliminary Report. In M. Otte, F. Biglari, and J. Jaubert (eds) *Iran Paleolithic*, 29–38. Oxford, BAR Publishing.

Boyle, K., Gamble, C., and Bar-Yosef, O. (2010) *The Upper Palaeolithic Revolution in Global Perspective*. Cambridge, McDonald Institute for Archaeological Research.

Brantingham, P.J. and Kuhn, S.L. (2001) Constraints on Levallois Core Technology: A Mathematical Model. *Journal of Archaeological Science* 28 (7), 747–761.

Coon, C.S. (1951) *Cave Exploration in Iran 1949*. Museum Monographs, the University Museum. Philadelphia, University of Pennsylvania.

Coon, C.S. (1957) *The Seven Caves*. New York, Knopf.

Dennell, R. (2017) Human Colonization of Asia in the Late Pleistocene: The History of an Invasive Species. *Current Anthropology* 58 (S17), S383–S396.

Dibble, H.L. (1984) The Mousterian industry from Bisitun cave (Iran). *Paléorient* 10 (2), 23–34.

Dibble, H.L. and Holdaway, S.J. (1993) The Middle Paleolithic Industries of Warwasi. *The Paleolithic Prehistory of the Zagros-Taurus* 29, 75–99.

Fu, Q., Li, H., Moorjani, P., Jay, F., Slepchenko, S., Bondarev, A.A., Johnson, P., Aximu-Petri, A., Prüfer, K., Filippo, C. de., Meyer, M., Zwyns, N., Salazar-Garcia, D., Kusmin, Y., Keates, S., Kosintsev, P., Razhev, D., Richards, M., Periston, N., Lackmann, M., Douka, K. Higham, T., Slatkin, M., Hublin, J.-J., Reich, D., Kelso, J., Viola, T.B., and Pääbo, S. (2014) Genome Sequence of a 45,000-year-old Modern Human from Western Siberia. *Nature* 514 (7523), 445–449.

Ghasidian, E. (2014) *Early Upper Palaeolithic Occupation at the Ghār-e Boof Cave, A Reconstruction of Cultural Traditions in Southern Zagros Mountains of Iran*. Tübingen, Kerns Verlag.

Ghasidian, E. (2018) In search of the oldest inhabitants of Mazandaran. Unpublished report to Iranian Centre for Archaeological Research, Tehran, Iran.

Ghasidian, E. (2019) Rethinking the Upper Palaeolithic of the Zagros Mountains. *PaleoAnthropology*, 240–310.

Ghasidian, E., Heydari-Guran, S. and Lahr, M.M. (2019) Upper Paleolithic cultural diversity in the Iranian Zagros Mountains and the Expansion of Modern Humans into Eurasia. *Journal of Human Evolution* 132, 101–118.

Ghasidian, E., Ramzanpour, H., Moradian, M., and Heydari-Guran, S. (2020) Kiyasar 1 Rockshelter, In Search for Hominin Settlements in Mazandaran. *History and Archaeology of Mazandaran* 1 (2) (in Persian).

Ghasidian, E., Kafash, A., Kehl, M., Yousefi, M. and Heydari-Guran, S. (2023) Modelling Neanderthals' dispersal routes from Caucasus towards East. *PLOS One* 18 (2), e0281978.
Grün, R. and Stringer, C. (2000) ESR and U-series Analyses of Dental Material from Tabun C1. *Journal of Human Evolution* 39, 601–612.
Hajdinjak, M., Fu, Q., Hübner, A., Petr, M., Mafessoni, F., Grote, S., Skoglund, P., Narasimham, V., Rougier, H., Crevecoeur, I., Semal, P., Soressi, M., Talamo, S., Hublin, J.-J., Gušic, I., Kučan, Ž., Rudan, P., Golovanova, L., Doronichev., V., Posth, C., Krause, J., Korlević, P., Nagel, S., Nickel, B., Slatkin, M., Patterson, N., Reich., D., Prüfer, K., Meyer, M., Pääbo, S., and Kelso, J. (2018) Reconstructing the Genetic History of Late Neanderthals. *Nature* 555 (7698), 652–656.
Harvati, K. (2010) Neanderthals. *Evolution: Education and Outreach* 3 (3), 367–376.
Heydari [Guran], S. (2004) Stone Raw Material Sources in Iran: Some Case Studies. In T. Stollner, R. Slotta, and A. Vatandoust (eds) *Persian Antique Splendor, Mining Crafts and Archaeology in Ancient Iran*, 124–129. Bochum, Deutsches Bergbau-Museum.
Heydari-Guran, S. (2014) *Paleolithic Landscapes of Iran*. Oxford, BAR Publishing.
Heydari-Guran, S. and Ghasidian, E. (2017) The MUP Zagros Project: Tracking the Middle–Upper Palaeolithic Transition in the Kermanshah Region, West-central Zagros, Iran. *Antiquity* 91 (355), e2.
Heydari-Guran, S. and Ghasidian, E. (2020) Late Pleistocene hominin settlement patterns and population dynamics in the Zagros Mountains, Kermanshah Region. *Archaeological Research in Asia* 21, 00161.
Heydari-Guran, S. and Ghasidian, E. (2021) Consistency of the 'MIS 5 Humid Corridor Model' for the Dispersal of Early Homo sapiens into the Iranian Plateau. In A. Abar and J. Köhler (eds) *Pearls, Politics and Pistachios: Essays in Anthropology and Memories on the Occasion of Susan Pollock's 65th Birthday*, 219–237. Heidelberg, Propylaeum.
Heydari-Guran, S., Benazzi, S., Talamo, S., Ghasidian, E., Hariri, N., Oxilia, G., Asiabani, S., Azizi, R., Naderi, R., Safaierad, R., Hublin, J.-J., Foloey, R., and Lahr, M. (2021) The Discovery of *In Situ* Neanderthal Remains in the Bawa Yawan Rockshelter, West-Central Zagros Mountains, Kermanshah. *PLOS One* 16 (8), p.e0253708.
Hublin, J.-J. (1998) Climatic Changes, Paleogeography, and the Evolution of the Neanderthals. In T. Akazawa, K. Aoki, and O. Bar-Yosef (eds) *Neanderthals and Modern Humans in Western Asia*, 295–310. New York, Plenum Press.
Inizan, M.L., Reduron-Ballinger, M., Roche, H., and Tixier, J. (1999) *Technology and Terminology of Knapped Stone*. Nanterre, C.R.E.P.
Kehl, M., Vlaminck, S., Köhler, T., Laag, C., Christian, R., Tsukamoto, S., Frechen, M., Sumita, M., Schmincke, H.-U., and Khormali, F. (2021) Pleistocene Dynamics of Dust Accumulation and Soil Formation in the Southern Caspian Lowlands – New Insights from the Loess-Paleosol Sequence at Neka-Abelou, Northern Iran. *Quaternary Science Reviews* 253, 106774.
Kolobova, K.A., Roberts, R., Chabai, V., and Derevianko, A. (2020) Archaeological Evidence for Two Separate Dispersals of Neanderthals into Southern Siberia. *Proceedings of the National Academy of Sciences* 117, 2879.
Krause, J., Orlando, L., Serre, D., Viola, B., Prüfer, K., Richards, M., Hublin, J.-J., Hänni, C., Derevianko, A., and Pääbo, S. (2007) Neanderthals in Central Asia and Siberia. *Nature* 449, 902–904.
Krijgsman, W., Tesakov, A., Yanina, T., Lazarev, S., Danukalova, G., Van Baak, C.G.C., Agusti, J., Alçiçek, M. C., Aliyeva, E., Bista, D., Bruch, A., Büyükmeriç, Y., Bukshianidze, M., Flecker, R., Frolov, P., Hoyle, T.M., Jorissen, E.L., Kirchser, U., Koriche, S.A., Kroonenberg, S.B., Lordkipanidze, D., Oms, O., Rausch, L., Singarayer, J., Stoica, M., van de Velde, S., Titov, V.V., and Wesselingh, F.P. (2019) Quaternary Time Scales for the Pontocaspian Domain: Interbasinal Connectivity and Faunal Evolution. *Earth-Science Reviews* 188, 1–40.
Mahforouzi, A. (2003) Preliminary Report on the Survey and Excavation in Eastern Mazandaran (with appendices by S. Shidrang, S. Heydari-Guran, E. Ghasidian, R. Naderi and M. Mashkour). *Archaeological Reports 2*. Iranian Centre for Archaeological Research, Tehran (in Persian).
Malaspinas, A.-S., *et al.* (2016) A Genomic History of Aboriginal Australia. *Nature* 538 (7624), 207–214.

Marinova, E. *et al.* (2018) Pollen-derived Biomes in the Eastern Mediterranean–Black Sea–Caspian-Corridor. *Journal of Biogeography* 45 (2), 484–499.

McBurney, C.B.M. (1964) Preliminary Report on Stone Age Reconnaissance in North-Eastern Iran. *Proceedings of the Prehistoric Society* 30, 382–389.

McBurney, C.B.M. (1968) The Cave of Ali Tappeh and the Epipalaeolithic in NE Iran. *Proceedings of the Prehistoric Society* 34, 385–413.

Meignen, L. (2019) The Mousterian lithic assemblages from Kebara Cave. In L. Meignen and O. Bar-Yosef (eds) *Kebara Cave, Mt. Carmel, Israel, the Middle and Upper Paleolithic Archaeology Part II*, 1–126. American School of Prehistoric Research Bulletins 51. Cambridge, Peabody Museum Press.

Olszewski, D.I. and Dibble, H.L. (1994) The Zagros Aurignacian. *Current Anthropology* 35 (1), 68–75.

Ramzanpour, H. (2020) Techno-typological analysis of Paleolithic artefacts from the Southeastern Caspian Sea based on attribute and chaînes opératoire. Ph.D. dissertation. Azad Islamic University, Tehran (in Persian).

Ramzanpour, H. (2022) *Preliminary Report on the First Season of Excavation at Shoupari Cave*. Unpublished Report to Iranian Centre for Archaeological Research, Tehran (in Persian).

Smith, P.E.L. (1986) *Paleolithic archaeology in Iran*. The American Institute of Iranian Studies Monograph. Philadelphia, The University Museum, University of Pennsylvania.

Solecki, R.S. (1963) Prehistory in Shanidar Valley, Northern Iraq: Fresh insights into Near Eastern prehistory from the Middle Paleolithic to the Proto-Neolithic are obtained. *Science* 139 (3551), 179–193.

Stringer, C. and Hublin, J.-J. (1999) New Age Estimates for the Swanscombe Hominid, and Their Significance for Human Evolution. *Journal of Human Evolution* 37, 873–877.

Tostevin, G.B. (2012) *Seeing Lithics: A Middle-Range Theory for Testing for Cultural Transmission in the Pleistocene*. American School of Prehistoric Research Monograph Series. Oxford and Cambridge, Peabody Museum and Oxbow Books.

Vahdati Nasab, H. (2009) Report on the Second Season of Paleolithic Survey into Gilan Province. *Archaeological Research Modarres* 1 (2) (in Persian).

Vahdati Nasab, H., Berillon, G., Jamet, G., Hashemi, M., Khaksar, S., Anvari, Z., Guérin, G., Heydari, M., Kharazian, M.A., Puaud, S., Bonilauri, S., Zeitoun, V., Sévêque, N., Darvishi Khatooni, J., and Asgari Khaneghah, A. (2019) The Open-air Paleolithic Site of Mirak, Northern Edge of the Iranian Central Desert (Semnan, Iran): Evidence of Repeated Human Occupations During the Late Pleistocene. *Comptes Rendus Palevol* 18 (4), 465–478.

Vahdati Nasab, H., Nikzad, M., Jayez, M., Hashemi, M., Knapp, Z., Sykes, N., Khalili, Z., Farima, B., Nasab, D., and Olszewski, D., *et al.* (2020) Komishan Cave: A Mesolithic and Later Settlement on the Southeastern Shore of the Caspian Sea, Iran. *Ancient Near Eastern Studies* 57, 97–125.

Vahdati Nasab, H. and Hashemi, M. (2016) Playas and Middle Paleolithic Settlement of the Iranian Central Desert: The Discovery of the Chah-e Jam Middle Paleolithic Site. *Quaternary International* 408, 140–152.

Vahdati Nasab, H., Clark, G.A., and Torkamandi, S. (2013) Late Pleistocene Dispersal Corridors Across the Iranian Plateau: A Case Study from Mirak, a Middle Paleolithic Site on the Northern Edge of the Iranian Central Desert (Dasht-e Kavir). *Quaternary International* 300, 267–281.

Vlaminck, S., Kehl, M., Christian, R., Oliver, S.F., Lauer, T., Lehndorff, E., Frechen, M., and Khormali (2018) Late Pleistocene dust dynamics and pedogenesis in Southern Eurasia – Detailed insights from the loess profile Toshan (NE Iran). *Quaternary Science Reviews* 180, 75–95.

Yanina, T. (2014) The Ponto-Caspian region: Environmental Consequences of Climate Change During the Late Pleistocene. *Quaternary International* 345, 88–99.

Yanina, T., Sorokin, V., Bezrodnykh, Y. and Romanyuk, B. (2018) Late Pleistocene Climatic Events Reflected in the Caspian Sea Geological History (Based on Drilling Data). *Quaternary International* 465, 130–141.

Chapter 2 Prologue

A history of excavations at Shahr-i Sokhta – The Burnt City, a UNESCO World Heritage site

The site of Shahr-i Sokhta (meaning 'Burned City' in Farsi) is located in southeastern Iran, south of the city of Zabol in the province of Sistan and Baluchistan and in the southern part of the basin of Helmand/Hirmand River. One of the major urban centers that developed in the late 4th millennium BCE in southeastern Iran, Shahr-i Sokhta was first discovered by Sir Aurel Stein in the 1920s but had to wait until 1967 to be excavated by a team of Italian archaeologists led by Maurizo Tosi from IsMEO (now IsIAO). Tosi and his team excavated Shahr-i Sokhta from 1967 until 1978 when the Islamic Revolution in Iran halted all international archaeology projects. Under the direction of S.M.S. Sajjadi, an Iranian team of archaeologists from the Iranian Cultural Heritage Organization began in 1997 a new round of archaeological investigations, still ongoing, at the site. One of the most studied archaeological sites in this part of the country (Sajjadi *et al.* 2003), Shahr-i Sokhta preserves the extensive remains of a mud-brick urban center. In addition to residential areas, the site also consists of an extramural cemetery, pottery workshop area, lithic industry area, and metal working area (Tosi *et al.* 1984).

The results from archaeological investigations demonstrate that by the end of the Chalcolithic period in southern Iran many of the smaller settlements in this region were abandoned and their number reduced, but at the same time there was a growth in the size and population of sites including Susa, Shahr-i Sokhta, and Malyan. Human communities began to condense, leading to the formation of urban-scale settlements (Sumner 2003). This process continued and accelerated during the Early Bronze Age.

In Sistan, southeastern Iran, Shahr-i Sokhta grew from 10–15 ha in the late 4th millennium to about 120 ha in the mid-3rd millennium BCE, becoming one of the largest urban centers in the region. The rise of urban life in the region led to a surge in connectivity and created new inter-regional flows of goods, ideas, and people, in turn contributing to the development of a distinctive, material culture. The chapter contributed by **Sajjadi and Moradi** sheds new light on Shahr-i Sokhta's interconnections during this era. As it grew, the archaeological record at Shahr-i Sokhta shows increased connections to Pakistani Baluchistan, Central Asia, the Proto-Elamite culture in Southwestern Iran, and Southern Mesopotamia. Some scholars argue that Shahr-i Sokhta could represent 'the north-western cultural boundary of the Indus core area' (Cortesi *et al.* 2008). The spread of Shahr-i Sokhta-style objects in its immediate neighboring regions demonstrates that it had become a culturally dominant site in Southeastern Iran (Thornton 2012). Whether Shahr-i Sokhta's dominance was also political is a matter of further research. The rise of urban life also occasioned the rise of the countryside as it transformed to meet urban subsistence needs.

The discovery of a large workshop for lapis lazuli at Shahr-i Sokhta suggests that a monopoly on the lapis lazuli trade from its source in Afghanistan to Mesopotamia was the basis for the rise of Shahr-i Sokhta. Evidence of lapis lazuli and other semi-precious stones in large workshops and also rich graves in the cemetery of Shahr-i Sokhta indicated that people in Shahr-i Sokhta engaged in craft production (Tosi and Piperno 1973; Tosi *et al.* 1984). In areas related to workshops and manufacturing activities at Shahr-i Sokhta, archaeologists have uncovered numerous devices for record-keeping, control over storage, and tracking goods and commodities. These include stone and metal stamp seals, cylinder seals, clay sealings, clay and stone counters, clay discs, and tally disks. In addition, archaeologists had uncovered a Proto-Elamite tablet during 1970s excavations (Tosi *et al.* 1984), discussed in the following chapter.

Differential amounts of lapis lazuli in burials in the extramural cemetery at Shahr-i Sokhta provide evidence for social inequality and even possibly social stratification (Sajjadi *et al.* 2003). However, the hierarchical structure at Shahr-i Sokhta is not as crystal clear in the material culture as it was in the highly stratified societies of Early Dynastic Mesopotamia or the Old Kingdom Egypt (Pittman 2013). And while Shahr-i Sokhta demonstrates some important urban features such as administrative buildings, separate workshop areas and artisan neighborhoods, and residential areas, it lacks some other features such as public buildings, monumental structures, and city walls (Biscione 1979; Thornton 2012).

Shahr-i Sokhta started to decline in the last quarter of the 3rd millennium BCE. The cause of its decline is not clear but a number of hypotheses have been proposed. For example, it is argued that around 2300/2200 BCE a dramatic increase in seaborne trade led to the decrease of overland lapis lazuli trade, which in turn led to the decline of Shahr-i Sokhta by the end of the 3rd millennium BCE (Thornton 2012). The decline is also attributed to 'a crisis in the structure of urban social organization and hierarchy' (Pittman 2013), and others argue that Shahr-i Sokhta became abandoned in the early 2nd millennium BCE due to climate and water course changes. It seems that urban life at Shahr-i Sokhta ended at around 1800 BCE (Tosi *et al.* 1984).

In 2014, Shahr-i Sokhta was inscribed in the list of UNESCO World Heritage sites based on three criteria: 1) it is an urban center that represents a transitional period from village to an urban life with major socio-cultural and economic developments in the late Chalcolithic through the Early Bronze Age; 2) as an urban center it provides plenty of evidence for interregional contacts with other contemporary urban centers in the form of metal objects, stone vessels, gems and pottery, and lapis lazuli (Shahr-i Sokhta was demonstrably in contact with major complex societies of the time such as Southern Mesopotamia and Southwest Iran, the Indus Valley, the southern shores of the Persian Gulf, the shores of the Oman Sea, and Central Asian societies); and 3) Shahr-i Sokhta also provides a great example of urban planning with specialized areas for residential mud-brick structures, separate cemetery, and workshop areas, all of which indicate the existence of urban organization and management.

In the following chapter, Sajjadi and Moradi provide information about an important and newly discovered Proto-Elamite tablet from Shahr-i Sokhta and also shed more light on the inter-regional connections of the city.

Bibliography

Biscione, R. (1979) The Burnt Building of Period Shahr-i Sokhta IV. An Attempt of Functional Analysis from the Distribution of Pottery Types. In G. Gnoli, G. and A. Rossi (eds) *Iranica,* 291–306. Naples, Instituto Universitario Orientale.

Cortesi, E., Tosi, M., Lazzari, A., and Vidale, M. (2008) Cultural Relationships Beyond the Iranian Plateau: The Helmand Civilization, Baluchistan and the Indus Valley in the 3rd millennium BCE. *Paléorient* 34 (2), 5–35.

Pittman, H. (2013) New Evidence for Interaction between the Iranian Plateau and the Indus Valley: Seals and Sealings from Konar Sandal South. In S.A. Abraham, P. Gullapalli, T. Raczek, U. Rizvi (eds) *Connections and Complexity New Approaches to the Archaeology of South Asia*, 63–86. New York, Routledge.

Sajjadi, S.M.S., Foruzanfar, F., Shirazi, R., and Baghestani, S. (2003) Excavations at Shahr-i Sokhta. First Preliminary Report on the Excavation of the Graveyard 1997–2000. *Iran* 41, 21–97.

Sumner, W.M. (2003) *Early Urban Life in the Land of Anshan: Excavations at Tal-e Malyan in the Highlands of Iran.* Philadelphia, University Museum of Archaeology.

Thornton, C.P. (2012) Iran. In D.T. Potts (ed.) *A Companion to the Archaeology of the Ancient Near East*, 596–606. Oxford, Wiley-Blackwell.

Tosi, M. and Piperno, M. (1973) Lithic Technology Behind the Ancient Lapis Lazuli Trade. *Expedition* 16, 15–23.

Tosi, M., Pracchia, S., and Macchiarelli, R. (1984) IRAN: The Joint ICAR/IsMEO Delivering Program: A Constrained Return to Shahr-i Sokhta. *East and West* 34, 466–482.

Chapter 2

Shahr-i Sokhta 2021: Excavation at Area XID

Seyyed Mansur Seyyed Sajjadi and Hossein Moradi

Abstract

After a hiatus of more than 18 years, excavation at Shahr-i Sokhta, a Bronze Age site located in the southeast of Iran, resumed in November 2019 in the Eastern Residential Area of Shahr-i Sokhta (ERA) with excavation in area XDV (Rooms 88 and 88a). In the 2021 season, after the COVID cessation, Rooms 27 and 28 in XID were excavated down to virgin soil, revealing a total of 11 cultural and nine structural layers. The upper layers of Room 27 in XID related to the expansion phases of Sistan (Period II) dated to 2500–2800 BCE and include Layers 1–5, while the floor of Layer 5 forms a large room or courtyard 2 m wide and possibly 4 m long.

During these new excavations in the ERA, local materials were found alongside Proto-Elamite cylinder seal impressions, figurines, ear-shaped handle jars in the Jemdet Nasr style, and cultural materials of neighboring regions such as Southern Turkmenistan, Nal, Quetta, and Kerman, as well as a Proto-Elamite style tablet discovered in area XID, Layer 6–11, linking the Proto-Elamite period that existed in Sistan between 3300–2900 BCE with this structure.

In Layer 8, archaeologists found mudbricks of a deconstructed kiln coated with thick cream plaster and with three rectangular holes. It is important to note that not a single piece of beveled-rim bowl pottery was found in all excavated areas of Shahr-i Sokhta. Excavations in Rooms 27 and 28 revealed virgin soil at a depth of 510 cm from the base point at the edge of the trench, which appears to be the deepest point excavated throughout the ERA. The only painted buff-ware in Layer 11 has no parallel in the Shahr-i Sokhta pottery collection.

Introduction

Shahr-i Sokhta is an ancient Bronze Age site in southeastern Iran, located 57 km south of Zabol (Fig. 2.1). After more than 40 years of excavation (Tosi 1983; Sajjadi 2003; Sajjadi and Moradi 2017), archaeologists identified four cultural periods and 11 construction phases, extending from the second half of the 4th millennium BCE to the second half of the 3rd millennium BCE.

Efforts to illuminate the dark spots of Period I – the earliest settlement – at Shahr-i Sokhta are hampered by the 5 m of archaeological deposits above those of this period. Throughout the Sistan plain, Shahr-i Sokhta is the only area where we can access the early stages of the formation of the culture of the southern Helmand delta and the Sistan plain. Shahr-i Sokhta participated in two main interaction domains during the late 4th millennium BCE: Jemdet Nasr and southern Turkmenistan/Quetta valley. The former was part of a trans-regional system for trading goods and financial documents in western Asia that passed through a west–east strip.

Square X is located at the eastern side of the site (Fig. 2.1), the area had been the heart of the city, and indeed of the southern Helmand delta in Sistan, for more than 1000 years of occupation. Squares XIB (Room 88) and XDV (Room 88a) are separate spaces in the western part of the House of Stairs. The Square XDV (Room 88a) is located at the western edge of the Eastern Residential Area (ERA) and XID is located in the north of XIB on the other side of Street 1 (Plate 2.1; Table 2.3).

After the seventh excavation campaign at Shahr-i Sokhta in November 1975, carried out by the Italian Archaeological Mission in Iran under direction of M. Tosi (Amiet and Tosi 1978), the evidence for the beginning phase of settlement in Iranian Sistan was limited to a less than 20 m^2 trench at the ERA of Shahr-i Sokhta in areas XDW and XDV. In that excavation, the cultural material of Period I, pottery in particular, was collected only on the surface, and other kinds of materials including seals and seal impressions were collected only in excavations within the ERA. Moreover, in other parts of the site, including the Central Quarters west of the ERA on the other side of the central depression (Salvatori and Vidale 1997; Sajjadi and Moradi 2017), the Craftsmen's Quarter (squares EWK and EWL), and the Northern Residential Area or Monumental Area (Sajjadi and Moradi 2014), the absence of any stratified material earlier than Phase 7 (ca. 2700 BCE) has been confirmed by long time excavations. Recently, archaeological surveys around Shahr-i Sokhta have revealed five sites with pottery related to Period I (more Phase 9) (Moradi *et al.* 2022).

After an 18-year hiatus from excavations, in 1997 exploration at Shahr-i Sokhta was started again in the residential areas by the Iranian Archaeological expedition under direction of S.M.S. Sajjadi from the Iranian Center of Archaeological Research (ICAR) (Sajjadi and Moradi 2019, 717) (Plate 2.1). The new excavations at the ERA looked for more evidence of Period I and the formation phase of the site. Since November 2018, new excavations continue the research in the ERA in squares XIB, XDV, and XID. XIB and XID had previously been excavated down to layers related to Periods II–III

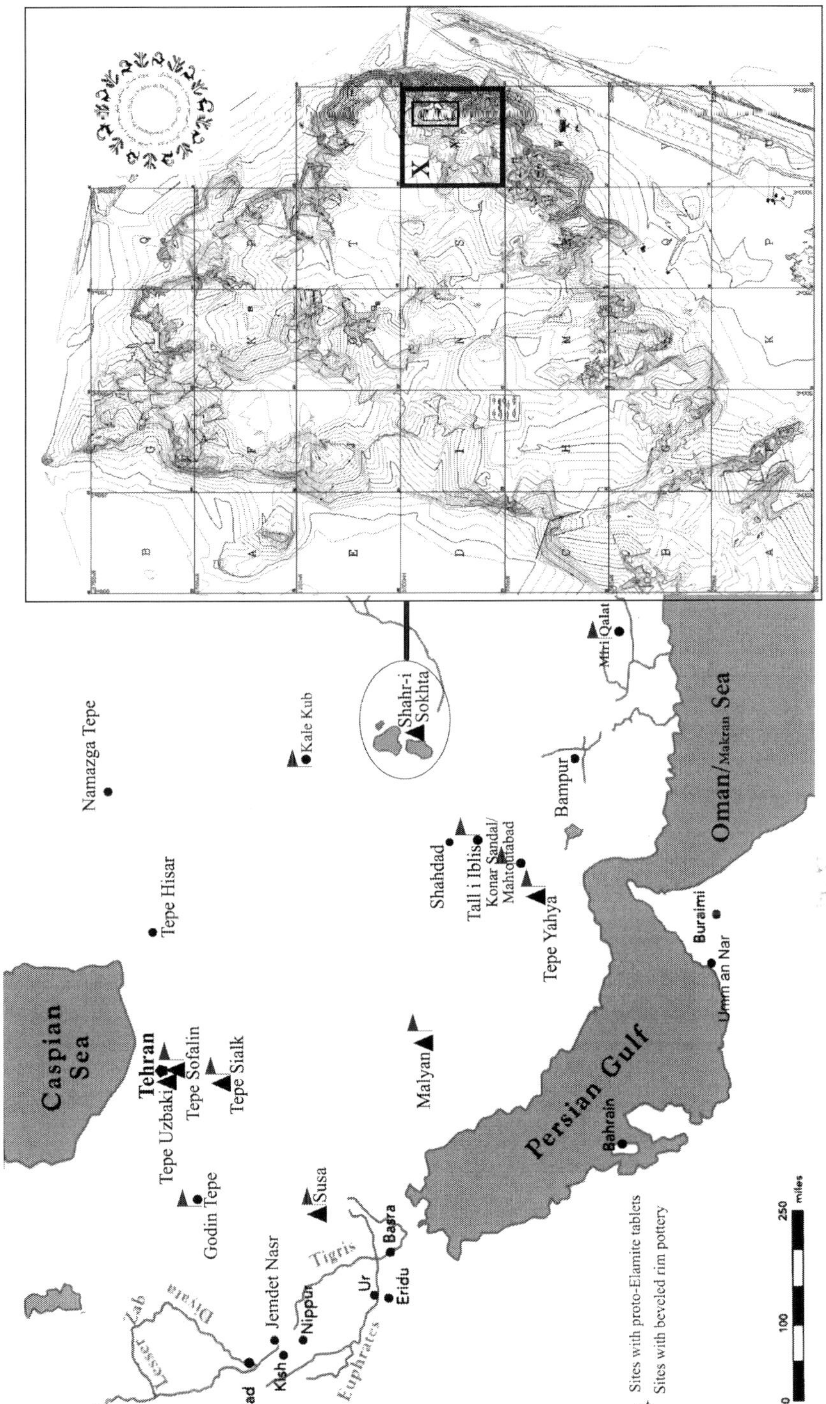

Fig. 2.1: The archaeological map of Iran and its neighbors in the late 4th millennium BCE and in the left the topographical map of Shahr-i Sokhta with focus on Square X and the Eastern Residential Area.

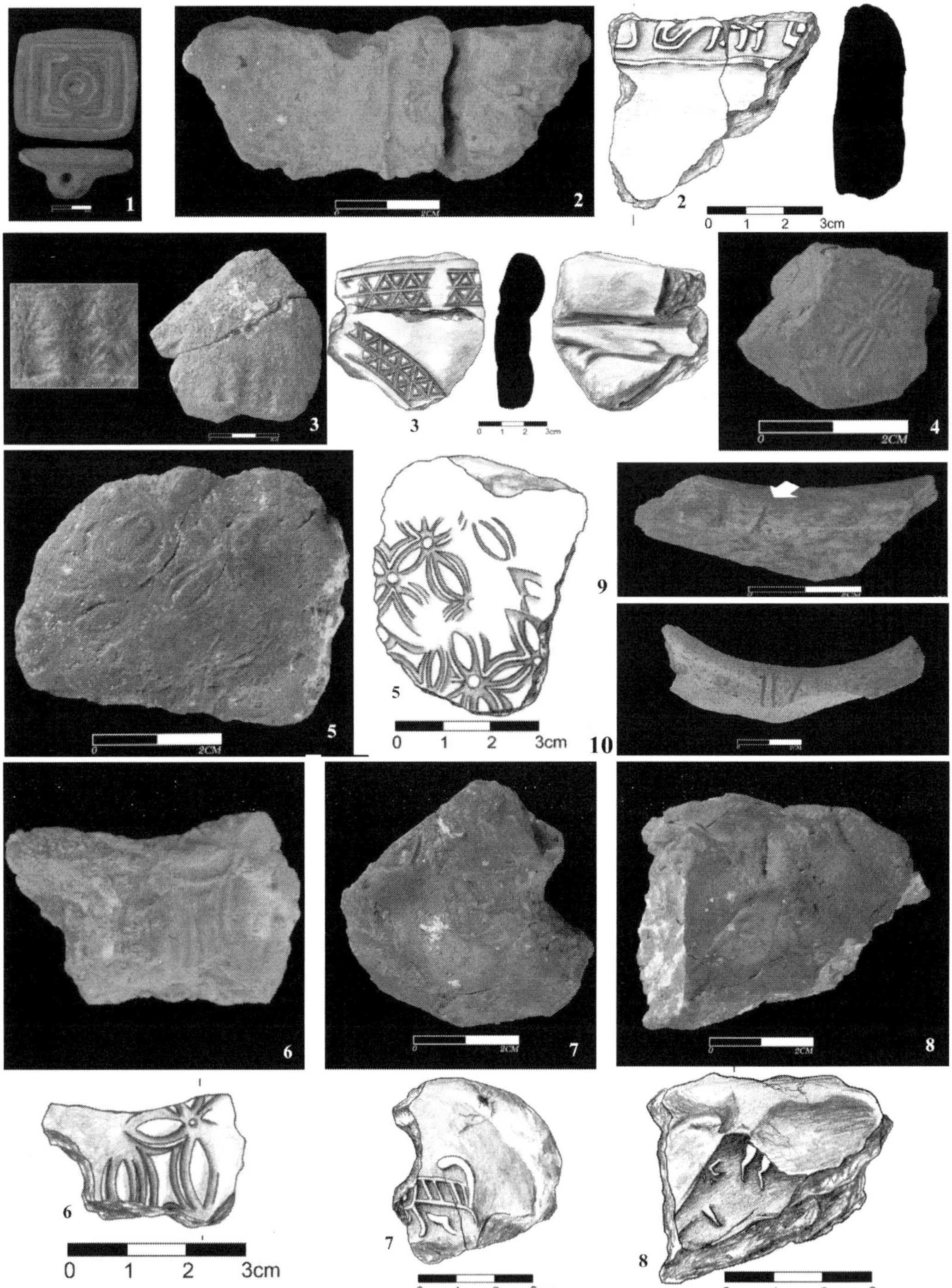

Fig. 2.2: Cylinder seal impressions found in Room 88 and 88a in the ERA.

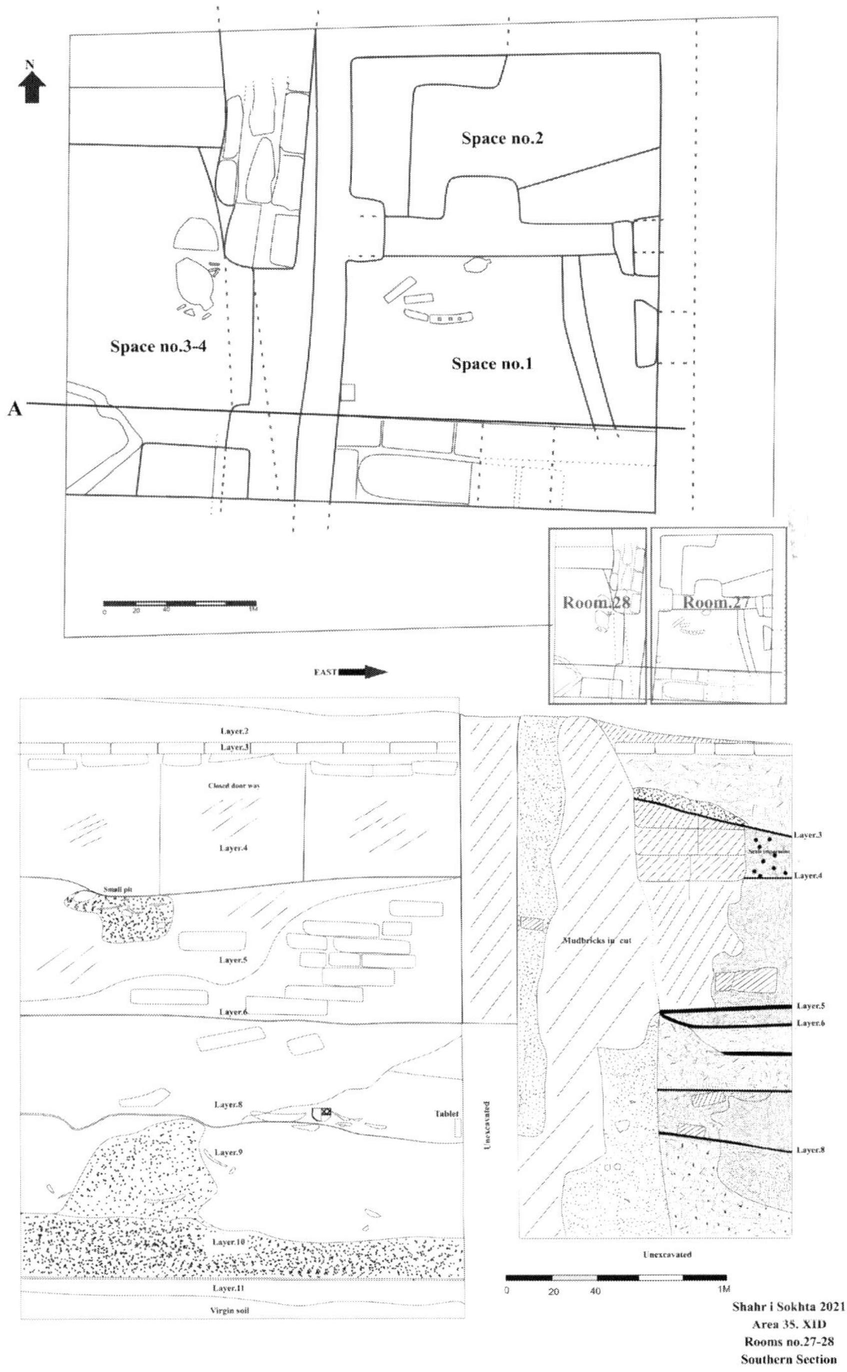

Fig. 2.3: Map of structures in Rooms 27 and 28 at XID at the top and stratigraphical section of the southern side of Rooms 27–28 at the bottom.

(2700–2500 BCE) between 1968–1974, and the XDV was re-excavated to re-examine the old data from this area.

In November 2019, excavations in Rooms 88 in XIB and 88a in XDV revealed seven construction phases (Moradi 2022, 143–159). Layers 3 to 4 of the trenches were related to Phases 9 and 10 of Period I, ca. 3300–3000 BCE,[1] and consist of rooms with narrow lined walls supported with small buttress walls (Moradi 2022). With the local materials in these rooms, archaeologists found Proto-Elamite cylinder seal impressions (Fig. 2.2; Table 2.3), figurines, ear-shaped handle jars in the Jemdet Nasr style, and cultural materials of neighboring regions such as Southern Turkmenistan, Nal, Quetta, and Kerman (Moradi 2021, 213–217). In the 2021 season, Rooms 27 and 28 in area XID of the ERA were excavated down to virgin soil, revealing a total of 11 cultural and nine structural layers (Fig. 2.3).

Stratigraphy and study of cultural evidence of the Proto-Elamite period in XID

Excavations in Rooms 27 and 28 revealed virgin soil at a depth of 510 cm from the base point at the edge of the trench, which appears to be the deepest point excavated throughout the ERA (Fig. 2.3).[2] We maintain that Layers 1–4 in these rooms are not connected to Proto-Elamite period, and based on the pottery assemblages and seal impressions, may be linked to early Period II. The first layer shows extensive use of the footprint of the structure first built in Layer 4. In the second layer is a room with plastered walls, standing on the remains of Layer 4. The third layer is a short period of use in Room 27 after the completion of the residence. The fourth layer is a room consisting of narrow walls with thick plaster and two buttress walls. One of the most important finds in Layer 4 is a collection of 27 stamp seal impressions whose designs are classified into two types – stepped shapes and petal motifs (Fig. 2.4). According to typological comparisons, seals with stepped-shaped decoration are common in Period II and III and they are used by more than one person or office (Ferioli *et al.* 1979, figs 8–9). The second type, petal motifs, are also found in the archaeological context of Period II (Ferioli *et al.* 1979, 28, no. 4) and there are a lot of examples of this kind of motif on stone, bone, and metal seals. It appears that the oldest seal used in XID was a flat, square, stamp-seal with a stepped decoration. No other Iranian site of the 4th millennium, including Susa, has yielded anything quite like it, although at Shahr-i Sokhta, in a later assemblage (Period II), as well as at Mundigak III and IV, plaque-shaped stamp-seals in chlorite have been found with a quite similar decoration (Amiet and Tosi 1978, 25). The function of the sealings, their use in administrative systems and the exchange of commodities, has not yet been studied. Many sealings have been thrown away in the garbage dump, leaving many questions unanswered.

The pottery assemblages of Layers 1–4 are related to late Period I or early Period II in the Shahr-i Sokhta sequence. Ceramics were made on a fast wheel and are often decorated with composite geometric motifs with thin and hatched lines. However,

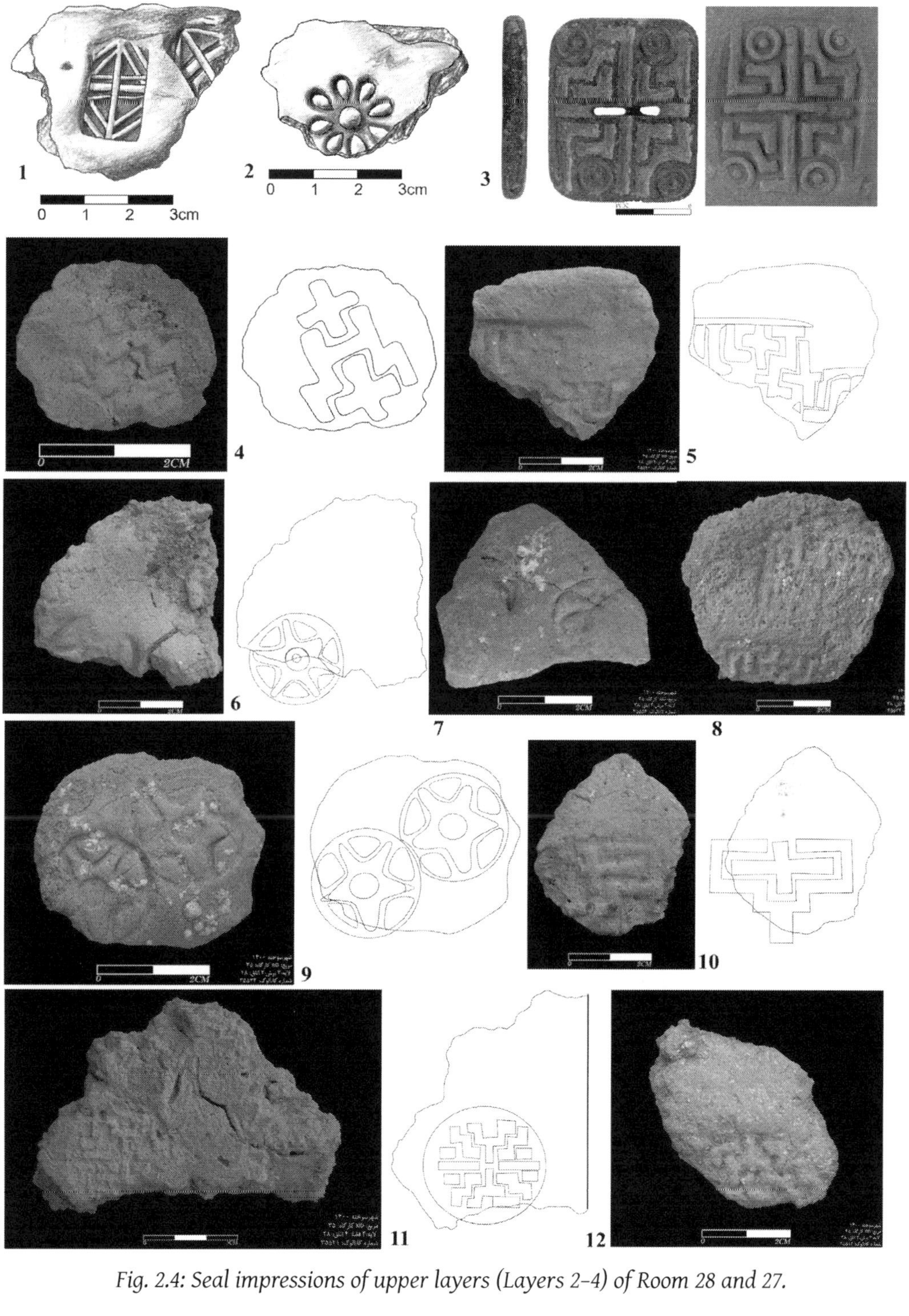

Fig. 2.4: Seal impressions of upper layers (Layers 2–4) of Room 28 and 27.

Table 2.1: The cultural sequences of Shahr-i Sokhta and adjacent areas.

Shahr-i Sockhta	*Layers in XID*	*Tepe Yahya*	*Bampur valley*	*Susa*	*Mesopotamia*	*BCE*
Site abandoned		?	Site abandoned	Middle Elam	Isin-Larsa	1600
						1700
						1800
IV.0	No evidence		Bampur VI	Old Elam	Ur III	1900
GAP					Akkad	2000
IV.1			Bampur V			2100
IV.2		IVB	Bampur IV.3		ED I–III	2200
III.3			Bampur IV.2			2300
III.4	1		Bampur I–IV.1			2400
						2500
II.5	2					2600
II.6	3–4					2700
II.7						2800
GAP		IVC		Susa III (Proto Elamite)	Jemdet Nasr	2900
I.8	5		No evidence			3000
I.9	6–7–8					3100
I.10	9–10			Susa II	Uruk	3200
?	11	Ali Abad VA	Chah Husseini Horizon			3300
						3400
						3500

in Layer 4, some simple patterns painted with thick lines can be seen, showing the continuation of the style of Period I at the end of Phase 9 (Table 2.1). Layer 5 pottery includes wide mouth bowls with festoon motifs under the rim, globular jars with small rims attached to the body, and fragments with solid geometric motifs and evidence for manufacture on a slow pottery wheel on the body. There are no seal impressions in this layer. Given that Phase 9 is a long cultural period in the sequence of the Shahr-i Sokhta, Layer 5 can be considered as part of the earlier stage of this phase.

In Layer 6, the patterns and forms of the pottery are comparable to standard forms and motifs of Namazgah III and Quetta wares, as well as wide mouth bowls with parallel bands on the body interior. Pottery is not decorated with linear simple and hatched motifs, but instead the predominant motif is the festoon hanging under the rim made with light brown lines. The number of motifs related to southern Turkmenistan and Quetta also increases in this layer (Fig. 2.5: 1–13; Table 2.2). Similar pottery from cuts 10–14 in area XDV had previously been obtained by Italian Expedition (Amiet and Tosi 1978, figs 10–12) and dated to 3200–3000 BCE (Salvatori and Tosi 2005, fig. 1). Other similar pottery was found in the new excavations of the ERA in Layer 3 of

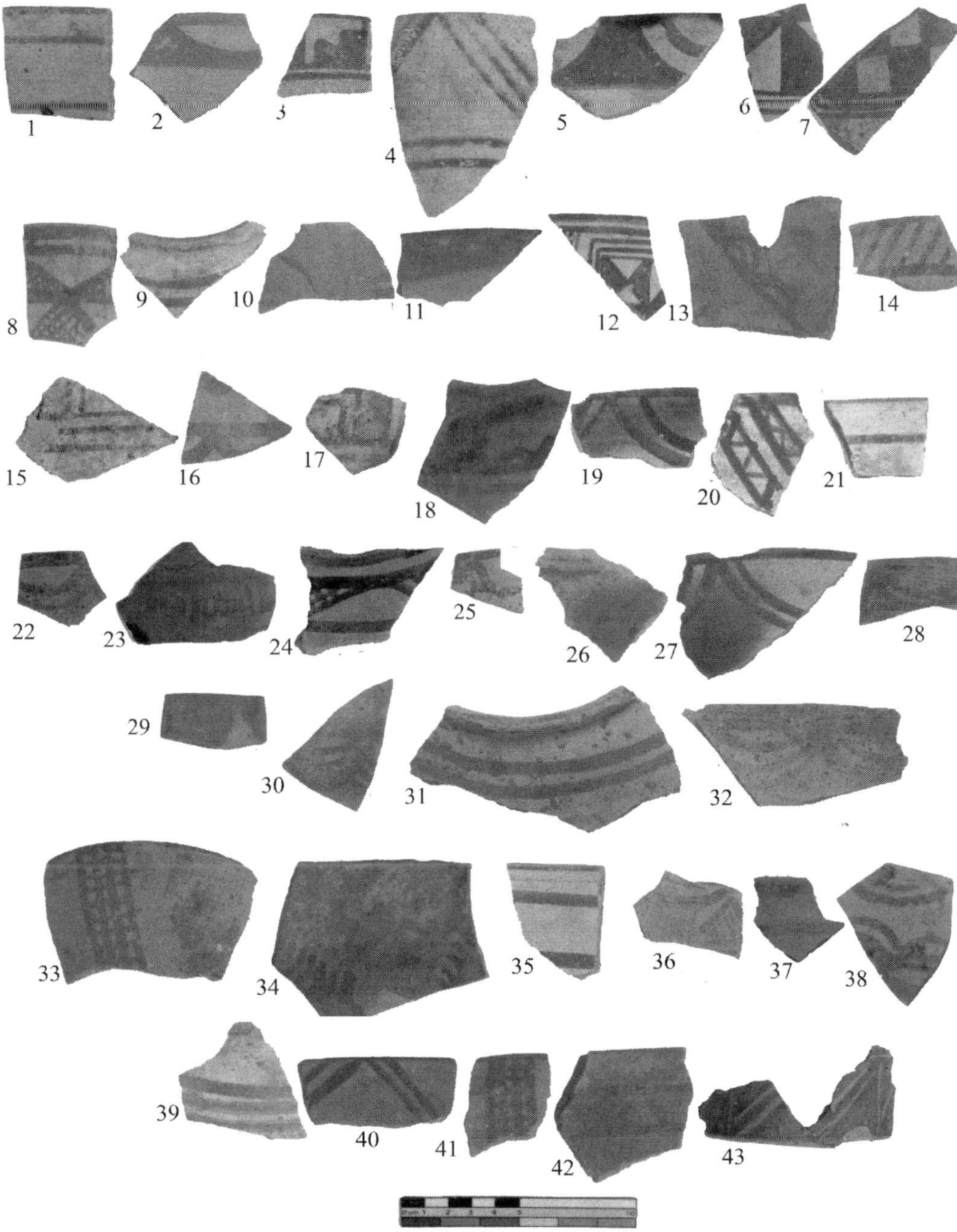

Fig. 2.5. Pottery of Layers 6–11 of Room 27.

Table 2.2: Details of shards illustrated in Figure 2.5.

No.	*Room*	*Layer*	*Paste*	*Motif color (Mf)*	*Cover*	*Details*
1,2,3		6	Reddish			1: Buff slip
4,5,6,7		6	Buff		Buff slip	No.7: Mf is dark brown/ No slip
8			Reddish	Light brown		
9,11,12,16,20,21,22,23			Buff			Nos.12,20,21: Buff slip
10,13,14			Gray			Nos.14: Mf is dark
15,17	27	7	Buff	Black-Red	Buff slip	Bichrome
18			Poor gray	Dark		
19			Buff	Dark brown		
24			Reddish		Buff slip	
25,26,27,28,31			Buff	Light brown		Nos.25,27,31: Mf: Dark Brown Nos.27,31 Cover: buff slip
29,30,32		8	Gray	Dark/black		No.29: Mf is dark/black
33,34	28		Reddish			No.34: fabric is gray
35			Buff	Light brown	Buff slip	
36,37,38		9	Poor gray			No.37: Mf is dark brown
39,40		9	Buff		Buff slip	
40	27	10	Buff	Dark brown		
41,42		10	Reddish	Light brown		No.42: fabric is buff
43		11	Buff	Dark brown	Buff slip	

Room 88 and Layers 3–5 of Room 88a (Moradi 2022, fig. 21), which according to the new chronology can be dated between 3300–3000 BCE.

Excavations by the Italian mission in 1975 yielded materials including a fragment of cylinder-seal with animal decoration which is specifically Proto-Elamite, a tablet inscribed in Proto-Elamite script, and a series of sealing fragments in unfired clay, each bearing a different seal impression (Amiet and Tosi 1978, 25; Pittman 1997, 145). Many of them belong to the Mesopotamian *koine* of the Jemdet Nasr period and the beginning of the following period (Amiet and Tosi 1978, 25). Among them there was only one example that could be related more specifically to Elam (Amiet and Tosi 1978, fig. 32, no.19). A large number of sherds has been recovered from the layers of Phase 10. Buff Ware predominates with a high incidence of painted surfaces in red/ brown, brown, and black (Amiet and Tosi 1978, 21–22).

The new excavations, in particular of Rooms 88 and 88a in XIB and XDV (Fig. 2.6) (Moradi 2022, figs 8, 16), revealed a large number of Uruk/Proto-Elamite seal impressions. Seal impressions found in the Proto-Elamite layers of Rooms 88 and 88a

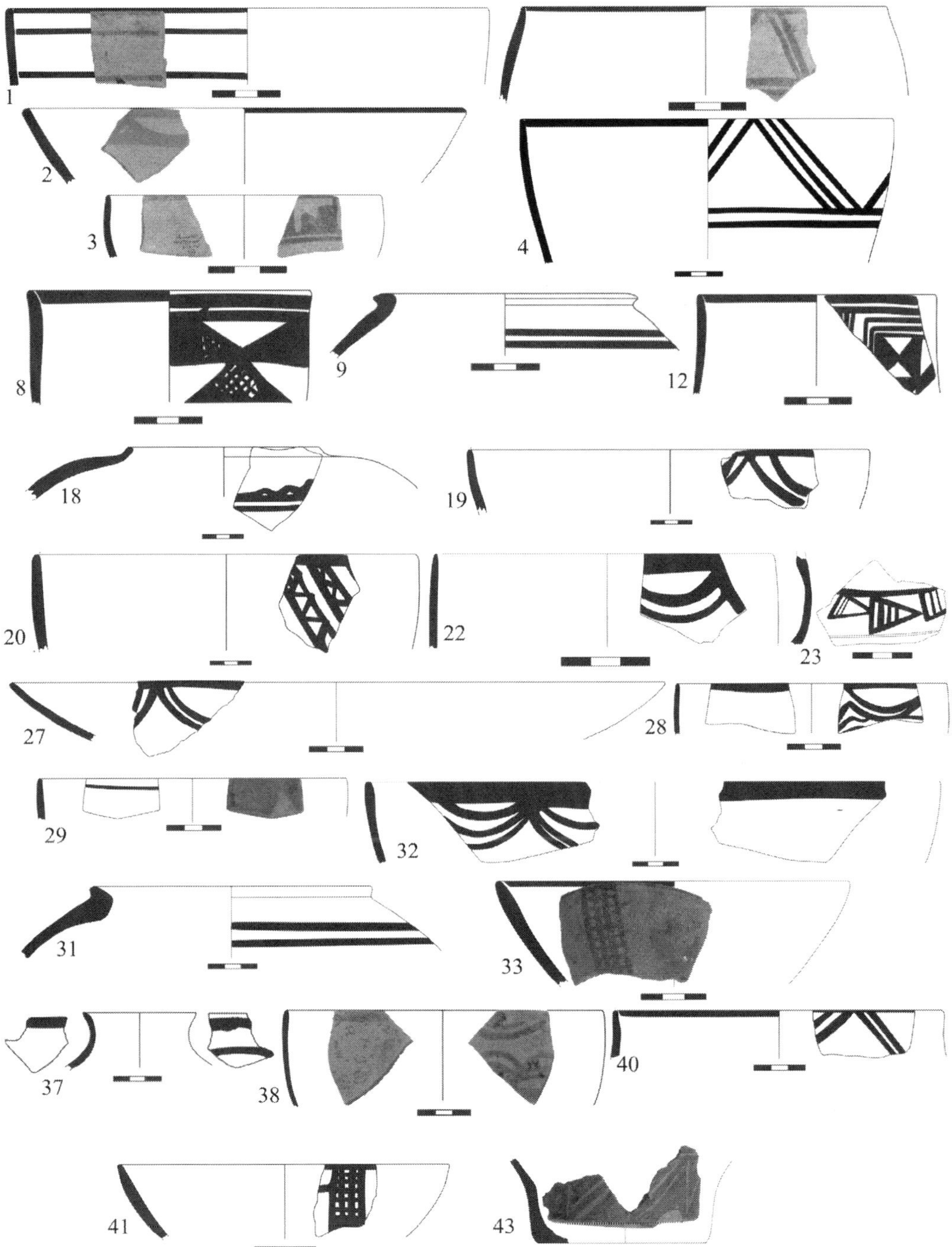

Fig. 2.6. Designs on pottery shown in Figure 2.5.

Table 2.3: Details of cylinder seal impressions shown in Figure 2.2.

No.	Area	Square	Room	Space	Layer	Cut	Details
1					1	9	Stamp seal
2		XDV	88A	2	4	9	Cylinder seal/ zoomorphic motif
3						15	Cylinder seal/ geometric motif
4					5	19	
5	35					8	Cylinder seal/quatrefoil motif
6						9	
7						11	Cylinder seal/ zoomorphic motif ?
8		XIB	88	1	3	11	
9						7	A rim jar with tow incised lines
10						4	A rim jar with three incised lines

are mostly quatrefoil (petals) motifs (Fig. 2.6: 4–6), which are common cylinder seal designs throughout this period in the Middle East. Archaeological evidence for this type of cylinder seal comes from Susa (Amiet 1972, pl. 26), Tell Malyan (Pittman 1997, fig. 4a), the Oman peninsula (Amiet 1975, 426), Tepe Yahya (Pittman 2001, fig. 10.29), and Mesopotamia (Frankfort 1955, pl. 8.51). These motifs have been found on cylinder seals from the Period I graves at Shahr-i Sokhta (Sajjadi 2009, 239) (Fig. 2.7: 5–6). Some scholars argue that the petaled design was the name of or symbol for an institution and did not designate an individual (Damerow and Englund 1989, 16). However, due to its broad geographical distribution, its many combinations with other signs and motifs, the duration of such motifs on seals including later stamp seals (Fig. 2.7, 8–10), and the presence of the seals among burial objects (Fig. 2.7, Table 2.4) in the cemetery, it is likely that this motif can be interpreted as amuletic or relating to the protection of goods.

The seventh and eighth layers form a relatively thick floor 4 m deep in Room 27 (Figs 2.3, 2.8).[3] This floor is connected by two eastern and western narrow walls. Both walls are connected to the floor of Layer 8 forming a large room or courtyard 2 m wide and possibly 4 m long.

Mud-bricks from a deconstructed kiln, coated with thick cream plaster and with three rectangular holes, were found in Layer 8 (Figs 2.8, Plate 2.3). The holes were probably used as channels for the passage of air to ignite and feed the fire (Figs 2.8, Plate 2.3: 2). Throughout this area, a thick layer of coal and ash can be seen, suggesting that it was probably used as a refuse pit or large landfill. The pottery in this layer appears to be in line with the traditions of Layer 6, with a decrease in solid patterns

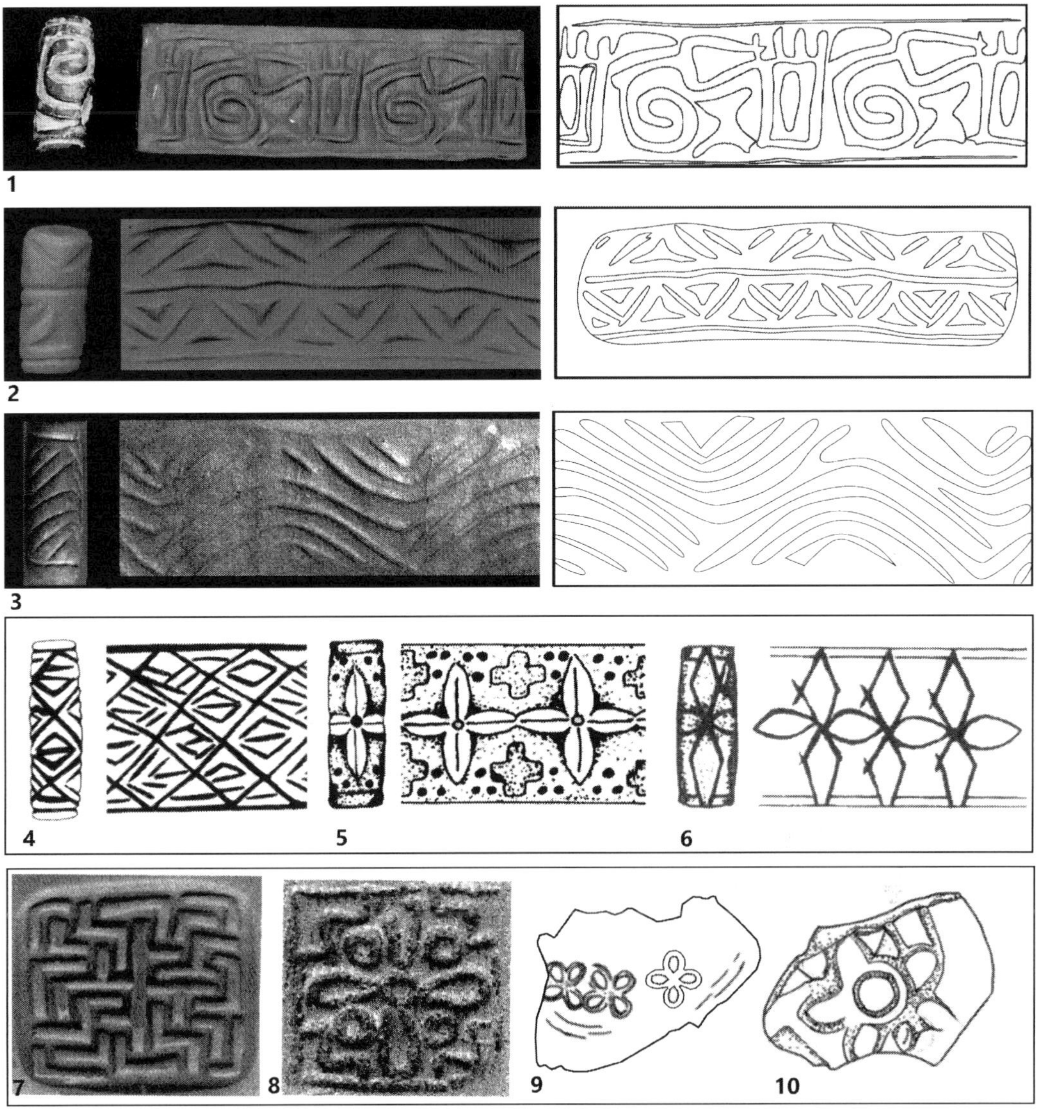

Fig. 2.7. Seals and seal impressions found in burials and residential areas of Shahr-i Sokhta (After Sajjadi 2009).

and increase in the variety of pottery in terms of fabric. Painted red and gray ware are visible. It appears that due to the probable use of slow wheels, the wide mouth forms of pottery are common in this layer. The fabric of the pots is fine, and their geometrical motifs are reminiscent a simplified motives from Quetta or Namazga III wares (Biscione 1974, 134) (Fig. 2.5: 25–35). A special example of pottery of this layer (Plate 2.2) is a kind of bichrome globular jar with stepped patterns painted with red

Table 2.4: Details of seals and sealings in Figure 2.7.

No.	*Location*	*Details*
1	Graveyard	Grave no.6708
2		Grave no.1610
3		Grave no.6005
4		Grave no.3208
5		Grave no.3203
6		Grave no.3105
7		Grave no.4310
8		Grave no.4602
9–10	Residential areas	Area no.23, Residential Area

and black colors (Plate 2.2: 9, 11). Similar containers have been found in the layers related to Phase 10 (Vidale 2011, fig. 2). Fragments of large animal bones, such as cattle, occur more in this layer than the upper layers. Six groups of cultural materials have been classified based on the results of excavation in the ERA, and are linked to spheres of interaction at Shahr-i Sokhta during Period I: 1. local cultural materials of Shahr-i-Sokhta, 2. pottery of southern Turkmenistan and Quetta valley, 3. Khurab/Emir Gray type, 4. Proto-Elamite cultural materials and pottery similar to Jemdet Nasr, 5. Nal and Central Pakistani Baluchistan pottery, 6. the pottery of Kerman, Bampur, and Makran (Moradi 2022, 164).

The tablet of XID

One of the important objects of this layer of area XID is a tablet found inside the western section of the trench (Fig. 2.8, Plate 2.3: 8). The location of this tablet is next to the debris of the kiln, suggesting that like the kiln debris, it was probably dumped from somewhere else (Plate 2.3: 8). This is the only object discovered with a seal impression from Rooms 27 and 28 in layers related to the Proto-Elamite period. However, other indicators of Proto-Elamite culture, such as beveled-rim pottery and typical numerical tablets, have not been found yet in these layers (Plate 2.3).

Historically, this was the second tablet found at Shahr-i Sokhta, and its type is unknown. Previously, in 1975, a tablet of the more common type had been found in cut 12 of XDV (Fig. 2.10), associated with a small group of seals, seal impressions, and the ceramic assemblage (Amiet and Tosi 1978, 24, fig. 16). This previous tablet is roughly rectangular, pillow-shaped, with straight sides, as is recurrent at Susa 16–13. The inscription runs from left to right and is restricted to a single line, along the top edge of one face (Fig. 2.10). The first sign recalls 322 h, known at Susa from three different texts, twice as an isolated item followed by the digit 1, and once grouped with sign 32, which might reproduce ideographically a tree or a branch. The second sign is still to be properly identified. It is followed by the numeral 5, written in the standard calligraphy of Susa. Anyhow we are not able to establish the meaning of the group of two signs here (Amiet and Tosi 1978, 24).

While the tablet found earlier has clear links to Susa-style Proto-Elamite tablets, the new one has fewer similarities with those both in the dimensions and signs (Fig. 2.9a). It is rectangular in shape with curved edges, and measures 128 mm in

Fig. 2.8. Archaeological context of Layer 8 in Room 27. 1: The Eastern plastered wall (no.35071). 2: Remains of deconstructed kiln. 3: Globular broken jar. 4: The floor. 5: Small black jar. 6: Stone object. 7: Shard of a big globular jar. 8: Tablet. 9: Painted buff bowl.

length, 80 mm in width, and 30 mm in thickness. On it are three types of signs (Fig. 2.9). The first sign is a collection of 30 rectangular holes arranged in five rows, four rows with seven holes and one row with two holes. However, due to the length of the fracture, it seems that the number of holes in each row was originally greater before it was broken (Fig. 2.9c). And based on the broken shape of the tablet, its overall dimensions, as well as the appearance of the cylinder seal impression on it, it can be assumed that the original number of holes in each row was 10 (Fig. 2.9c), making the total number of original holes 45, likely the count (or less likely the volume) of the goods or items traded. The second sign is composed of three dashed lines across the top of the tablet, parts of which have disappeared over time.

The third sign is the cylinder seal impression at the bottom of the tablet and under the numerical holes (Fig. 2.9d). This seal impression is in the style of Uruk/Proto-Elamite cylinder seal motifs and the reversed lobe pattern is repeated on it, likely indicating the identity of the trader of the goods. Although there is no evidence for the use of this identical seal from coincident sites in Iran and Mesopotamia, patterns of reversed lobes similar to this seal impression have been found in the Proto-Elamite layers from Tepe Sofalin (Hesari and Yousefi Zoshk 2010, fig. 4 bottom) (Fig. 2.12: 1).

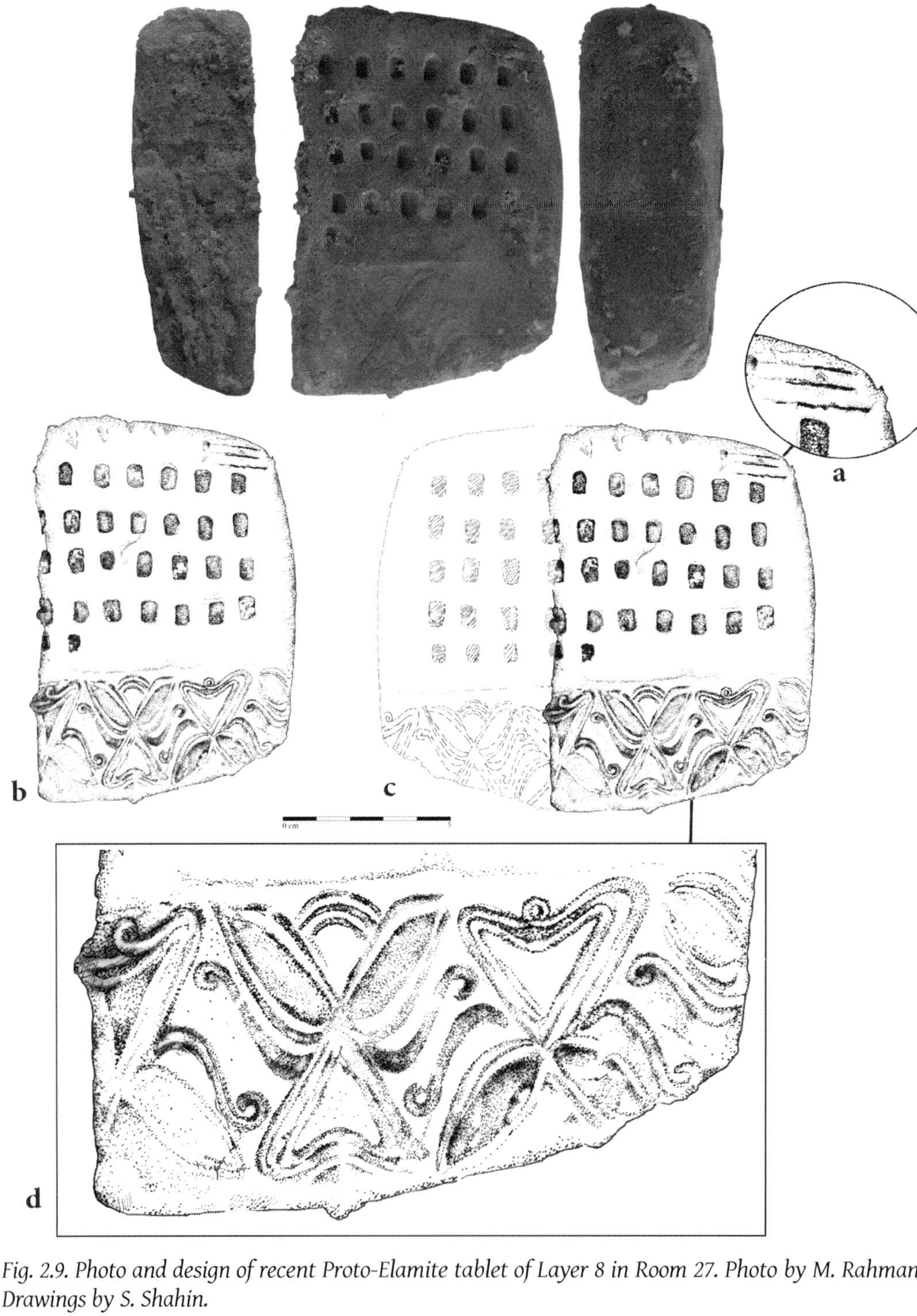

Fig. 2.9. Photo and design of recent Proto-Elamite tablet of Layer 8 in Room 27. Photo by M. Rahmani, Drawings by S. Shahin.

Also from Tepe Sofalin, a cylinder seal with quatrefoil petals motif similar to the effect of XDV seals was found (Hesari and Yousefi Zoshk 2010, fig. 4 top) (Fig. 2.12: 2). More clay fragments that looked like parts of a blank tablet were found below, perhaps discarded while the tablet was being created (Fig. 2.4: 3).

Fig. 2.10. Proto-Elamite tablet of Shahr-i Sokhta found in 1975 (After Amiet and Tosi 1978, photo by Haleh Helali).

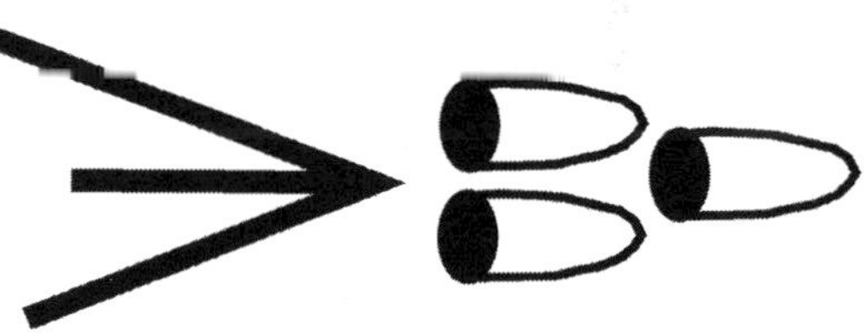

Fig. 2.11. Proto-Elamite signs M388 and M72, comparable to Babylonian SAL and KUR.

Since the discovery of the first Proto-Elamite tablet in Susa in 1901 (Dahl 2005, 7), a total of 1775 tablets had been found at eight different sites (Desset 2016, 69), the most recent example from Shahr-i Sokhta being No.1776. The earlier tablet at Shahr-i Sokhta was found in square XDV during the excavations of the 1970s (Amiet and Tosi 1978, fig. 16). It bears only numerical signs and a signature, which in this respect is comparable to the example of Chogha Mish (Dahl 2005, 81–82). This finding is typologically consistent with common tablets of this period and is comparable to other samples that were found at other sites in the central plateau of Iran. In areas such as Susa (Le Brun 1978, fig. 37), Tell-e Ghazair (Caldwell 1971, cited in Dahl *et al.* 2013, 358), and Tall-e Malyan (Sumner 1988, 308–311) in southwest Iran, Tepe Yahya (Damerow and Englund 1989), Tepe Sialk of Kashan (Ghirshman 1938, pls. XXXI: 1, XCII), Tepe Sofalin of Varamin (Dahl *et al.* 2012, figs 5–12), and Tepe Uzbeki (Madjidzade, cited in Dahl *et al.* 2013, 358), tablets follow a standard form, indicating the relative complexity of a regional system of trade in the second half of the 4th millennium BCE throughout the Iranian plateau.

But so far, tablets similar to the second tablet of Shahr-i Sokhta, from square XID, have not been found in any of the areas from which similar examples were obtained in terms of general shape and signs. And while the new tablet of Shahr-i Sokhta is similar, there are also significant differences between it and the ca. 1500 tablets of

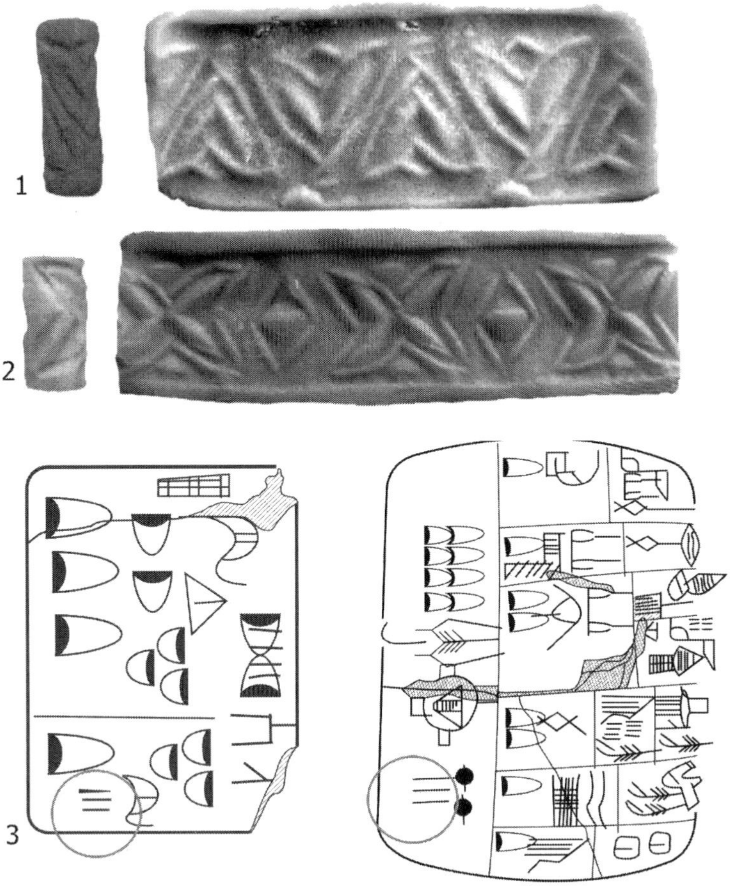

Fig. 2.12. Top: Cylinder seals from Tepe Sofalin (After Hesari and Yousefi Zoshk 2010). Bottom: The Uruk tablets with three parallel lines (shown by a circle) that may indicate enslaved people, domestic animals, or low status workers (after Englund 2011).

Proto-Elamite origin. The first difference is the size of the tablet. All Proto-Elamite tablets are classified according to their size into three main groups, the third group being very large, thick, and flat tablets classified as group x, all published in MDF 17 (Dahl *et al.* 2013, 366). The dimensions of the group x vary but the largest one is 250 × 152 × 60 mm, and many of the fragments are between 70 × 60 mm,[4] similar to the Shahr-i Sokhta tablet from XID. This group of tablets is not very prominent, and in Susa they were probably excavated from a layer higher than Layers 17a and 16 (Dahl *et al.* 2013, 365–366, fig. 11). The dimensions of the broken tablet from Shahr-i Sokhta are 128 × 80 mm. Hypothetically, we have reconstructed this tablet to be square in shape with dimensions of approximately 12.5 × 12.5 cm (Fig. 2.9). It possibly had a 1:1 ratio, in contrast to the 3:2 ratio in contemporaneous Proto-Elamite and Uruk tablets (Damerow and Englund 1989, 11).

The second difference is in the rectilinear shape of the holes made on it. Other similar tablets use circular or semicircular-shaped holes as numerical signs, rather than rectangular. Despite this difference, comparisons can be made with respect to size and arrangement of these holes. The first interesting point is that in the lower row, which has fewer marks, smaller holes – almost half the size of the upper holes – are used. Based on comparison to the signs on contemporaneous tablets, especially those employing the sexagesimal system where smaller holes were used to calculate smaller numbers (Englund 2001, 8–9, fig. 4), it is possible that these smaller holes were used in the same way. The reconstructed number of these holes – four of the five rows of holes probably originally had 10 marks each – is compatible with the decimal system, which is used only for Proto-Elamite tablets (Englund 2001, 112; Fig. 2.9). While generally Proto-Elamite tablets used the same method (sexagesimal system) for counting and measuring as the Babylonian examples, but for counting domestic animals and lower-class workers they also used a decimal system, which was adapted from the sexagesimal system (Englund 2011, 46–47).

We believe that the three dashed lines at the top of the tablet indicate the use at Shahr-i Sokhta of a sign known in the Uruk/Proto-Elamite writing system (Fig. 2.9a, c). The use of three parallel dashed lines as a token of goods occurs in two tablets from Uruk IV (Englund 2011, figs 2.8b and 2.9b) (Fig. 2.12: 3), which were used for the exchange or management of domestic herds or labours (Englund 2011, 47). The most widely used signs on Proto-Elamite tablets for this purpose are M388 and M72, which are comparable to the SAL and KUR symbols in Babylonian tablets. Two three-line signs that meets at one point (Fig. 2.11) in Tablets 11–13 from Tepe Yahya, correspond to the SAL and KUR signs in the Uruk tablets (Fig. 2.12: 3), and were used to denote animals or slaves and low status workers (Damerow and Englund 1989, 29–30). The first sign looks like the three parallel dashed lines on a Shahr-i Sokhta tablet. It should be emphasized again that the volume of bone remains of large animals, probably cows, increased significantly in the layers of Period I, both in squares XIB and XDV and in Layers 7–11 in XID. It is possible that such symbols were related to the exchange of animals.

So far, no beveled-rim bowls have been found as an indicator of the Proto-Elamite period in the Shahr-i Sokhta. Pottery vessels of Layers 7 and 8 of XID are made with a slow wheel. Common forms in this layer include examples of medium sized, spherical jars with patterns of parallel stripes on the body, along with painted and simple wide mouth bowls (Fig. 2.5:14–35, Table 2.2). On the inner body of wide bowls, patterns such as stripes or hanging wavy lines under the inner edge can be seen, common features of the pottery of Period I (Figs 2.5: 25, 27, 30; 2.6: 27). A grey jar (Fig. 2.8: 5; Plate 2.3: 5) and a buff ware bowl with linear motifs belonging to Namazga III are among the samples found on the floor of Layer 8 (Fig. 2.8; Plate 2.3: 9). Quetta Ware patterned pottery is also obtained from the upper sections of Layer 7, which, along with two bi-chrome fragments (Plate 2.2; Table 2.5), is similar to the pottery tradition

Table 2.5: Details of shards shown in Plate 2.2.

No.	Room	Layer	Fabric	Motif	Details
1			Reddish	Light brown	Jemdet Nasr type
2,3			Buff	Dark brown	Local type
4			Gray	Dark	Baluchistan type
5,6,7,8	28	7–8	Buff	–	Local type/No.6: fabric is reddish
9			Buff	Red/Light brown	Bichrome
10			Reddish	–	Oval base
11			Buff	Red/Light brown	Jemdet Nasr type/ Bichrome

Table 2.6: Details of objects illustrated in Plate 2.4.

No.	Room	Layer	Cut	Fabric	Motif
1–2			4–5	Poor gray	Light brown/Brown
3	27	9	–	clay	–
4			9	Poor gray	Light brown
5–6		10	–	Clay/ Stone	5: clay slings/6: circle flat stones

of Phase 10. A number of smooth oval and flat stones that may have been used as weights (Ascalone 2019, 77), clay sling bullets (Plate 2.3: 11–12), two small jars, a cucumber shaped stone object (Fig. 2.8; Plate 2.3: 6), and a large broken grinding stone were also recovered from the floor of Layer 8.

Due to the evidence of severe burns on the floor of Layer 10 at a depth of 480 cm, it was assumed that the orange soil of Layers 9–10 was mainly part of the ancient debris and accumulation associated with the burned floor of Layer 10. The pottery in this layer is mostly unpainted and handmade. Examples of painted pottery include small jars and gray bowls associated with large pots (Fig. 2.5: 40–43). Grayish buff ware or light gray ware pottery is one of the findings of this layer, which indicates the incomplete control of heat of the kiln in which they were fired (Table 2.6; Plate 2.4: 2, 4). Generally speaking, painted pottery is rare (Fig. 2.5: 40, 43).

These layers yielded several clay anthropomorphic and zoomorphic figurines as gained from upper layers (Plate 2.4: 5, 6). The number of bones of large animals (probably cows) is impressive and may be related to the function of this space. The 11th layer is located on virgin soil and has fewer artifacts than the upper layers. The only painted buff-ware in this layer has no parallel in Shahr-i Sokhta pottery collection (Fig. 2.5: 41, 42).

Conclusion

The data from excavations in neighboring regions, as well as continuous excavation in the ERA at Shahr-i Sokhta confirm or complement previous findings and provide a broader understanding of the extent of regional interactions – particularly in the southern Helmand.[5] Although the effects of the Jemdet-Nasr/Proto-Elamite and Southern interaction domains are mostly evident in Shahr-i Sokhta in Period I Phases 9–10, it seems that the effects of the Proto-Elamite culture diminished at the end of Phase 10 and during Phase 9 the influence of southern areas like the Bampur valley, Nal and Quetta became more obvious at Sistan. While the newly discovered tablet is in line with some of the traditions of product management and goods exchange in the Proto-Elamite sphere, it also demonstrates local/indigenous traditions with no direct parallels in any area of West Asia. Secondly, it seems that at Shahr-i Sokhta, the integrated and global tradition of Susiana/Mesopotamian exchanges has been abridged and simplified in the southern Helmand Delta.

Also, despite the presence of beveled-rim bowl type pottery in all other areas where Proto-Elamite tablets were found, not even a single piece of beveled-rim bowl pottery was found in the relevant environments at Shahr-i Sokhta. Such a discovery demonstrates the limited impact of the Susiana/Mesopotamian traditions, perhaps related to the greater distance between Shahr-i Sokhta and these centers. It is not surprising that in the period of stabilization of Sistan culture, from 2900 BCE onwards (Phase 8), instead of forming a complex and practical mechanism in the management and exchange of goods as we see in Susa, Yahya, or Fars regions, we witness the prevalence of stamp seals with very simple geometric patterns and probably a restricted closed economy in a small area limited to the Sistan plain. Instead of cylinder seals with complex iconography as we see at Mesopotamia, Susa or Yahya, the use of stamp seals with simple geometric designs characterizes trade exchanges at the beginning of Period II at Shahr-i Sokhta (2800 BCE). At the beginning of the 3rd millennium BCE, as the relationship between Sistan and the west diminished, administrative technology at Shahr-i Sokhta changed as well. The use of writing for keeping economic documents diminished compared to Period I (3300–3000 BCE), replaced by a local tradition that used stamp seals.

Acknowledgments

We would like to thank Enrico Ascalone for his valuable comments, Saeed Parsaeian, Zahra Rajabion, Javad Mar'ashi, Tahereh Rahim Khani, and Reyhane Salimi for collaborating in excavation, Media Rahmani, Sareh Amini, Setareh Shahin, and Nahid Zamani for the artistic designs and photography of the data.

Notes

1 The article on reviewing and correcting the chronology of Shahr-i Sokhta and Sistan plain based on the latest carbon-14 tests in Shahr-i Sokhta will be published soon.

2 The depth of the virgin soil in Room 88a is about 470 cm measured regarding this starting point.

3 Layer 7 was considered as a separate layer only because it had a different color from Layer 6 and was composed of heated orange soil.

4 Special thanks to Francois Desset.

5 Hirmand in Persian.

Bibliography

Amiet, P. (1972) *Glyptique susienne des origines à l'époque des perses achéménides. Cachets, sceaux-cylindres et empreintes antiques découverts à Suse de 1913-1967. 2 vols, MDAFI 43.* Paris, P. Geuthner.

Amiet, P. (1975) A Cylinder Seal Impression Found at Umm an-Nar. *East and West* 25, 425–426.

Amiet, P. and Tosi, M. (1978) Phase 10 at Shahr-i Sokhta: Excavation in Square XDV and the Late 4th Millennium BC Assemblage of Sistan. *East and West* 28, 9–41.

Ascalone, E. (2019) Gli oggetti dell' area 33 a Shahr-i Sokhta. In E. Ascalone and S.M.S. Sajjadi (eds) *Scavi e ricerche a Shahr-i Sokhta*, 75–114. Tehran, Pishin Pazhouh.

Biscione, R. (1974) Relative Chronology and Pottery Connections between Shahr-i Sokhta and Mundigak, Eastern Iran. *Memorie dell'Istituto Italiano di Paleontologia Umana* 2, 131–145.

Caldwell, J.R. (1971) Ghazir, Tell-i. *Reallexikon der Assyriologie und vorderasiatischen Archäologie* 3, 348–355.

Dahl, J. (2005) Animal Husbandry in Susa During the Proto-Elamite Period. *SMEA* 47, 81–134.

Dahl, J., Morteza Hesari, L. and Yousefi Zoshk, R. (2012) The Proto-Elamite Tablets from Tape Sofalin. *Iranian Journal of Archaeological Studies* 2 (1), 57–73. [Persian]

Dahl, J., Petrie, C., and Potts, D.T. (2013) Chronological Parameters of the Earliest Writing System in Iran. In C. Petrie (ed.) *Ancient Iran and its Neighbours - Local Developments and Long-range Interactions in the Fourth Millennium BC*, 353–378. British Institute for Persian Studies Archaeological Monographs. Oxford, Oxbow Books.

Damerow, P. and Englund, R.K. (1989) *The Proto-Elamite Texts from Tepe Yahya.* Peabody Museum of Archaeology and Ethnology, Harvard University. Cambridge, MA, Harvard University Press.

Desset, F. (2016) Proto-Elamite Writing in Iran. *ARCHEO-NIL, Revue de la société pour l'étude des cultures prépharaoniques de la vallée du Nil* 26, 67–134.

Englund, R.K. (2001) The State of Decipherment of Proto-Elamite, The Cuneiform Digital Library (CDLI), Version, 21. August 2001, PREPRINT 18 3.

Englund, R.K. (2011) Accounting in Proto-Cuneiform. In K. Radner and E. Robson, *The Oxford Handbook of Cuneiform Culture*, 32–50. Oxford, Oxford University Press.

Ferioli, P., Fiandra, E., and Tusa, S. (1979) Stamps Seals and the Functional Analysis of their Sealings at Shahr-i Sokhta II–III (2700–2200 B.C.). In J. E. Lohuizen-de Leeuw (ed.) *South Asian Archaeology* 1975, 7–32. Leiden, Brill.

Frankfort, H. (1955) *Stratified Cylinder Seals from the Diyala Region (Oriental Institute Publications vol. LXXII).* Chicago, University of Chicago Press.

Ghirshman, R. (1938) *Fouilles de Sialk Près de Kashan 1933, 1934, 1937 Vol.1.* Paris, Museé du Louvre.

Hesari, M. and Yousefi Zoshk, R. (2010) Emergence of Pre-Governmental Institutions in Central Iranian Plateau: Ruling Lords in the Proto-Elamite Period at Pishva's Tepe Sophalin. *Journal of Archaeological Studies* 1 (2), 1–22. [Persian]

Le Brun, A. (1978) Suse, chantier 'Acropole 1'. *Paléorient* 4 (1), 177–192.

Moradi, H. (2021) Cultural Dynamics of the Second Half of the Fourth Millennium BC and the Roots of Early Urbanization in Southeastern Iran (3500–3000 BC). *JARCS* 12 (4), 211–228.

Moradi, H. (2022) Excavation in Square X: ERA of Shahr-i Sokhta: Pottery Traditions and Cultural Interactions During Period I. In E. Ascalone and S.M.S. Sajjadi (eds) *Excavation and Researches at Shahr I Sokhta 2*, 143–182. Tehran, Pishin Pajouh.

Moradi, H., Sarhaddi Dadian, H., Saadatian, M., Marashi, M.J. and Keikha, M. (2022) Archaeological Survey on the East and Southeast Areas of Shahr-i Sokhta: Some Evidence for Making Chronology during the Third and Early Second Millennium BC. In E. Ascalone and S.M.S. Sajjadi (eds) *Excavation and Researches at Shahr i Sokhta 3*, 233–266. Tehran, Pishin Pajouh.

Pittman, H. (1997) The Administrative Function of Glyptic Art in Proto-Elamite Iran: A Survey of the Evidence. *Sceaux d' Orient et leur employ. Res Orientalis* 10, 133–161.

Pittman, H. (2001) Glyptic art of Period IV. In C.C. Lamberg-Karlovsky and D.T. Potts (eds) *Excavations at Tepe Yahya, Iran 1967–1975. The Third Millennium (American School of Prehistoric Research Bulletin 45)*, 231–246. Cambridge, MA, Peabody Museum of Archaeology and Ethnology.

Sajjadi, S.M.S. (2003) Excavations at Shahr-i Sokhta. Preliminary Report on the Excavations of the Graveyard, 1997–2000. *Iran* 41, 21–97.

Sajjadi, S.M.S. (ed.) (2009) *Excavation at Shahr-e Sokhta, Second Preliminary Report on Excavation of the Graveyard (2001-2003)*, with contributions by F. Foruzanfar, R. Shirazi and R.M. Zaruri. Tehran, ICHHTO, Cultural Heritage, Handicrafts and Tourism Organization of Sistan and Baluchistan Province. [Persian]

Sajjadi, S.M.S. and Moradi, H. (2014) Excavation at Buildings Nos.1 and 20 at Shahr-i-Sokhta. *International Journal of the Society of Iranian Archaeologists* 1 (1), 77–90.

Sajjadi, S.M.S. and Moradi, H. (2017) Shahr-i Sokhta 2014–2015 Excavations. The New Results in Areas 1, 20, 26 and 28. *Studi di Aerotopografia Archeologica Archeologia Aerea* 9/15, 149–167.

Sajjadi, S.M.S. and Moradi, H. (2019) The Report of 17th Season Excavation at Shahr i Sokhta. In R. Shirazi and S. Hoorshid (eds) *Short Articles of 17th Annual Meeting of Archaeology of Iran*, 716–721. Tehran, ICAR. [Persian]

Salvatori, S. and Tosi, M. (2005) Shahr-i Sokhta Revised Sequence. In C. Jarrige and V. Lefevre (eds) *South Asian Archaeology 2001, Proceeding of the 16th International Conference of the European Association of South Asian Archaeologists*, 281–292. Paris, Éd Recherche sur les Civilisations.

Salvatori, S. and Vidale, M. (1997) *Shahr-i Sokhta 1975-1978: Central Quarters Excavations, Preliminary Report*. Roma, Istituto Italiano per l'Africa e l'Oriente.

Sumner, W.M. (1988) Malyan, Tall-e (Anšan). *Reallexikon der Assyriologie* 7, 306–320.

Tosi, M. (ed.) (1983) *Prehistoric Sistan I (IsMEO Reports and Memoirs XIX, 1)*. Rome, IsMEO.

Vidale, M. (2011) A Vessel for Building another Vessel. A Technical Template of the Late 4th Millennium BCE in the Central-Eastern of the Iranian Plateau? *Iranian Journal of Archaeological Studies* 1 (2), 9–16.

Chapter 3 Prologue

The history and prehistory of the Silk Road

The following chapter by Ali Vahdati and his colleagues is part of a larger project, the Iran–China Joint Expedition, under the aegis of China's 'Belt and Road Initiative' (BRI), a massive infrastructure project to recreate the historic Silk Road for the 21st century. The earlier Silk Road(s) emerged during the Han Dynasty (220 BCE–220 CE) in China and the Parthian period in Iran (247 BCE–224 CE). These routes passed overland through Central Asia (modern Afghanistan, Turkmenistan, Tajikistan, Kyrgyzstan, Kazakhstan), South Asia, through Western Asia (Iran, etc.), into Europe, stretching over 4000 miles. Maritime networks stretched from the east coast of China, around the coast of Southeast and South Asia, around the Arabian Peninsula to the coast of Africa, and north through Egypt to the Mediterranean Sea. Not a single 'road', the Silk Road describes multidirectional and complex networks for moving finished goods, raw materials, foodstuffs, animals, peoples, technologies, and ideas over long distances. Silk was one of the major products moving westward, as were tea, gems, porcelain, gunpowder, perfumes, and spices. Goods moving east included horses and their accoutrement, glassware, grapevines and wine, camels, and enslaved people. These networks persisted until 1453 when the Ottomans restricted trade with Europe, forcing Europeans to search out alternative routes to access eastern markets (Millward 2013).

Iran was never integrated into the Ottoman Empire. Trade between Iran and the Far East continued, particularly the trade of Chinese blue and white ceramics. Persian tastes had long favored ceramics, particularly stone paste vessels, glazed in shades of cobalt, turquoise, and lapis lazuli (Froom 2020). In the 17th century, for example, Persian consumers preferred early Ming pottery of the type that had arrived in Southern Persia in the 15th century. Chinese potters in the ceramic production center of Jindezhen produced imitations of these earlier ceramics for export in Western Asia in a range of qualities. Potters in Iran also produced imitations of Chinese blue and white ceramics, and there is some evidence that the Persian imitations could compete with, and even pass as, Chinese examples (Rogers 1991). During the 17th century, inscriptions refer to ceramic workshops in Nishapur, Kubachi Ware, Kerman, and closer to the subject of this chapter, the city of Mashhad in Razavi Khorasan province of northeastern Iran (Watson 1991).

Of course, the roads, tracks, and waypoints that constitute the Silk Road did not miraculously spring into being in the 3rd century BCE. Millennia earlier, between 2500–1500 BCE, Iran was part of a wide network of interactions spanning Southwest and East Asia. During this period, top-down states and empires were arising in the broader region, to the west in Syro-Anatolia and Mesopotamia, around the Persian Gulf, in the floodplains of southwestern Iran, and the Indus Valley. The Chalcolithic and Bronze Ages in eastern Iran and Central Asia witnessed the development of different types of communities.

In southern Central Asia, the chronological period is referred to by the Namazga sequence, after the site of Namazga in Turkmenistan near the Iranian border. Namazga IV–VI comprises the Bronze Age in the region, with sites including examples of complex urban centers, like Altyn-tepe, with craft specialization and clear evidence of participation in long distance trade. These developments contributed to the Bactria-Margiana Archaeological Complex (BMAC, formerly 'Oxus Civilization'), with its large, urban settlements in Turkmenistan (ancient Margiana) and northern Afghanistan (ancient Bactria). BMAC urban sites depended on irrigation agriculture, animal husbandry, and craft production that often relied on imported, precious raw materials; marine shells from South Asia, lapis lazuli and tin from the mountains of Afghanistan and Tajikistan, semi-precious stones from southern Iran, and soft stone (chlorite, calcite) from the Iranian Plateau. Finished BMAC artifacts were found in all of these regions, indicating a pattern of exchange where these regions were exporting raw materials and importing finished goods from the BMAC centers, and from there distributing them in Elam and Mesopotamia. Critical to the success of the BMAC culture, the sources of raw materials are controlled by mobile pastoralists, as are many of the routes that linked the various regions in the exchange network. It has been argued that large settlements in Turkmenistan, like Gonur Tepe, connect the BMAC to the pastoralist Eurasian Steppe cultures, and from there to the Far East. Such centers were critical sites for interaction between nomadic pastoralists and farmers/city dwellers that promoted trade relationships (Frachetti and Rouse 2012).

These long-distance interactions took place through what Gregory Possehl has called the Middle Asian Interaction Sphere (MAIS), a 3rd millennium BCE pioneer network characterized in part by a distinctive material culture exemplified by soft stone objects – carved in an 'intercultural style' with animals in combat, composite creatures, and geometric motifs – found across Mesopotamia, the Persian Gulf, the Iranian Plateau, and Indus Valley (Possehl 2007). Further north in the vast Eurasian Steppe, Michael Frachetti has postulated a parallel network during the 3rd millennium along the Inner Asian Mountain Corridor that stretches through the foothills and highlands of the Hindu Kush, Pamir, Tian Shan, and Dzhungar Mountains, a network by which pastoralists 'contributed significantly to the growth and ideological shape of the urban political economies of the BMAC, the Indus Civilization (Harappans), and the Elamites of the Iranian Plateau—civilizations variously in dialogue with the empires of the Near East throughout the late 3rd and early 2nd millennium BCE' (Potts 1999; Frachetti and Rouse 2012).

With the dawn of the Iron Age in the region in the mid-2nd millennium, a new culture, named for the site of Yaz Tepe in Turkmenistan, emerged. The Yaz culture had distinctive painted pottery and different burial customs from the BAMC predecessors, with regional differences in pottery technology and architecture. The area within which this culture is found includes Bactria, Margiana, Sogdia in modern Uzbekistan, the Fergana Valley in the Tianshan mountains, and northern Iran, where we find Tepe Naderi (Buławka 2017; Lhuillier and Mashkour 2017).

The site of Tepe Naderi featured in this chapter has witnessed and participated in these networks over its long history, from the late 4th millennium BCE through the late Islamic era. While its earlier levels with Namazga IV pottery clearly indicate that it was within the BMAC sphere, this study shows that both the analysis of ceramics and of faunal and botanical remains link the site strongly to the Gorgan/Damghan region south of the Caspian Sea, illustrating the cultural shifts in the region over time. The persistence of these interactions over thousands of years is confirmed by the discovery of late Islamic blue and white stone paste ceramics, and indeed by the Chinese–Iranian partnership that produced these results.

Bibliography

Buławka, N. (2017) The Yaz I–III Settlement Pattern in the Serakhs Oasis, Southern Turkmenistan. *Iran* 55, 143–170.

Frachetti, M.D. and Rouse, L.M. (2012) Central Asia, the Steppe, and the Near East. In D.T. Potts (ed.) *A Companion to the Archaeology of the Ancient Near East*, 687–705. Oxford, Blackwell Publishing Ltd.

Froom, A. (2020) Between Sea and Sky: Blue and White Ceramics from Persia and Beyond at the Museum of Fine Arts, Houston. *Arts of Asia* September–November, 1–4.

Lhuillier, J. and Mashkour, M. (2017) Animal Exploitation in the Oases: An Archaeozoological Review of Iron Age Sites in Southern Central Asia. *Antiquity* 91, 655–673.

Millward, J.A. (2013) *The Silk Road: A Very Short Introduction*. Oxford, Oxford University Press.

Possehl, G.L. (2007) The Middle Asian Interaction Sphere. *Expedition* 49, 40–42.

Potts, D.T. (1999) *The Archaeology of Elam: Formation and Transformation of an Ancient Iranian State*. Cambridge and New York, Cambridge University Press.

Rogers, J.M. (1991) Chinese-Iranian Relations IV: The Safavid Period, 1501–1732. *Encyclopedia Iranica* V, 436–438.

Watson, O. (1991) Chinese-Iranian Relations XI: Mutual Influence of Chinese and Persian Ceramics. *Encyclopedia Iranica* V, 455–457.

Chapter 3

Iran–China joint archaeological excavations at Tepe Naderi, Shirvan, Northern Khorasan: Preliminary report of the 2016 and 2018 seasons

Ali A. Vahdati, Liangren Zhang, Tao Shui, Binbin Liu, Xin Jia, Homa Fathi, Margareta Tengberg, and Marjan Mashkour

Abstract

In 2016 and 2018, the Iran–China Joint Expedition carried out two seasons of fieldwork at Tepe Naderi, which is composed of an imposing tepe and a dilapidated adobe fortification wall enclosing it. The expedition implemented a multidisciplinary research strategy, comprising radiocarbon, archaeometric, archaeobotanical, and zooarchaeological studies so as to develop a robust understanding of the recovered materials. Beside two trenches (Tr. 1 and Tr. 2), the team opened 12 small test pits at the foot and along the periphery of the tepe to grasp the stratigraphy and formation of the tepe. Moreover, they performed geophysical and drilling surveys to delineate the boundary of archaeological deposits. The results of the two seasons of fieldwork suggest that Tepe Naderi was first settled during the late 4th millennium BCE (ca. 3500 BCE) and continued to be occupied intermittently until the Late Islamic period. Radiocarbon dates assign the tepe to the Late Chalcolithic, Bronze, and Iron Ages, and the lacustrine sediment around the tepe to later periods. It appears that throughout prehistoric times the site was closely associated with both the Namazga culture of southern Turkmenistan and the Burnished Grey Ware culture of the Gorgan/Damghan region, and the area of Shirvan, where Tepe Naderi is located, was a zone of cultural interactions between Central Asia and the Iranian Plateau from the 4th to the 2nd millennium BCE.

The upper Atrak valley in northeastern Iran, where Tepe Naderi is located, is flanked by two parallel mountain ranges, i.e., the Kopet Dagh to the north and Ala Dagh to the south, approximately 60 km long and 30 km wide, with an average altitude at the valley floor of 1200–1300 m, and a maximum elevation of approximately 3080 m above sea-level at the peak of the highest mountain in the vicinity, Shah-e Jahan (Fig. 3.1). In addition to the Atrak River and the tributaries flowing from small lateral

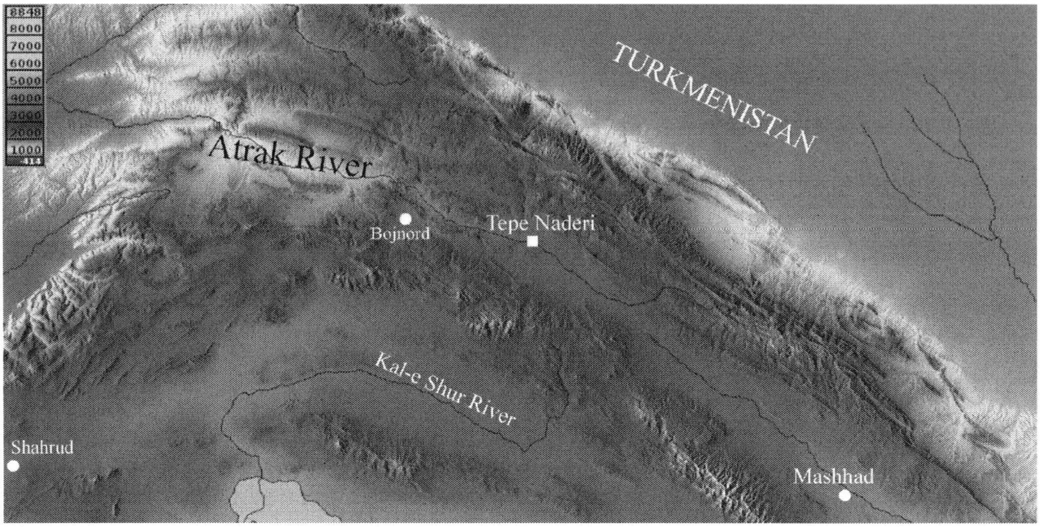

Fig. 3.1: Map of Northern Khorasan showing location of Tepe Naderi in the upper Atrak valley.

valleys, a series of deep wells and a network of now largely disused *qanat* galleries (an underground aqueduct system for conducting water from an aquifer to the surface) bring water further away from the rivers and streams for cultivation, on which agriculture in the region is highly dependent.

While the upper Atrak River and the lateral streams are suitable for the development of permanent settlements, the uplands are rich in pasture and favorable for the development of semi-sedentary pastoralist and agro-pastoral communities (Papoli-Yazdi 1991; Vahdati 2021). Until the recent past, the population centers in the valley had been functioning as small markets, exchanging agricultural goods for pastoral products (Fisher 1968, 66–67). Moreover, the valley is a natural corridor connecting the Mashhad plain to the east to the plain of Gorgan to the west along the course of Kashaf-Rud and Atrak rivers, and a particularly important east–west caravan route through the ages. Furthermore, thanks to some passes in both the Kopet Dagh and Ala Dagh Mountains, the valley has access to the main branches of the 'Silk Road' that connects Central Asia and the Iranian Plateau (Venco Riccardi 1980, 52). It could be postulated that such a geographical position has had facilitated contacts both with the region of Gorgan and southern Turkmenistan at least from the 4th millennium BCE, giving rise to the formation in the valley of important population centers such as Tepe Naderi, Tepe Devin, Tepe Yam, and other archaeological sites.

The upper Atrak valley, a zone of crustal instability, has nevertheless experienced several violent earthquakes in the past two centuries. The most recent one, the 'Kopet Dagh earthquake' (May 1, 1929), was so severe as to destroy more than 80 villages as well as the citadel on Tepe Naderi (also known as Citadel of Old Shirvan, Arg-e Naderi, or Tepe Naderi), and cause up to 3200 casualties in the region (Ambraseys and Melville 1982, 76–77). Through-going joints[1] and cracks in an Early Bronze Age massive wall (Feature 39) at the base of the tepe, described below, could also be of seismic origin, which suggests a similar tectonic event in ancient time.

Recent field investigations in the intermontane valleys of North Khorasan province have suggested that the province was a contact zone between the two vigorous cultural regions, i.e., the Iranian Plateau and Central Asia, throughout its history (Venco Riccardi 1980, 52; Vahdati 2015, 277; 2018, 63–65). So far only six tepes with prehistoric sequences have been excavated at small scales in the province, however, more excavation is desirable for exposing diachronic cultural development and cross-regional interactions in ancient times.

Tepe Naderi (37°23′45.3″ N, 57°55′06.4″ E) is located in the upper Atrak valley, in the southwest of the modern city of Shirvan (Fig. 3.1). It is situated at the confluence of the Atrak river and its tributary Qoljoq (a seasonal stream), both of which are vital for the sustenance of agricultural lands and orchards in the region. The tepe is an imposing, 20 m tall, irregularly elliptical mound. It is girded by a huge fortification wall of the Safavid and Qajar periods (Plate 3.1).

In 2016 and 2018 the Iran–China Archaeological Joint Expedition carried out two seasons of fieldwork at Tepe Naderi. Apart from two trenches (Tr. 1 and Tr. 2), the expedition sunk a series of small test pits at the foot and along the periphery to grasp the stratigraphy and the formation of the tepe, performed geophysical and drilling surveys to delineate the boundary and the sedimentary deposition, all for the purpose of illuminating the formation of the site as a whole. In addition, the expedition implemented a multidisciplinary research program, comprising radiocarbon, archaeometric, archaeobotanical, and zooarchaeological studies, to obtain a robust understanding of the material remains from the two seasons of excavation. The results of the geophysical and drilling surveys and a ceramic study have been published elsewhere (Zhang *et al.* 2021; Ma *et al.* 2022); this paper will report some important materials from the excavations, archaeobotanical, and zooarchaeological studies.

Tepe Naderi

The town of Shirvan, where Tepe Naderi is located, is mentioned in the accounts of several 19th-century travelers. Colonel C.M. MacGregor (1879, 89–92), who visited Shirvan in 1875, and Eʿtemad-al-Salṭana (1884, 143–145) were particularly informative, providing detailed description of the town and its fortification. MacGregor (1879, 90–91) mentioned a fortification wall enclosing about 300 houses, a number of irregular, narrow alleys, and one main street leading from the western gate (*Darvazeh Quchan*) to the Khan's house and to a citadel built on the top of a high artificial tepe, which commanded a view of the entire town (Fig. 3.2). Without any doubt this high artificial tepe refers to Tepe Naderi. These observations are largely confirmed by the account of Muhammad Hasan Khan (Eʿtemad-al- Salṭana), who befell upon Shirvan in company with Nasir al-din Shah (1831–1896) of the Qajar Dynasty during his second royal tour of Khorasan in 1300 AH (1883 CE). He added that the fortification wall had 40 towers along its perimeter and a wide moat outside. He also described a variety of public buildings within it, including baths, mosques, ice houses, and 150 shops such as draperies, apothecaries, groceries, dyeing workshops, blacksmith shops, shoemaker's and tailor's shops. In addition, he also alluded to the citadel on the top of the high tepe on the western side of the town, and blocks of modest dwellings for about 1500 families who lived in the town (Eʿtemad-al-Salṭana 1884, 143–145).

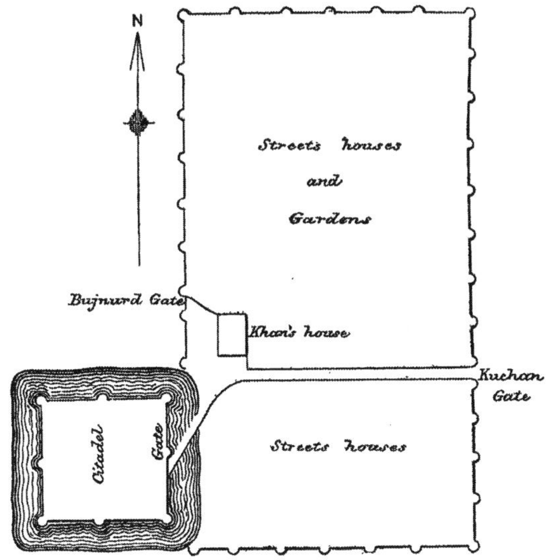

Fig. 3.2: Rough plan of the town of Shirvan sketched by MacGregor in 1875.

The citadel on the top of the tepe was already partly destroyed at the time of Nasir al-din Shah; the dwellings within the fortified wall were totally destroyed, probably during the major 'Kopet Dagh earthquake' of 1929. Later on, the local government cleared the ruins on the top and around the tepe and turned it into a park and agricultural field. The ruins of the citadel were thoroughly razed in the 1990s to make room for a television tower, which was relocated in 2017. Today only small segments of the fortification wall and a single tower are extant on the western and southern sides of the site.

Tepe Naderi was first recorded as an archaeological site in 1964 by E.O. Negahban during his survey in northern Khorasan. In 1976 the tepe was surveyed by an Italian team from Turin University. It was estimated to be approximately 2.5 ha in dimension, and its earliest occupation was dated to the Chalcolithic period (Venco Riccardi 1976). As the second largest tepe in the upper Atrak valley, it was not subject to a full-scale excavation until 2016, when the Iran–China Joint Expedition opened two trenches at the southern foot of the tepe to investigate the human-environment interactions during and after the site's formation (Plates 3.2, 3.3). In the course of the second season in 2018, an archaeobotanist and a zooarchaeologist from Muséum National d'Histoire Naturelle in Paris joined the expedition.

The excavation materials from the two trenches indicate that Tepe Naderi was first settled during the late 4th millennium BCE (F28, 5128±30 cal BP) and continued to be occupied intermittently till the late Islamic period. During the Late Chalcolithic and Bronze Age, the tepe was closely associated with both the well-known Namazga culture of southern Central Asia and the coeval Burnished Grey Ware culture of the Gorgan/Damghan region. While the red and buff painted pottery with distinctive zoomorphic and geometric motifs of the Namazga III–IV culture are prominent, the Burnished Grey Ware is absolutely dominant in the late 4th and 3rd millennium BCE layers, the pattern of which confirms that the area of Shirvan was a contact zone between Central Asia and the Iranian Plateau from the 4th to the 2nd millennium BCE (cf. Venco Ricciardi 1980, 52; Kohl 1984, 93, 105). The extent of Namazga V occupation at Tepe Naderi, if ever existed, is not yet evident, but there is no doubt that throughout the 2nd and the first half of the 1st millennium BCE the site was occupied by Namazga VI (BMAC) and Yaz cultures of the type known from the central and eastern piedmont zones of southern Turkmenistan.

Survey and excavation

At the beginning of fieldwork, a Real-Time Kinematic (RTK) apparatus was used to refine an existing topographic map of the tepe, and a drone was employed to take photographs to generate a 3D model of it. The tepe was then surveyed through surface collection and with the Chinese drill.[2] During the first season in 2016, a total of 67 points were bored: 37 at the foot of the tepe and 30 in the agricultural fields surrounding the tepe (Plate 3.2). As these surveys indicate, the tepe is elliptical, measuring 185 m east–west and 148 m north–south. In 2018, a geophysical survey with ground-penetrating radar and multi-electrode resistivity was undertaken to investigate the tepe and the area around it. The results of the mapping, drilling, and geophysical surveys have been reported elsewhere (Zhang *et al.* 2021). In addition, 12 small test pits were dug at random spots in the area around the tepe to define the spatial extent of off-tepe archaeological deposits, which is required for delineating the protection zone of the site Tepe Naderi.

Two trenches (Tr. 1 and Tr. 2) were cut at selected points (Plates 3.2, 3.3). Trench 1 was first sunk in the area to the south of the tepe, along the south–north axis. It was 29 m long and 2 m wide, and was divided into three 9–10 m-long sections (S1–3). In the second season of 2018, excavation was resumed in S1–3. The trench was excavated to the depth of 3 m in S2 and S3, and to the virgin soil, 8 m deep, in a 4 m-long segment of S1. As a result, Layers 3 and 4 were divided into five and four sub-layers because several features were found between them. The sub-layers of Layer 3 and Sub-layers 4-1 and 4-2 are horizontal sheets of silt, but Sub-layers 4-3 and 4-4 are slanting sheets of washout from the tepe (Fig. 3.3). During the second season, Trench 1 was extended northward up the slope of the tepe for 40 m, which was divided into eight sections;

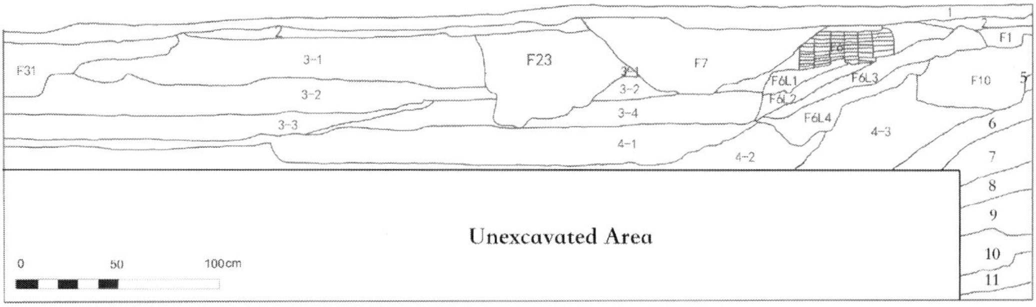

Fig. 3.3: Section drawing of Trench 1, showing succession and division of layers in S1–S3.

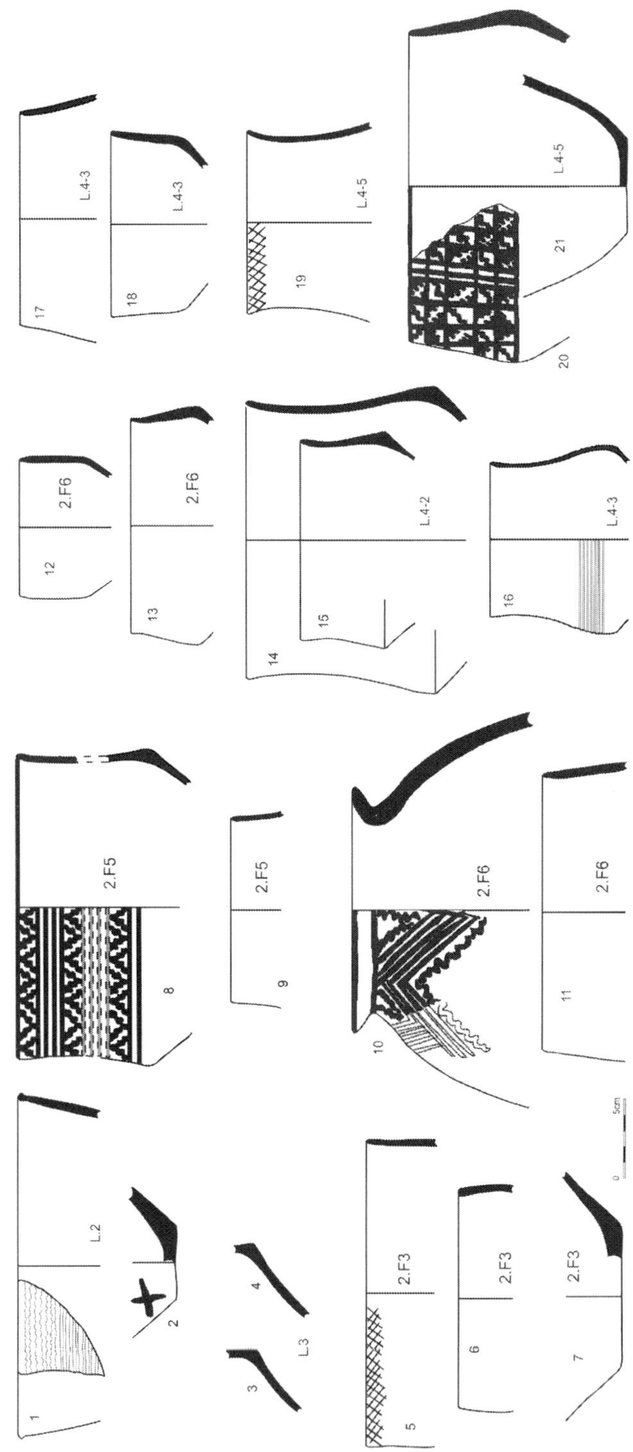

Fig. 3.4: Pottery from Trench 2, Layer 2 (1–2), 3 (3–4), 4 (14–22), F3 (5–7), F5 (8–9), and F6 (10–13).

Table 3.1: Cultural layers and features identified at Trenches 1 and 2 at tepe Naderi, and radiocarbon dates for some samples from the trenches analyzed at Beta Analytic Inc., Miami, Florida.

Table	*Location*	*Layer/feature*	*Chronology*	*Radiocarbon date (cal BP, 2 Sigma)*
L1	Trench 1	depositional layer	Modern	
L2	Trench 1	depositional layer	Islamic period	
L3	Trench 1	depositional layer	Islamic period	
L4-1	Trench 1	depositional layer	Islamic period	
L4-2	Trench 1	depositional layer	Islamic period	
L4-3	Trench 1	depositional layer	Islamic period	
L4-4	Trench 1	depositional layer	Islamic period	
L5	Trench 1	depositional layer	Late Iron Age, Yaz III	
L6	Trench 1	depositional layer	Late Iron Age	2225±90
L7	Trench 1	depositional layer	Early Bronze Age, NMZ IV	4672±144
L8	Trench 1	depositional layer	Early Bronze Age, NMZ IV	4669±146
L9	Trench 1	depositional layer	Early Bronze Age, NMZ IV	
L10	Trench 1	depositional layer	Early Bronze Age, NMZ IV	
L11	Trench 1	depositional layer	Late Chalcolithic, NMZ III	
L4-1	Trench 2	depositional layer	Early Bronze Age, NMZ IV	
L4-2	Trench 2	depositional layer	Early Bronze Age, NMZ IV	
L4-3	Trench 2	depositional layer	Early Bronze Age, NMZ IV	4104±120
L4-4	Trench 2	depositional layer	Early Bronze Age, NMZ IV	
L4-5	Trench 2	depositional layer	Early Bronze Age, NMZ IV	4628±180, 4954±86
L5-1	Trench 2	depositional layer	Early Bronze Age, NMZ IV	4697±127
L5-2	Trench 2	depositional layer	Early Bronze Age, NMZ IV	4749±105
L5-3	Trench 2	depositional layer	Early Bronze Age, NMZ IV	
F39	Trench 1, S11	mud-brick wall	Early Bronze Age and Late Chalcolithic, NMZ IV–III	
F43	Trench 1, S10, S11	mud-brick wall	Early Bronze Age and Late Chalcolithic, NMZ IV–III	
Unit 1	Trench 1, S11	ash deposit	Late Chalcolithic, NMZ III	5069±199
F13	Trench 1, S7, S8	pit-house	Iron Age, Yaz-I/II	4735±108, 2752±27
F11	Trench 2	stone cluster	Early Bronze Age, NMX IV?	
F9	Trench 2	mud-brick wall	Early Bronze Age, NMZ IV	
F5	Trench 1, S3	bag-shaped pit	Late Islamic period	146±145, 180–250, 150–210

among them three sections (S4–6) were left unexcavated due to the time and budget constraint. Each of the five excavated sections (S7–11), however, was dug to a depth of about 3 m, in line with the step-trench method (Plate 3.3). A good number of dwellings were exposed in these sections.

Altogether 11 cultural layers and 10 features were discovered in Trench 1. Among the 11 layers recorded in S1, Layer 1 is modern; Layers 2–4 are of the Islamic period (11th–19th centuries); Layer 5 produces Iron Age pottery of the Yaz I–III culture; Layers 6 presents a mixture of Yaz culture pottery and Namazga VI (BMAC) sherds, with a radiocarbon date of 2225±90 cal BP (Table 3.1); Layers 7–10 exhibit Early Bronze Age pottery of the Namazga IV period; and Layer 11 contains late Chalcolithic pottery sherds similar to Namazga III. Among them, Layers 7 and 8 are radiocarbon dated to 4672±144 and 4669±146 cal BP (Table 3.1). The features identified in the three sections of Trench 1 (S1–3) are a series of pits (Features 1–3, 5, 7–9), a cluster of flat rocks, possibly a stone foundation of a house (Feature 4), a mud-brick wall (Feature 6), and a lime plastered house floor (Feature 10), all dating to the Islamic period.

Trench 2 was opened next to Trench 1 at the waist of the tepe, where a 3.4 m-high section had already been quarried in recent decades. A succession of architectural remains was thus exposed. The trench was 7 m long, but due to the irregular surface of the section across the length it was 0.5 m wide at the western end and 2.2 m at the eastern one. During the first season of excavation in 2016, because of time constraints, the section was only cleaned down to 1.5 m above the present-day ground level, revealing three layers and four features. In 2018 the excavation went down for another 1 m. Two major occupational layers were found, each of which comprises three sub-layers, labeled 4-1, 4-2, 4-3, 5-1, 5-2, and 5-3. Each of these sub-layers, with minor differences, consist of loose sandy soil, ashes and animal dung, lime conglomerates, and mud-brick fragments. The associated pottery is comprised of a variety of buff and red painted wares, sometimes with very fine and intricate geometric designs known as carpet or tapestry style (Fig. 3.4: 8, 20; Plate 3.4: 1–5), alongside the highly polished grey ware with burnished and/or incised decorations (Plate 3.4: 6–10), suggesting an Early Bronze Age date for these layers. Polished grey ware is, again, numerically dominant in these layers. Four radiocarbon dates from sub-layers 4-5, 5-1, and 5-2 place these layers within the range of 4628±180 cal BP and 4954±86 cal BP (2 Sigma, 95.4% probability), respectively (Table 3.1).

Features

As a result of the two seasons of excavation, a great number of features, including foundational pits, mud-brick walls, and semi-subterranean dwellings, which date from the Early Bronze Age to the late Islamic period, were found in Trench 1 and Trench 2. This is not the place to report all of them; it suffices to offer a few outstanding examples; in some cases, a description of pottery wares from them and radiocarbon dates of bone or charcoal samples are presented.

F39

A massive mudbrick wall at the base of the tepe. It is located in S11, beyond which lie Sub-layer 4-4 and Layers 5–11, i.e., the washout deposits from the tepe (Fig. 3.5). The wall is 320 cm wide and preserved to the height of nearly 2 m; it is oriented east–west, and extended beyond the trench. It is built with square and rectangular mudbricks of various sizes, including 21 × 21 × 10 cm and 35 × 20 × 11 cm, which are laid in the Flemish-bond style with a 1–3 cm thick clay mortar and covered with a 2–3 cm thick plaster on both surfaces. A long fissure, some 20 cm wide in the middle of the massive wall, shows a through-going joint; presumably it resulted from a severe earthquake after the occupation.

The wall seems to be part of a defensive structure that possibly surrounded the first settlement at Tepe Naderi during the Early Bronze Age. This hypothesis finds support in the electric resistivity survey of Tepe Naderi that discloses a wall-shaped anomaly at the same depth. The resistivity signature indicates that the wall stretches along the base of the tepe and serves as the rampart for it (Zhang *et al.* 2021). It is worth noting that all of the depositional layers immediately to the south of F39 sharply drop down, but the layers to the north of it are formed horizontally. One may infer that the wall was the perimeter protecting the residential area inside; beyond it, washout from the tepe formed

Fig. 3.5: The massive mud-brick wall (Feature 39) found in Tr.1-S11.

the slanting layers and sub-layers (Sub-layer L4-3, L4-4, Layers L5–L11) in S1. Among them Layer 8 is radiocarbon dated to 4669±146 cal BP (2 Sigma, 95.4% probability), whereas the ash deposit from S11-Unit 1, a feature abutting the wall to the north, is radiocarbon dated to 5069±199 cal BP (2 Sigma, 95.4% probability) (Table 3.1). All these dates place the wall well within the range of the Late Chalcolithic Age and the Early Bronze Age.

F43

A mudbrick wall (Feature 43) of a dwelling within the perimeter wall F39, it runs north–south from S11 into S10. The space inside it is filled with thick layers of ash deposit, S11-Unit 1, in which a considerable number of pottery sherds, sling balls made of sun-dried clay, and a few clay animal figurines are found. The above-mentioned radiocarbon date of the ash deposit from S11-Unit 1 is consistent with the chronology of the pottery wares from the same context. The overwhelming majority of the pottery from the ash deposit are polished grey wares (Fig. 3.6: 1–11, 16–19, 20–25); but buff and red painted wares are also abundant. The grey wares as a rule are highly polished on the surface, sometimes decorated with burnished or incised patterns comprised of

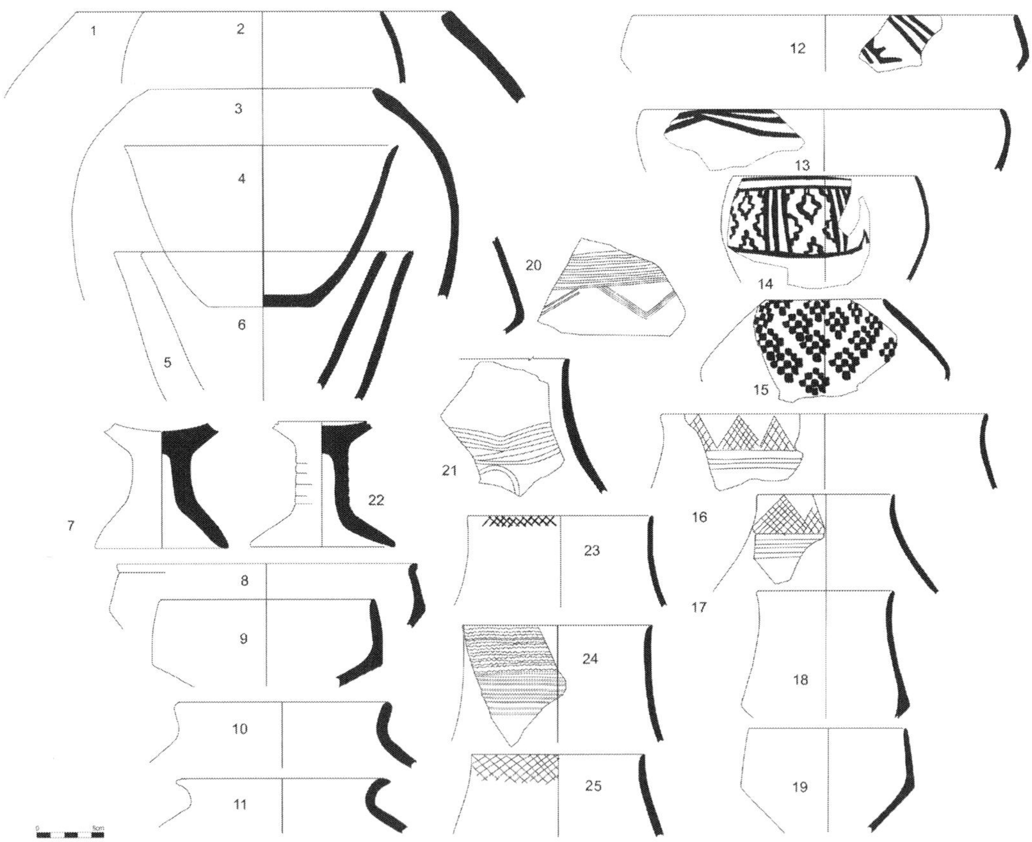

Fig. 3.6: Grey ware and painted pottery from the ash deposits of S11, unit 1 (1–19) and S10, Layers 7–9 (20–25), and S9, Layer 7 (26–28).

cross-hatching, undulating lines, oblique lines, and the like (Fig. 3.6: 16–17, 20–25). The most frequent forms are biconical beakers with sharp carination in the body (Fig. 3.6: 18–21, 23–25), flaring bowls (Fig. 3.6: 4–6), pedestal bowls (Fig. 3.6: 7, 22), and round-bodied jars (Fig. 3.6: 1–3), most of which find parallels in the early 3rd millennium BCE layers of Ak-depe in southern Turkmenistan (Masson 1976, 103–109), Shah Tepe (Arne 1945, pl. XLIV–XLVI) and Tepe Hissar (Schmidt 1937, pl. XXXVIII, H4260, H2562) in northeastern Iran. The buff and red wares are sometimes decorated with black or dark-brown geometric designs, i.e. nets, parallel lines, stepped lozenges, maltese crosses, zigzags (Fig. 3.6: 12–15, Plate 3.5: 1–7, 9–10), and rarely zoomorphic motifs featuring spotted leopards (Plate 3.5: 8). These are characteristic motifs of the Late Chalcolithic and Early Bronze Age of Central Asia frequently found at Kara-depe, Ak-depe, Altyn-depe, Khapuz-depe, Namazga-depe, and Ulug-depe in southern Turkmenistan (Masson 1961, 203, pls 26–27; 1988, pls IV, XXV, XXVII; Kircho *et al.* 2008).

F13

A unique structure, identified as a pit-house, is located at the waist of the tepe in S7 and S8. Irregular in plan, it has a straight wall in the south and two recesses in the north (Figs 3.7, 3.8). The western and eastern walls of the house are located outside of S7 and S8. The house is semi-subterranean, some 50 cm deep in the south but

Fig. 3.7: Semi-subterranean structure with platform, F13, Tr.1–S7.

82 cm deep in the north. The floor is 164 cm wide, but with the recesses it is 278 cm. Both the southern and northern walls are plastered with a fine, washed clay covering that has a whitish-green appearance. The floor of the structure is flat and very well smoothed. Against the southern wall there is a complex 'fireplace' consisting of a 10 cm-high rectangular platform, slightly tapering northwards and oriented 15° northeast, 120–130 cm long and 68–90 cm wide. On the platform there are three earthen stands installed in a triangular arrangement, located approximately 36–42 cm from each other. The stands are portable and two of them are found almost intact. They are in the form of rectangular pillars with rounded angles, 16 × 10–8 cm, concave on top, with traces of a loop at the center, fired dark red and stained with black soot. The three stands may have been used as a tripod to hold up a cooking vessel. Under the southwestern stand was found a small, plain greyish red, flat-bottomed cup with single vertical handle (broken), almost intact, 10 cm high and 6 cm in diameter, and which had been subjected to high temperatures in use. To the south of the three stands there is a round hole, 13 cm in diameter at the opening but slightly narrower at the bottom. The interior is fired red, apparently under high temperature, but the function of the hole, as well as the whole installation is not yet known precisely.

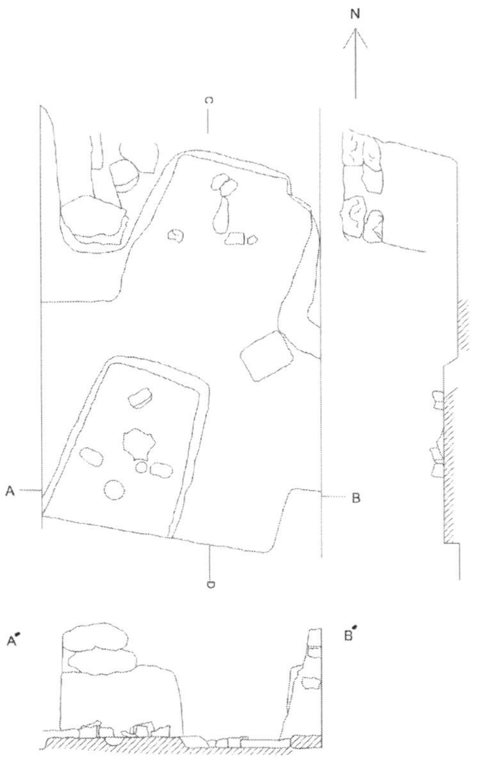

Fig. 3.8: Plan of F13, Tr.1, S7.

In one recess of the northern wall, another set of three stands is found; two stands are poorly preserved. They are oval-shaped, 10 cm long; rectangular, 6 cm; and rectangular, 12 × 8 cm. Again, each item is set 36–46 cm apart from the others. There is some evidence showing that the whole structure is intentionally filled in a single episode with layers of dark, greenish rounded pebbles, ashes, and soft soil, possibly after the house ceased to be functionally occupied. A similar situation has been reported from Bandykhan II (Bektepa) in the Surkhandarya region of southern Uzbekistan, where a pit-house of Yaz II period was completely overlain by several 'sterile' layers of sand and clay, containing numerous rounded pebbles and stones of different sizes (Boroffka and Sverchkov 2013, 53). The pottery sherds found in the fill of F13 are mainly of the Early Iron Age Yaz I and II styles (Fig. 3.9). The pottery of Yaz I in Tepe Naderi is mainly handmade, medium- to coarse-tempered ware of

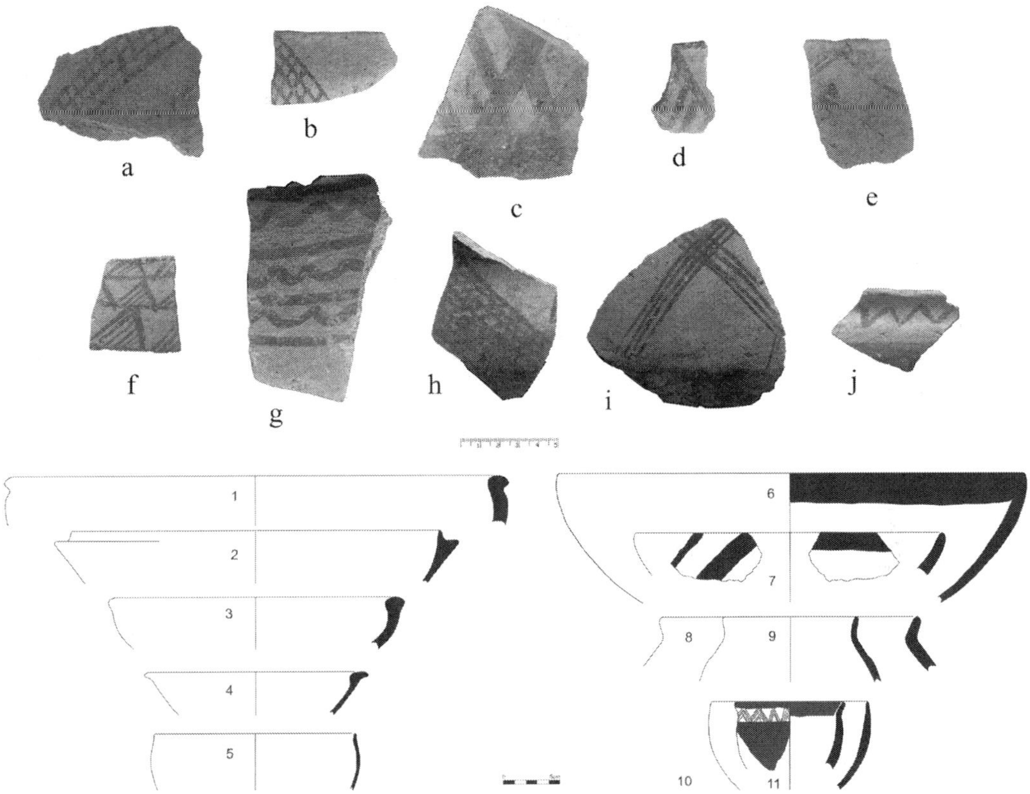

Fig. 3.9: Yaz pottery from Tr.1, S7 (1–4 from surface, a–b, 5 from Layer 1, c–e, 6–9 from Layer 2, 10–11 from Layer 3), and S8 (f, surface; g–j, Layer 2).

reddish paste with red or buff engobe decorated with dark-brown or red decorations. Painted motifs include a wide range of geometric patterns such as undulating lines, hatched and cross-hatched triangles, parallel crossing lines, and simple wide bands across the rim interior/exterior (Fig. 3.9: a–j, 6–11). Compared with that of the sites of south Central Asia and the plains of Jajarm-Esfarayen to the southern foothills of Alborz, the Yaz I pottery of Tepe Naderi (and the whole Atrak valley) is less coarse, finer in fabric, and better fired. The Yaz II pottery from Tepe Naderi is wheel-thrown, medium to fine-tempered ware of buff and reddish paste with plain surface. Two radiocarbon dates of animal bones extracted from the fill of F13 (Layer 2) are markedly discrepant, one 2752±27 cal BP (2 Sigma, 95.4% probability), and the other 4735±108 cal BP (2 Sigma, 95.4% probability) (Table 3.1), which probably results from the intrusive character of the earlier sample.

F11

A stone cluster, which constitutes the foundation of a dwelling under Sub-layer 4-3 in Trench 2, and intrudes into Sub-layers 5-1, 5-2, and 5-3. It is 1.4 m long north–south and 0.3–0.7 m wide east–west, comprising eight large boulders. The feature seems to extend beyond the western and northern walls of Trench 2, and it has a large patch of ashy deposit. There are very few pottery and bone fragments inside the feature, which makes it difficult to date.

F9

A mudbrick wall located in the east of Trench 2. It is found under Sub-layer 5-1. The wall is built of a single row of mudbricks, five courses high, 2.4 m long, 0.2 m wide, and 0.6 m high. The surface is not coated with straw-tempered clay, nor are the mudbricks laid in the English bond, but they are bound with mortar. The mudbricks are mostly regular, measuring 40–45 cm long, 20 cm wide, and 12 cm thick. Between the northern wall of Trench 2 and F9, a large number of pottery sherds, animal bones, gypsum clumps, and a large patch of ashy deposit are found in Sub-layers 5-2 and 5-3. For the moment the excavators ascribe this deposit to the occupation time of F9, which dates to the early 3rd millennium BCE. Among the pottery sherds, most are grey wares, and a small number of them are thick light buff painted wares. Among these, there are several pieces of grey perforated fragments and a red clay spout of a vessel. In addition, several fragments of gypsum objects are found.

F5

Located in S3 of Trench 1, it cuts into the sub-layers of Layers 3 and 4. First discovered in 2016, the feature is a bag-shaped pit, 116 cm wide at the opening, 296 cm at bottom, and 248 cm deep (Plate 3.6). In 2018, the bottom of the pit, which is leveled and plastered with gypsum, was found. Many plain and glazed pottery wares, particularly dozens of blue-white stonepaste wares, along with animal bones, stone tools, eggshells, and chicken bones are uncovered in the fill. A calibrated radiocarbon date of a piece of animal bone places this pit within the range of 146±145 cal BP (2 Sigma, 95.4% probability), or the Qajar period. This is consistent with two thermoluminescence dates of two pottery samples, 180–250 and 150–210 BP (Table 3.1). A study of the blue-white stonepaste wares discloses a complex history of the trade of blue-white porcelain from China to West Asia and the production of imitations in Syria, Iraq, Turkey, and Iran since the 14th century (Ma *et al.* 2022).

Test pits

Test pits, all 1 × 1 m, are traditionally accepted as the most effective way of exploring the spatial extent of archaeological deposits of ancient sites in Iran. During the second season, the joint expedition opened 12 test pits randomly in the area around the tepe to define the boundary of the protection zone. These pits show that the area within the fortification wall of the Islamic period is comprised of thick lacustrine (lake) sediment containing abundant animal bones and pottery sherds, which is consistent with layers L3 and L4 in Trench 1. The area outside the wall, further away from the tepe, is likewise composed of thick lacustrine sediment but devoid of artifacts. In line with the results of drilling and geophysical survey, this finding indicates that Tepe Naderi was intermittently surrounded by still water surface, into which silt and cultural artifacts washed from the tepe were deposited. Tepe Naderi is located in a small basin with a small outlet; when rainstorm occurs, a water surface can be formed around the tepe. The fortification wall, therefore, fortuitously marks the boundary of the site of Tepe Naderi.

Preliminary results of the faunal and botanical analyses

Large assemblages of animal and plant remains were recovered during the excavation of Tepe Naderi. The detailed study of the animal bone assemblages is currently ongoing in the Bioarchaeology Laboratory of the University of Tehran. Several thousands of generally well-preserved bone remains were recovered from the two trenches. Uncovered from successive occupational layers, they provide a valuable dataset to explore agropastoral activities diachronically. The bulk of faunal remains belong to small herbivores, mainly domestic sheep and goat. Cattle remains are also present in lower numbers, as are equids. Remains of horse, donkey and possibly their hybrids, all present on the Iranian Plateau during the 3rd millennium BCE are expected to be identified. These animals were important in agricultural activities, long-distance trade, and movement of human communities. Remains from wild animals, including gazelles, wild sheep, and wild goats, further provide information on the availability of natural resources in the surrounding areas. Gazelle was hunted in steppe habitats while wild goats and sheep were hunted in highlands or foothills.

In parallel to animal bones, plant remains (wood, seeds, and fruits) were collected from different sections of the trenches during the excavation in 2018. Flotation was implemented to dirt from the two trenches for the purpose of extracting charred plants, which were then dried before a preliminary study undertaken in the field with a binocular loupe. Bronze Age contexts in Trench 2 (Sub-layer 4-1) yielded barley and free-threshing wheat, as well as a series of wild pulses and grasses. Plant remains were abundant in the Islamic period contexts in both trenches with the presence of numerous grape seeds as well as cereal (barley and wheat) grain and chaff. Millet grains were attested in the later levels but they need both closer examination and radiocarbon dating.

Even though the bioarchaeological studies are still at the initial stage, the preliminary results highlight the importance of the assemblages for understanding the organization of agropastoral activities as well as the exploitation of the wild animal and plant biodiversity in a region where very little information exists so far. In Northern Khorasan province, the nearest sites for which we have comparable zooarchaeological and archaeobotanical assemblages are Tepe Damghani, Tepe Chalow, and Shahrake Firouzeh.

Conclusion

As a result of the two seasons of fieldwork, the Iran–China Joint Expedition has not only documented many features and artifacts, but also gained a better understanding of the formation of Tepe Naderi and its cultural interaction with contemporaneous sites in southern Central Asia and the Iranian plateau. The earliest features so far discovered are the massive wall F39 and the adjoining walls to the north, all dated to the last centuries of the 4th millennium BCE. As suggested by the geophysical survey data, the wall F39 extends at least along the entire southern and western periphery of the tepe. This wall may have served as a defensive perimeter of the early Bronze Age settlement. Inside the wall, mud-brick dwellings were revealed. Beyond the wall lies a vast lowland, situated about 8 m below present ground. Over time this area was filled with layers of lacustrine sediment. The earliest Layers 8–11, which date to the first and the second quarter of the 3rd millennium BCE, yield painted and grey wares similar to the Namazga IV pottery wares.

Of the upper layers, Sub-layers 4-2 and 4-1 and Layer 3, which are lacustrine sediments, fill up the vast area around the tepe horizontally. Over 3 m thick within S2 and S3 of Trench 1, these sediments spread out beyond the fortification wall of the Islamic period, at least in the area to the south of the tepe. This is repeatedly corroborated by the drilling, geophysical surveys, and testing pits. It appears that a body of still water, as results of seasonal flooding, was formed several times during the Islamic period in this area to make the tepe practically an island. This observation is confirmed by local inhabitants' memories of the old days with flashfloods and subsequent submergence of the dwellings near the tepe. Upon the surface of Layer 3, 8 m above the pristine ground, several features dating to the Islamic period were found. The expedition was able to dig to the bottom of one pit and found numerous blue-white stonepaste wares of the Qajar period, recalling the history of vibrant exchange of blue-white porcelain wares between West Asia and China since the 14th century.

Acknowledgments

The fieldwork at Tepe Naderi (2016, 2018) was done under the auspices of the Research Institute of Cultural Heritage and Tourism (RICHT), Iranian Center for Archaeological Research (ICAR) and the provincial office of Cultural Heritage and Tourism in Northern Khorasan Province. We would like to thank Drs H. Choubak and R. Shirazi, former directors of the Iranian Centre for Archaeological Research for their constant support of the project. It was funded by the SPIC program of Nanjing University and a grant from the State Administration of Cultural Heritage, China. Part of the bioarchaeological activities was also funded by the Program ATM-Orient Spread of the National Museum of Natural History of Paris. The study of animal bone was performed partly at the site and mainly at the Bioarchaeology Laboratory of the University of Tehran. We thank Dr Haeedeh Laleh and Dr Ahmad Aliyari for their help and support. Last, but not least, we would like to thank Dr Raffaele Biscione from the

Institute of Technologies applied to Cultural Heritage (ITABC), Rome, for reading and commenting on the earlier draft of the paper, and Dr Kyle Olson from Washington University, St Louis for proofreading the text.

Notes

1 Through-going joints, as a type of damage pattern supposedly of seismic origin, are distinctively regular in form, spacing, and orientation cutting across few adjacent (mud-)bricks in a wall.

2 The Chinese drill, a coring tool, is customarily used by Chinese archaeologists to investigate the dimension and stratigraphy of a site, be it a settlement or a cemetery, but rarely used outside of China.

Bibliography

Ambraseys, N.N. and Melville, C.P. (1982) *A History of Persian Earthquakes.* Cambridge, Cambridge University Press.

Arne, T.J. (1945) *Excavations at Shah Tepe, Iran.* Stockholm, The Sino-Swedish Expedition Publication 27.

Boroffka, N.G.O. and Sverchkov, L. (2013) The Jaz II and III Period Pottery. Classification and Chronology Viewed from Bandikhan, Southern Uzbekistan. In M. Wagner (ed.) *Pottery Chronology of the Early Iron Age in Central Asia*, 49–74. Warszawa, Kazimierz Michałowski Foundation, Institute of Archaeology, University of Warsaw.

E'temad-al-Salṭana, M.H. (1884) *Matla' Alshams.* Tehran.

Fisher, W.B. (1968) Physical Geography. In W.B. Fisher (ed.) *The Cambridge History of Iran I: The land of Iran*, 3–110. London, Cambridge University Press.

Kircho, L.B., Fedorovna Korobkova, G., and Masson, V.M. (2008) *Tekhniko-tekhnologicheskij potencial eneoloticheskogo naselenija Alatyn -Depe kak osnova stanovlenija rannegorodskoj civilizacii.* Saint-Petersburg, Evropejskij Dom. [Russian]

Kohl, P.L. (1984) *Central Asia. Paleolithic Beginnings to the Iron Age. Paris,* Editions Recherche sur les civilizations.

Ma, Y., Li, Z., Zhang, L., Wu, J., Xiong, Y., Vahdati, A., and Zhang. J. (2022). A Scientific Study of Late Islamic Blue-white Stonepaste Wares of Iran. *Archaeometry* 64 (5), 1110–1123.

MacGregor, C.M. (1879) *Narrative of a Journey through the Province of Khorassan and on the N.W. Frontier of Afghanistan in 1875.* London, W.H. Allen & Co.

Masson, V.M. (1961) The First Farmers in Turkmenia. *Antiquity* 35, 203–213.

Masson, V.M. (1976) *Pervobytnyj Turkmenistan.* Ashkhabad. [Russian]

Masson, V.M. (1988) *Altyn-depe.* Philadelphia, University Museum Monograph 55.

Papoli-Yazdi, M.H. (1991) *Le nomadisme dans le nord du Khorasan.* Paris/Tehran, Institut français de recherche an Iran.

Schmidt, E.F. (1937) *Excavations at Tepe Hissar, Damghan.* Philadelphia, The University of Pennsylvania Museum of Archaeology and Anthropology.

Vahdati, A.A. (2015) Preliminary Report on the Archaeological Survey in Esfarāyen County, Northeastern, Iran. *Archäologische Mitteilungen aus Iran und Turan* 47, 261–287.

Vahdati, A.A. (2018) The Early Iron Age in Northern Khorāsan. In J. Lhuillier and N. Boroffka (eds) *A Millennium of History: The Iron Age in Central Asia (2nd and 1st Millennia BC)*, 51–66. Archaologie in Iran und Turan, 17/ Memoires de la Delegation Archeologique Francaise en Afghanistan, XXXV. Berlin, D. Reimer.

Vahdati, A.A. (2021) Newly Found Rock Painting Sites in the Upper Atrak Valley, Northern Khorasan, North-eastern Iran. *Archaeological Research in Asia* 28, 100317.

Venco Ricciardi, R. (1976) Prospection au Khorassan (Vallee de l'Atrek)-Rapport sommaire, 1976. Unpublished Report Archived in the Document Center of the Iranian Ministry of Cultural Heritage and Tourism.

Venco Ricciardi, R. (1980) Archaeological Survey in the Upper Atrak Valley (Khorassan, Iran), Preliminary Report. *Mesopotamia* 15, 51–72.

Zhang, L., Liu, W., Guo, Z., Qiao, Y., Qin, J., Shui, T., and Vahdati, A.A. (2021) Brief Report on the Archaeological Survey at Tepe Naderi, Iran. *Kaoguxue Jikan* 24, 215–227. [Chinese with English Abstract]

Chapter 4 Prologue

The excavations of the ceremonial center of Persepolis

The chapter by Ahmad Ali Asadi *et al.* presents the results of archaeobotanical studies on materials recently excavated in drainage channels at the Achaemenid Persian site of Persepolis, modern Takht-e Jamshid, in the Marv Dasht plain in Southwestern Iran. This site, a ceremonial center and capital for the Achaemenid Empire (539–330 BCE), was constructed on a massive, manmade terrace at the base of a mountain called Kuh-e Rahmat and has been the focus of archaeological work for more than a century. One of several capitals for the Achaemenid Empire – others being Babylon, Susa, Pasargadae, and Ecbatana – the site, known as Pârsa in Old Persian, and called 'Persepolis' in Greek, had monumental buildings on its terrace, and a large outer town. Its proximity to the ritually significant site of Naqsh-e Rustam – which would become the dynastic necropolis for the Achaemenid ruler Darius I (522–486 BCE) and his descendants – and its grand and elaborately decorated architecture suggests that when it was built 'Persepolis would appear to have been viewed as a kind of mirror-image of the concept of Achaemenid Persian kingship. This is how Darius and his successors almost certainly viewed the splendor of their "home capital" and, if we keep in mind the comprehensive burning of Persepolis by Alexander in 330 BC, the very presence of the site would appear to have held similar connotations for the Macedonians' (Stronach 2012, XXI). Inscriptions at the site attribute the foundation to Darius I (r. 522–486 BCE) and the completion of many structures to Darius' son Xerxes (486–465 BCE).

The site

The earliest phase of this ambitious construction project involved leveling a natural outcrop to create a massive, multi-level terrace, which was then topped by a large, single entranced, mudbrick building. The excavators called this structure the Treasury, concluding it had served as a repository for tribute, spoils of war, and documents on clay tablets, although most of the portable, valuable objects stored there were removed when the site was ransacked by Alexander of Macedon's Army in 330 BCE.

Closer to the center of the platform was an enormous, columned audience hall referred to as the Apadana (columned or hypostyle hall in Old Persian), containing gold and silver foundation tablets in stone boxes in two corners. This intimidating space, where one presumably could encounter the king, had a ceiling supported by columns 24 m tall, and was approached by a double, reversing staircase on the north and east sides. Both staircases are elaborately carved with images of the king and court receiving visitors and tribute from all the lands encompassed by the empire. It was in this early stage of construction that builders carved into the living rock of the terrace – under and around these buildings – channels for carrying water and draining runoff. The 12 ha fortified citadel includes the Terrace and areas to the east, and the city was 50 ha in total.

Walls and towers fortified the citadel. The north-eastern tower contained a group of 30,000 tablets, many with seal impressions, called the 'Persepolis Fortification Tablets' which has been extensively studied by textual experts and art historians. A smaller cache of tablets, the Persepolis Treasury Tablets, was found in the Treasury. Most of these clay tablets were written in Elamite using cuneiform signs, a small number were written in the Aramaic language and script, and a few are uninscribed. Other languages represented in the archive include Greek, Old Persian, Babylonian, and Phrygian (Stolper and Tavernier 2007). These tablets document the activities of the administrators and Achaemenid court, payments to construction workers – including those from Syria, Egypt, and Ionia (Western Greece), and mention 'travelers and other individuals referred to as Indians, Babylonians, Carians, Arabs, Greeks, Egyptians, etc., who were involved in the construction activities outside Persepolis' (Mousavi 2012, 48). Dated tablets range from 509 BCE to 457 BCE.

Buildings on the terrace begun by Darius but completed by his son include the Tachara, or winter palace, and north of the Apadana the monumental Gate of All Lands, consisting of a four pillared hall with winged bulls, and a trilingual (Elamite, Old Persian, Babylonian) cuneiform inscription. Xerxes then initiated construction of the Hadish, a larger palace between the Treasury and the Apadana, expanded the Treasury, and reconstructed the area to its west to create an L-shaped building with red plastered floors. While earlier excavators called this structure the 'Queen's Quarters', or 'Harem', there is no Achaemenid era evidence for such a structural type, and more recently Ali Mousavi has suggested that the building accommodated visiting delegations (Mousavi 2012, 24).

Xerxes' successor, Artaxerxes I Makrochaeir (465–424 BCE), initiated the last major construction projects at the site, adding the Palace of Artaxerxes I and the Hall of One Hundred Columns. Nearly a century later, a descendent, Artaxerxes III Ochus (358–338) added tombs for himself and his father. His son Artaxerxes IV Arses (337–336 BCE), along with Darius III Codomannus, started construction of a gate in the north area of the terrace that was unfinished at the time of the site's capture by Alexander in early 330 BCE.

Alexander of Macedon had defeated the Persian Army in the west, and he took Persepolis without force. For unknown reasons – but attributed in Classical sources to revenge for the Persian sack of Athens in 480 BCE, or general drunkenness, or the instigation of an Athenian *hetaira* (courtesan) named Thais – the armies of Alexander of Macedon burned and vandalized much of the site in 330 BCE. They thoroughly ransacked the Treasury, removing portable objects of precious metal to fund further military campaigns (Mousavi 2012, 65–70). Parts of the city continued to be inhabited for a while, but for the most part the site lay in ruins and largely abandoned for millennia, while a new Persian capital arose 5 km north in Istakhr.

Excavation history

The visible ruins and soaring columns of massive Achaemenid structures at the sites of Persepolis and Pasargadae, and the inscriptions and rock reliefs at Naqsh-e Rustam, were well known locally. In the millennia that had passed since the monumental complex was destroyed, it had become untethered from the memory of its creation and its cultural milieu. The enormous, close-jointed stones that characterize its construction were considered a work of supernatural origin. By the 11th century CE locals referred to the site as the Takht-e Jamshid, or throne of Jamshid, and attributed its construction to Jamshid, a mythological ruler immortalized in Ferdowsi's *Shahnameh*. These ruins were much visited by European envoys to the Safavid court en route to the capitals of Shiraz, Isfahan, and Tehran as early as the late 16th–early 17th centuries CE.

During the 18th–19th centuries Western travelers produced engravings of ruined buildings and the sculpture and cuneiform inscriptions that decorated them. These images circulated widely in Europe (Sancisi-Weerdenburg 1991). Missions sent by the British and French governments to strengthen relations with Persia in light of Ottoman trade restrictions included artists like Sir Robert Ker Porter, whose careful draftsmanship produced the earliest measured drawings of the monuments, and artist and architects Eugène Flandin and Pascal Coste, who published illustrations of monuments across Persia (Porter 1821; Coste and Flandin 1843–1854). The French held exclusive rights to excavate in Persia from 1894–1927, and focused their excavations on the site of Susa (Mecquenem 1947; Mousavi 2013). Following the abolition of the French monopoly in 1927 and the creation of the Antiquities Law of 1930, the German archaeologist Ernst Herzfeld, who had been working in Mesopotamia, came to Iran to excavate and photograph the site of Pasargadae, and then moved on to the site of Persepolis. Here he led a team from the University of Chicago from 1931–1934 (Herzfeld 1941). He and his partner, Friedrich Krefter, excavated numerous monumental buildings at Persepolis, investigated the underground water channels discussed in this chapter, and discovered the Persepolis Fortification Tablets in a tower (Herzfeld 1941; Stolper and Tavernier 2007). In the 1930s, with the rising tide of anti-Semitism in Europe, Herzfeld was forced into exile in the US.

The Chicago Persepolis expedition replaced Herzfeld with Erich Schmidt, a German-American archaeologist and pioneer of aerial photography of archaeological excavations (Schmidt 1939; 1940; 1953; 1957; 1970). As World War II brought the excavations to a close, cases of artifacts destined for Chicago were tragically lost when the freighter carrying them was torpedoed in 1942 in the Caribbean Sea (Mousavi 2012).

When the American team left Persepolis in 1939, the government of Iran took over administration and excavation of the site, and continued excavations, the results of which are summarized by Ali Mousavi (2012). The renowned archaeologist Ali Sami was appointed director of the excavations in 1941, a position he held until 1961. In addition to extensive restorations, Sami focused excavations on the northern part of the Terrace where he explored structures abutting the Hall of One Hundred Columns. He also explored the underground water channels, and functionally restored them to prevent further erosion of the site.

Between 1964 and 1979, an Italian team worked with Iranian archaeologists to restore the site, with special attention to the Gate of All Lands, the Tachara, the Hadish, the Apadana, and the Hall of 100 columns, and the tomb of Artaxerxes III. Alongside restoration efforts, Iranian Archaeologist Ali-Akbar Tadjvidi expanded the focus of the work from the monumental buildings on the Terrace to the study of Achaemenid urban planning. While Persepolis was named a UNESCO World Heritage site in 1979, excavation lagged in the wake of the Iranian revolution. In 1991, when then-President Rafsanjani lauded Persepolis for its significance to national pride, the site was established as a focal point for interest in Iran's pre-Islamic past. Later efforts under the aegis of the Parsa-Pasargadae Research Foundation secured a buffer zone around the site, and with international collaborators conducted geomagnetic surveys, ceramic analysis, and dredged the channels. Numerous Iranian projects in the 2000s, some still unpublished, explored beyond the monumental buildings to examine the town itself (Mousavi 2012, 210–216).

This chapter provides an example of the more recent archaeological activity at Persepolis, and of the trend toward laboratory based archaeometric and archaeobotanical research in Iranian archaeology. The authors of this study analyzed archaeobotanical samples taken from Terrace channels that still provide essential drainage at the site, and compared the materials they identified to other evidence – textual, art historical, and archaeological – to clarify what is known about the natural vegetation and horticultural practices at the site, as well as the way different foodstuffs were processed. The samples from the channel residue contained seeds, fruit, charcoal, chaff, and some roots, and are likely dated to the period before the destruction of the site. They have been identified as the seeds of date, almond, elm, and plane trees, with some evidence for wild catchfly (Silene sp.) and seeds in the buckwheat family seeds. Faunal samples include dozens of freshwater snails, indicating periods when the channels held standing water or connected to a reservoir. Finally, given that the Fortification Tablets record that wages to royal staff were paid in grain, it is indeed surprising that there were no cereals amongst the samples. While this could indicate that grain processing happened elsewhere, future excavations in unexplored channels might provide more information.

Bibliography

Coste, P. and Flandin, E. (1843–1854) *Voyage en Perse, Entrepris par Ordre de M. le Ministre des Affaires Etrangères, D'après les Instructions Dressées par l'Institut (6 vols.).* Paris, Gide et J. Baudry.

Herzfeld, E. (1941) *Iran in the Ancient East.* Oxford, Oxford University Press.

Mecquenem, R. de (1947) *Contribution à l'étude du palais achéménid à Suse, in: Mémoires de La Mission Archéologique En Iran* 30. Paris, Presses universitaires de France.

Mousavi, A. (2012)*Persepolis.* Boston and Berlin, Walter de Gruyter.

Mousavi, A. (2013)The History of Archaeological Research in Iran: A Brief Survey. In D.T. Potts (ed.) *The Oxford Handbook of Ancient Iran,* 3–16. Oxford, Oxford University Press.

Porter, R.K. (1821) *Travels in Georgia, Persia, Armenia, Ancient Babylonia, &c. during the Years 1817, 1818, 1819, and 1820.* London, Longman, Hurst, Rees, Orme, and Brown.

Sancisi-Weerdenburg, H. (1991) Through Travellers' Eyes: The Persian Monuments as Seen by European Visitors. In H. Sancisi-Weerdenburg and J. Drijvers (eds) *Through Travellers's Eyes: European Travellers on the Iranian Monuments: Achaemenid History VII,* 1–35. Leiden, Nederlands Instituut voor het Nabije Oosten.

Schmidt, E.F. (1939) *The Treasury of Persepolis and Other Discoveries in the Homeland of the Achaemenians.* Chicago, University of Chicago Press.

Schmidt, E.F. (1940) *Flights over Ancient Cities of Iran.* Chicago, University of Chicago Press.

Schmidt, E.F. (1953) *Persepolis I. Structures, Reliefs, Inscriptions.* Chicago, University of Chicago Press.

Schmidt, E.F. (1957) *Persepolis II. Contents of the Treasury and Other Discoveries.* Chicago, University of Chicago Press.

Schmidt, E.F. (1970) *Persepolis III: Royal Tombs and Other Monuments.* Chicago, University of Chicago Press.

Stolper, M. and Tavernier, J. (2007) From the Persepolis Fortification Archive Project, 1: An Old Persian Administrative Tablet from the Persepolis Fortification. *ARTA* 1, 1–28.

Stronach, D. (2012) Forward. In A. Mousavi, *Persepolis,* xxi–xxiv. Boston and Berlin, Walter de Gruyter.

Chapter 4

Identification of plant remains found at the underground channels of Persepolis

Ahmad Ali Asadi, Zohreh Shirazi, and Sharareh Ghasemi

Abstract

*Most of the archaeological research at Persepolis took place in the middle of the last century, with little attention to environmental issues. In the period since the destruction of Persepolis, all its channels, especially near their exits in the southeastern corner of the Terrace, have filled with building debris and other sediments containing plant remains important for understanding environmental conditions at Persepolis during the site's lifetime. Therefore, the aim of this article is to shed more light on the vegetation around Persepolis in the Marvdasht plain and local diet based on these data. Some sediment and deposits were sampled and floated from this channel. The obtained seeds, fruits and charcoal were studied at the Archaeobotanical Laboratory of the World Heritage Base of Shahr-i Sokhta. The results indicate the presence of date stones in the southern channels of the Treasury and in the trench excavated alongside the southern wall of the Terrace. These findings are in parallel with other archaeological, iconographic, and linguistic evidence already identified at Persepolis. It seems that date palm was imported to Persepolis from southern regions of Fars. No evidence of cereals has been found among the studied materials. The fact can be explained in two ways: cereals may have been transported to the Terrace as processed material (as flour or bread) rather than raw grain, as is attested by written sources, or the archaeobotanical sampling has not been sufficient. It should be added that around Persepolis evidence for cultivated trees such as almond (*Amygdalus *sp.), plane tree (*Platanus *sp.), and elm (*Ulmus *sp.) has been identified. These facts, along with other palynological (relating to particles) data, indicates a great diversity of arboricultural activities during the Achaemenid period.*

The symbolic capital of the Achaemenid Empire, Persepolis is located in the Fars province in southwestern Iran. The majority of archaeological excavations at this site were carried out from the 1930s until the 1940s by Ernest Herzfeld and Erich Schmidt of the Oriental Institute of the University of Chicago. Following this work, the Iranian archaeologist Ali Sami continued excavations at the site for more than 12 years. Although Herzfeld and Sami also published some results of their excavations (Herzfeld 1941; Sami 1951; 1960), it was Schmidt who, with three volumes of Persepolis I (1953), Persepolis II (1957), and Persepolis III (1970), created the most important books on Persepolis and its excavations. During this era, archaeology focused largely on recovery of architecture and other monuments, particularly those decorated in relief. More interdisciplinary investigations, including scientific studies, were often neglected, as they were at Persepolis. As a royal site, Persepolis was studied for its special architecture and artistic style, seen in columned halls and carved orthostats.

At this time, archaeobotany was largely overlooked. While tablets from Persepolis frequently refer to the agricultural products that served as rations for workers and employees (Hallock 1969), no attempt was made to identify evidence of these products in Persepolis. The first project including such archaeobotanical data occurred during the excavations of the Persepolis channels beginning two decades ago (Askari Chaverdi 2008, 70). In addition to studying the architecture and layout of the channels, excavators turned their attention to the contents of the canals, especially focusing on plant and faunal remains. During the excavation season in the summer of 2014 (Asadi 2014), mainly performed on the channels of the Treasury building, a subgroup of the archaeobotanical team evaluated the excavated deposits. In the following, the details of these studies and their results are described. Therefore, the aim of this article is to shed more light on the vegetation around Persepolis in the Marvdasht plain and the local diet based on these data.

Environmental characteristics of Marvdasht Plain

The Fars region is a part of the south and southeastern Zagros mountains. From a geomorphological point of view, the north and northwestern parts of Fars are formed by inter-connected mountains and deep valleys while the south and southwestern parts consist of plains (including Marvdasht, Shiraz, and Kazerun). These plains are irrigated by the Kur River and the Khoshk river (Khodaghloi *et al.* 2017). In terms of precipitation, the region is influence by low pressure system from northern Africa as well as the dry climatological conditions of the Iranian plateau. The average annual precipitation is 314 mm/year and the average annual temperature is 27.86°C (82.15°F).

Based on the climatic and geographical conditions, the vegetation of Fars can be categorized as Steppe, Semi-Steppe, and Steppe-Forest ecoregions. The Steppe ecoregion (eastern and southern Fars) included plant species like tamarisk (*Tamarix*), milkvetch (*Astragalus*), goosefoot (Chenopodiaceae), licorice (*Glycyrrhiza glabra*), harmel (wild rue) (*Peganum harmala*), and Mugwort (*Artemisia*). Semi-steppe ecoregion is found in semi-arid regions with species such as Red Feathers (*Echium amoenum*), Tragacanth gum/gond katira (*Tragacanth*), asafoetida (*Ferula assa-foetida*), common thistle (*Cirsium vulgare*), basilisk (*Prangos ferulacea*), liquorice (*Glycyrrhiza glabra*), yarrow (*Achillea millefoliun*), camelthorns (*Alhagi*), common fumitory (*Fumaria officinalis*), *Acanthophyllum* species, Milkvetch (*Astragalus*), and trees and shrubs like tamarisk, willow (*Salix*), plane (*Platanus*), pine (*Pinus*), cypress, and ash (*fraxinus*). Nowadays, these vegetation patterns have been destroyed due to agriculture and pastoral activities. The Steppe-forest (also known as dry forest) includes trees such as oak (*Quercus*), almond (*Amygdalus*), cypress, fig (*Ficus carica*), pistachio (*Pistacia*), hawthorn (*Crataegus*), and Christ's thorn jujube (*Ziziphus spina-christi*). These forests are not dense, and they are in danger of disappearing because of locally low precipitation and anthropogenic impact (Ghasemi 2015, 22–23). Marvdasht plain is a part of this ecoregion and benefits from a diversified vegetal cover in the mountainous region and lowland.

Persepolis channels

The channels of Persepolis constitute an important part of this royal site (Plate 4.1). The plan of these structures shows a relatively complex network of several key channels, as well as smaller channels, reaching the entire surface of the Terrace. As parts of the Terrace are located directly on the bedrock, the drainage system of Persepolis was either carved from the natural rock of the mountain or, in some areas, were created with stone blocks.

The drainage system of Persepolis, according to its functional purpose, was accessible through an entrance gate in the southeast of the Hall of One Hundred Columns and through hatches located in the courtyards as well as inside of the mudbrick walls. The latter hatches were connected to the roof of the buildings by a system of pottery pipes. All of the channels at Persepolis ended at an outlet in the southeast corner of the terrace. The water in the channels evacuated from this outlet to the southern area of the terrace.

Fig. 4.1: Deposited layers within the southern channel of the Treasury building. Photograph by Morteza Homayoun.

As Schmidt, the site's main excavator, pointed out, the founder and architects of Persepolis were well aware of the destructive effects of winter rainfalls. Therefore, to protect the buildings, which were mainly built from mudbrick, they created a network of channels to quickly drain the water from roofs and yards to prevent possible flood damage to the structures (Schmidt 1953, 39). The construction of these channels began simultaneously with preparing the Terrace site for the construction of buildings. Based on the relationship between the architecture and the channels, and the method of digging the channels, the construction of their main courses and major channels must have been finished immediately before, or simultaneously with, the construction of the earliest palaces. After the destruction of Persepolis, these channels were filled with debris, and stopped flowing.

Excavations in the channels

As archaeological excavations Persepolis resumed in 2003, excavations were carried out to identify the southeastern channels on the terrace, during which their main outlet was identified (Askari Chaverdi 2008, 70–71). In addition, the lead author of this text found the channels located under the Treasury building and excavated the northeast area of the Terrace (i.e. the so-called Building of Unfinished Gate) and the courtyard of the Tachara Palace (also known as the Palace of Darius) (Plate 4.2). This archaeological work has continued up to recent years (Asadi 2012; 2014; Asadi and Mansouri 2017; Asadi and Mohammadzadeh 2021). In addition to mapping the network of channels, another aim of these excavations was to restore the function of these structures to drain rainwater which had been flooding the Treasury building.

Stratification of the deposited soils in the ancient drainage systems is almost completely different from the stratification methods in the usual residential sites. The main difference is that the drainage systems normally are not a place of residence, and unlike in a residence, sediment in a channel accumulates over shorter time periods. In conventional sites, the highest layers or strata are dated to the latest settlement periods and the lower levels represent the earlier phases. In drainage systems, due to various reasons, sediment accumulates in different ways. Based on these facts, the following method was employed in the excavation of Persepolis channels. At each area selected for the excavation, first and after the initial cleaning, a precise section-drawing of the sediments inside the channel was created. Then, based on stratigraphic observations of phases of sedimentation in the channel, the excavation started by removing the soil from the upper layers and then the lower parts of the sediments until it ended at the bottom of the channel. Using this method, some of the stratigraphic units (SU) were located on top of each other and some of them were next to each other. Distinguished by color, texture, and cultural materials (pottery, carved stones, bones, special objects, etc.), a separate unit number was assigned to each SU.

Excavation season of 2014

During the 2014 excavation season, excavators focused on three areas: the channels beneath the Treasury building, the channel in the southern courtyard of the Tachara Palace, and an area near the southern wall of the Terrace (Asadi 2014). In the following year, the excavations in these three locations were evaluated and their archaeological deposits analyzed.

Our excavation showed that all the channels under the Treasury building at Persepolis lead to a hatch located in room 82 of the Treasury building. By the end of the excavation, the results showed a junction of two perpendicular channels under the hatch in room 82 (Plate 4.2, Fig. 4.1): one channel (Eastern channel) extends eastward and then turns 90° to continue southward. The second channel (Southern channel) extends directly toward the south and finally ends at the south wall of the Terrace. During the excavation of the Southern channel, sediments were of particular interest. Here a distinct layer of grey soil combined with large amounts of ash and charcoal was gradually discovered in the channel. This layer gradually became thicker, and the percentage of charcoal and ash increased, as the channel extended toward the south, i.e., its terminus (Plate 4.2). Samples were extracted for archaeobotanical studies.

Fig. 4.2: Location of the southern wall trench of the 2014 excavation season. Photograph by Morteza Homayoun.

There is sufficient evidence that the obstruction of the Southern channel by sediments took place after the Treasury building ceased to be used, when Persepolis was captured by Alexander and his army in the year 330 BCE and, according to the sources, set on fire (Asadi 2021,165). In support of this, Schmidt noticed traces of fire during his excavations of the Treasury building (Schmidt 1953, 171–200).

Excavations in the Southern channel of the Treasury building continued for 39 m to the south and resulted in the discovery of a new outlet. Having excavated the length of the channel, a trench was opened next to the southern side of the Terrace wall in order to locate the exterior of the newly discovered outlet (Fig. 4.2). The upper layers of this trench included some of the dumped soils of earlier excavations at Persepolis. A small amount of these soils was extracted for archaeobotanical studies, to determine the relationship to samples from the Terrace buildings.

Fig. 4.3: Deposited layers within the channel of southern Tachara Palace, Photograph by Younes Zare.

Another goal of the excavation season of 2014 at Persepolis was to excavate a part of the channel located in the southern Tachara Palace (Palace of Darius) (Fig. 4.3). During the excavation of this channel, numerous Achaemenid period artifacts were found, suggesting that this channel filled with debris from the destruction of surrounding buildings. Samples of the soil in this channel were collected for archaeobotanical purposes.

Material and method

The studied plant remains for this research were collected from three excavated trenches at the above-mentioned channels at Persepolis: the southern courtyard of the Tachara Palace (TSCT), the southern channels of the Treasury (TSC) and the trench alongside the Southern Wall of the Terrace of Persepolis (SWT). The samples from these trenches ranged between 20 and 70 kg. Deposits located in the southern channels of the Treasury included a great quantity of ashes and charcoal. In total, 140 kg of deposits were sampled from channels for archaeobotanical studies. The technique used to extract plant remains from sediments was flotation.

In this method, which is based on differentiating the density of soil particles, plant remains, and water molecules, a series of sieves with 1–2 mm holes were used. Archaeobotanical data obtained from flotation consisted of seeds, fruits, charcoal, and in some cases chaff and plant roots. The archaeobotanical analyses of the materials were conducted in the Archaeobotanical Laboratory of the World Heritage Base of Shahr-i Sokhta, Iran. The initial examination of the plant remains (charred) showed that they are in a good state of preservation for laboratory and microscopic studies. The study involves different stages including separation of various types of plant remains (seeds, fruit, and charcoal) done under a binocular stereomicroscope (80X, model NSZ-810), followed by microscopic observation to identify seed and fruit remains using the above-mentioned binocular stereomicroscope and comparison to seed and fruit descriptive atlases based on their morphology (Jacomet 2006; Struwe 2009; Zohary *et al.* 2012; Parkinson *et al.* 2015; Mackizadeh Tafti and Sharifi Ashourabadi 2017). The last stage involves microscopic observation of the anatomical structure of charcoals using a metallurgical microscope (1000X, model NMM800TR) and comparison to wood descriptive atlases and reference collections based on the three section: Transversal Section (TS), Tangential Longitudinal Section (TLS), and Radial Longitudinal Section (RLS) (Paulssen 1964; Hejazi 1979; Niloufari 1986; Wheeler *et al.* 1989; Neumann *et al.* 2000; Pajouh and Schweingruber 2001). Only the date stones were photographed by a camera (Canon) connected to our stereomicroscope. Other remains were not photographed due to their microscopic size.

Fig. 4.4: Date stone found in the southern channels of the Treasury of Persepolis. Photograph by Zohreh Shirazi.

Results

Identified taxa

Plant remains obtained from the channels of Persepolis include 66 charcoals and 11 seeds. All these data were studied by microscope in order to identify the anatomical and morphologic characteristics of the samples. The obtained results are as follow (Table 4.1):

1. From 70 kg of sediments collected from the channels of the southern courtyard of the Tacara Palace, only a small amount of almond charcoal (*Amygdalus* sp.) has been identified.

Table 4.1: Results of archaeobotanical studies in the excavation season of excavation in the channels of Persepolis.

Waterways/ Channels	*Type of deposit*	*Weight of deposits before flotation (kg)*	*Identified Taxa*	*Vegetal ecoregion*
TSCT: Southern courtyard of the Tacara Palace	Compact clay layer combined with ash and charcoal	70	Charcoal: Almond (16 fragments)	Steppe-Forest
TSC: The southern channels of the Treasury	Compact clayey layer combined with ash and charcoal	50	Charcoal: Almond (12 fragments), Elm (4 fragments), plane tree (16 fragments) Seed: date stone (8 fragments)	Steppe-Forest, Hygrophilous, Fruit
SWT: Trench alongside the southern Wall of the Terrace of Persepolis	Compact clayey layer combined with ash and charcoal	20	Charcoal: Almond (12 fragments), Elm (2 fragments), plane tree (4 fragments) Seed: one Intact date stone, silene (1 seed), Polygonaceae (5 seeds)	Steppe-Forest, Hygrophilous, Fruit, Weed

2. Other plants identified from 50 kg of deposits coming from the southern channels of the Treasury include almond, elm (*Ulmus* sp.), plane tree (*Platanus* sp.), and date palm (*Phoenix dactylifera*) (Fig. 4.4).
3. Finally, from 20 kg of sediments collected from the trench alongside the southern wall of the Terrace of Persepolis, we identified the vestiges of almond, elm, and plane tree charcoals alongside date stones and seeds of wild plants such as catchfly (*Silene* sp.) and buckwheat family (Polygonaceae).

Discussion

Among the plant remains collected from the southern channels of the Treasury and the trench alongside the southern wall of the Terrace of Persepolis, we have identified date stones (fragmentary and intact) (Fig. 4.4). The geographic origin of date palm is believed to be Baluchistan, Saudi Arabia, and North Africa. Today different varieties of *Phoenix dactylifera* are cultivated in tropical and subtropical regions of southern Iran such as Khuzestan, southern parts of Fars, Kerman, Baluchistan, and Yazd (Sabeti 1994, 509). In the surrounding regions of Fars, charred stones and charcoal of date palm have been reported elsewhere from the Bronze Age site of Konar Sandal south (Mashkour *et al.* 2013, 129). Moreover, the motif of date palm appears frequently on chlorite objects from the Jiroft (Perrot and Majidzadeh 2005, 129), perhaps reflecting the importance of this tree in the local subsistence economy. It seems that the environmental conditions of Jiroft Plain with permanent water resources (*Halil Rud*) and a hot and humid climate provided a suitable environment for cultivation of the date palm. This evidence, along with the remains of charred date stones related to Period VII (5400–4800 BCE) at Gaz Tavileh in the Dowlat Abad Plain, indicate that the date palm had been domesticated in the southeastern part of the Iranian Plateau during the Bronze Age and was part of the landscape in the region (Costantini 1985, 211). Tablets from Persepolis documented the extensive use of the date palm in daily life during the Achaemenid period in the mid-1st millennium BCE (Garrison 2014, 95–103; 2017, 362) (Plate 4.3). These tablets also mentioned the cultivation of other plants including rice, flax, sesame, and horticultural products such as almond, fig, walnut, pistachio, and grape in the fertile regions of the Empire (Koch 1992, 229). The date palm was frequent in southern Fars, and it seems that it has been cultivated in southern Fars for nutritional purposes.

In the trench alongside the southern wall of the Terrace at Persepolis, a small number of seeds of annual and perennial herbaceous plants such as catchfly (*Silene* sp.) and members of the Buckwheat family (Polygonaceae), typical for this temperate and subtropical region, were identified. Previously, *Silene* sp. and *Polygonum* sp. were reported respectively from Tal-i Mushki and Tal-i Jari in contexts dated back to the Neolithic period (Miller and Kimiaie 2006). Recently, these taxas have been identified from samples in early (6370–6200 BCE) and late phases (6200–6000 BCE) at Hormangan in Fars (Kazemi 2021). The presence of wild taxa at Persepolis could be related to their natural growth in the area. This phenomenon could be useful for better understanding of vegetal cover in the area and possibly the plants and grasses of the small gardens existing on the Terrace of Persepolis. It is also conceivable that these were weeds transported with edible seeds needed by the staff and soldiers settled on the Terrace.

Carbonized almond has been identified from the channels of the southern courtyard of the Tachara Palace, the Southern channel of the Treasury, and the trench alongside the southern wall of the Terrace of Persepolis. Archaeobotanical evidence for almonds has been reported from Neolithic sites at Fars such as Hormangan, Rahmat Abad, and from Chalcolithic transitional phases from Tol-i bashi (Tengberg and Kharanaghi 2016; Kazemi 2021). Palynological and sedimentological studies at Maharlou Lake in southern Iran indicate that during the Achaemenid period (550–330 BCE), almond, pistachio, and oak trees constituted the main elements of vegetal cover (Djamali *et al.* 2015; Saeidi *et al.* 2020).

Almonds grow among the species characteristic of the Irano-Touranian botanic region (Juniperetum and Pistacietum communii), with low precipitation and arid seasons. The distribution of *Amygdaletum* (almond) includes Azerbaijan in the north and continues south through Kurdistan, Luristan, Fars, Bakhtyari, Kerman, Baluchistan, down to the central Iranian deserts, and almost into the piedmonts of Alborz Mountains (Sabeti 1994, 44). Wild almond, oak, wild pistachio, cypress, are among the most famous forest trees in the petrified forest of Fars. Nowadays, various species of almond such as *Amygdalus Arabica*, *A. communis*, *A. elaeagnifolia*, *A. erioclada*, *A. glauca*, *A. haussknechtii*, and *A. scoparia* are distributed in Fars (Sabeti 1994).

Another tree species whose charcoal remains were identified in the Southern channels of the Treasury and the trench alongside the Southern Wall of the Terrace of Persepolis is Elm. Elm (*Ulmus* sp) belongs to the hygrophilous plant community that grows in mountainous regions with a moderate, humid climate and is adapted to clay soils. Two species of elm are attested in the northern (from Arasbaran to Gorgan) and western forests of Iran: *U. carpinifolia* and *U. glabra* (Sabeti 1994, 753–754). Archaeobotanical evidence for elm has been reported from Ali Tappeh Cave in Mazandaran, which dates to the Epi-Paleolithic period (Shirazi 2018), and from Shahr-i Sokhta dated to the 3rd millennium BCE (Shirazi 2019).

Fig. 4.5: Snail samples found in southern channels of the Treasury. Photograph by Zohreh Shirazi.

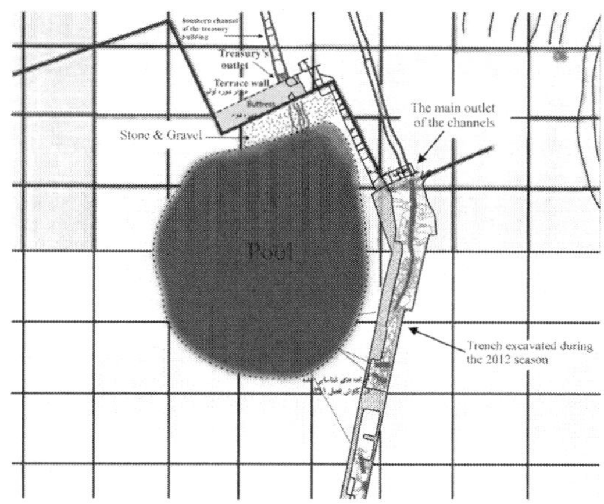

Fig. 4.6: Possible location of pool in the vicinity of the southern area of the Terrace (from Asadi 2021, 171).

Evidence for the Plane tree has also been identified in the southern channels of the Treasury and the trench alongside the Southern Wall of the Terrace of Persepolis. It has been reported elsewhere as an adapted species in semi-arid zones of Fars (Kazemi 2021, 19). At the present time, the geographical distribution of the plane tree consists of a vast region including the piedmont of Alborz in northern Iran (especially Kojour), Haraz Valley, Roudbar, Khoy, Hamedan, Harsin, Luristan, Bakhtyari, Marvdasht, Kazeroun, Kerman and Torbat Jam (Sabeti 1994, 521). Palynological evidence of the plane tree has been noted among samples from Almalou Lake in northwestern Iran and from Maharlou and Parishan Lakes, and according to radiocarbon dates they have been attributed to the Achaemenid period (Saeidi *et al.* 2020).

In addition to plant remains, other organic materials such as bones and animal remains were also found in the course of excavations. The collected bones have been studied separately and therefore have not been discussed in the present paper. However, it is interesting to note the presence of 75 freshwater snail shells of various sizes (Fig. 4.5). Most of these snails were extracted from the sediments obtained from channels of the Treasury. Since the presence of snails depends on permanent or seasonal waters, it can be concluded that water collected in permanent or temporary pools in some parts of the Persepolis channels. These data are particularly important because other evidence suggests a water reservoir (Fig. 4.6) in the southern part of the Terrace (Asadi 2021, 171).

Conclusion

Our archaeobotanical evidence, especially the charred date stones in the southern channels of the Treasury Building and the trench alongside the Southern Wall of the Terrace of Persepolis, provide information about vegetation cover and horticultural activities during the Achaemenid period, and confirms the available data derived from written sources and iconographic representations regarding the presence of date palm, probably local at southern Fars, in the royal stores at Persepolis. In addition, charcoal remains also indicate the cultivation of almond, elm, and plane trees around Persepolis. These facts are in accord with palynological data indicating a great diversity of arboriculture (such as plane tree, grape, walnut, pomegranate, and date palm) during the historical period in Iran, particularly during the Persian Empire.

It is interesting that there is little evidence of unprocessed cereals in the sediments collected from the channels of Persepolis, despite the fact of their frequent appearance in the Persepolis fortification tablets. In fact, it seems that there is no evidence for unprocessed grains on the terrace. Rather, it seems that somewhere outside the terrace, food was prepared for the employees and guards. A survey of the written sources on the fortification tablets indicates that barley was the main food resource, and wheat was cultivated in a small amount. It is reasonable to think that barley is more adapted to the climatological and pedological (soil) conditions of the Iranian Plateau. The lack of cereals, including barley, known to have been widely paid as wages to the workers and other royal staff at Persepolis, can be explained in two ways, a) the cereals and grains arrived at Persepolis and were used as processed materials (flour or bread) rather than unprocessed grain; b) the archaeobotanical sampling done during the excavation was insufficient. Finally, it is important to note that parts of the Persepolis channels have not been excavated and therefore further studies on the identification of archaeobotanical evidence will help to complete and correct the results of the present research.

Acknowledgments

The authors would like to express their gratitude to the members of the Persepolis channels Archaeological Excavation Group in 2014 and anonymous peer reviewers for their useful critiques and comments.

Bibliography

Asadi, A.A. (2012 [1391]) *Preliminary Report of Excavations Alongside the Main Outlet of Persepolis's Channels.* Persepolis Library, Unpublished Report. [Persian]

Asadi, A.A. (2014 [1393]) *Second Preliminary Report of Excavations at Persepolis's Channels.* Persepolis Library, Unpublished Report. [Persian]

Asadi, A.A. (2021) General Architectural System and New Related Findings in the Southeast of Persepolis Terrace. *Journal of Iran's Pre-Islamic Archaeological Essays* 4/1, 149–172. [Persian with an English abstract]

Asadi, A.A. and Mansouri, M. (2017 [1396]) *Preliminary Report on the Third Season of Excavations at Persepolis's Channels.* Persepolis Library, Unpublished Report. [Persian]

Asadi, A.A. and Mohammadzadeh, F. (2021 [1399]) *Preliminary Report on the Fourth Season of Excavations at Persepolis's Channels.* Persepolis Library, Unpublished Report. [Persian]

Askari Chaverdi, A. (2008 [1386]) Excavation at Persepolis Channels System/Kavosh dar A'braheha-yi Zirzamini-yi Takht-i Jamshid. *Bastanshenasi va Tarikh* 21/1 (41), 65–72. [Persian]

Costantini, L. (1985) Considerazioni su alcuni reperti di palma da dattero e sul centro di origine e l'area di coltivazione della *Phoenix dactylifera.* In G. Gnoli and L. Lanciotti (eds) *Orientalia Josephi Tucci Memoriae Dicata*, 209–218. Rome, IsMEO.

Djamali, M., Jones, M.D., Migliore, J., Balatti, S., Fader, M., Contreras, D., Gondest, S., Hosseini, Z., Lahijani, H., Naderi, A., Shumilovskikh, L.S., Tengberg, M., and Weeks, L. (2015) Olive Cultivation in the Heart of Persian Achaemenid Empire: New Insights into Agricultural Practices and Environmental Changes Reflected in a Late Holocene Pollen Record from Lake Parishan, SW Iran. *Vegetation History and Archaeobotany* 25, 255–269.

Garrison, M. (2014) The Royal Name Seals of Darius I. In M. Kozuh, W.F.M. Henkelman, C.E. Jones, and C. Wood (eds) *Extraction and Control: Studies in Honor of Matthew W. Stolper*, 67–104. Chicago, University of Chicago Press.

Garrison, M. (2017) *The Ritual Landscape at Persepolis.* Chicago, University of Chicago Press.

Ghasemi, S. (2015) Investigation on the Agriculture Process in the Fars Region According to Archaeobotanical Evidence Discovered at Toll-e Sabz from Neolithic to the Bronze Age. MA dissertation, Islamic Azad University of Marvdasht. [Persian]

Hallock, T.R. (1969) *Persepolis Fortification Tablets.* Chicago, University of Chicago Press.

Hejazi, R. (1979) *Principles of Wood Anatomy.* Tehran, Dehkhoda Publication. [Persian]

Herzfeld, E. (1941) *Iran in the Ancient East.* London/New York, Oxford University Press.

Jacomet, S. (2006) *Identification of Cereal Remains from Archaeological Sites* (2nd ed.). Basel, Archaeobotany Lab IPAS, Basel University.

Kazemi, S. (2021) Reconstruction of Fars's Subsistence Economy During the Second Half of the Seventh Millennium BCE Based on the Plant Remains of Hormangan. MA Dissertation, University of Tehran. [Persian]

Koch, H. (1992) *Es kündet Dareios der König, vom leben im persischen Grossreich.* Mainz, Zabern.

Kodaghloi, M., Fayaz, M., Shirani, K., Taghi Faezi, M. and Yazdani, M (2017) Project for recognition of ecological region of country: Vegetal types of Fars province. Tehran. Research institute of Forests and rangeland. [Persian]

Mackizadeh Tafti, M. and Sharifi Ashourabadi, E. (2017) *Atlas of the Seeds of Medicinal Plants.* Tehran, Research Institute of Forests and Rangelands. [Persian]

Mashkour, M., Tengberg, M., Shirazi, Z., and Majidzadeh, Y. (2013) Bio-archaeological Studies at Konar Sandal, Halil Rud Basin, Southeastern Iran. *Journal of Environmental Archaeology* 18/3, 222–246.

Miller, N. and Kimiaie, M. (2006) Some Plant Remains From the 2004 Excavations of Tall-e Mushki, Tall-e Jari A and B, and Tall-e Bakun A and B. In A. Alizadeh (ed.) *The Origins of State Formation in Prehistoric Highland Fars, Southern Iran: excavation at Tall-e Bakun*, 107–118. Chicago, University of Chicago Press.

Neumann, K., Détienne, P., Schweingruber, F.H., and Schoch, W. (2000) *Wood of the Sahara and the Sahel.* Bern/Stuttgart/Wien, Eidg. Forschungsanstalt WSL, Birmensdorf, Verlag Paul Haupt.

Pajouh, D.P. and Schweingruber, F.H. (2001) *Atlas des bois du nord de l'Iran description anatomique et identification microscopique des essences principales.* Tehran, University of Teheran Publication.

Parkinson, H., Mangold, J., and Menalled, F. (2015) *Weed Seedling Identification Guide.* Bozeman, Montana State University Extension.

Paulssen, L.M. (1964) *Identification of Active Charcoals and Wood Charcoals.* Copenhagen/Oslo, Universitets Forlaget.

Perrot, J. and Madjidzadeh, Y. (2005) L'iconographie des vases et objets en chlorite de Jiroft (Iran). *Paléorient* 31/2, 123–152.

Sabeti, H. (1994) *Forests, Trees, and Shrubs of Iran.* Yazd, Yazd University Press. [Persian]

Saeidi, G., Andam, S., Nelle, D.O., Naderi Beni, A., Haghighifard, M., Brisset, E., and Poschlod, P. (2020) Vegetation History of the Maharlou Lake Basin (SW Iran) with Special Reference to the Achaemenid Period (550–330 BC). *Vegetation history and Archaeobotany* 30, 595–610.

Sami, A. (1951 [1330]) Twelve Years of Excavations of Persepolis Research Foundation in Different Historical Area/Kavoshha-yi Davazdah Sale-yi Bongh-i Elmi-yi Takht-i Jamshid Dar Noghat-i Mokhtalef-i Tarikhi, Gozareshha-yi Bastanshenasi Vol.2. Shiraz, Takht Jamshid Scientific Institute. [Persian]

Sami, A. (1960 [1338]) Excavation and Restoration at Pasargadae and Persepolis from 1951–1960/ Hafari va Khak bardari va Taamirat Pasargad Va Takht-i Jamshid Az Sal-e 1331 Ta 1338 Khorshirdi, Gozareshha-yi Bastanshenasi Vol.4. Tehran, Idārah-i Kul-i Bāstān'shināsī. [Persian]

Schmidt, E.F. (1953) *Persepolis I: Structures, Reliefs and Inscriptions*, Chicago, University of Chicago Press.

Schmidt, E.F. (1957) *Persepolis II. Contents of the Treasury and Other Discoveries.* Chicago, University of Chicago Press.

Schmidt, E.F. (1970) *Persepolis III: Royal Tombs and Other Monuments.* Chicago, University of Chicago Press.

Shirazi, Z. (2018) Charcoal Studies at Ali Tappeh Cave (Mazandaran), An Introduction to the Herbal Sources in the Epipaleolithic Period in the Eastern Alborz. *Pazhouhesh-ha-ye Bastanshenasi Iran* 8/18, 7–24. [Persian with a long English abstract]

Shirazi, Z. (2019) Vegetal Evidence of Southern Sistan During the Third Millennium BCE Based on the Vegetal Remains from Shahr-i Sokhta. In E. Ascalone and S.M.S. Sajjadi (eds) *Scavi e ricerche a Shahr-i Sokhta*, 273–320. Tehran, Iranian Center for Archaeological research. [Persian with English and Italian abstract]

Struwe, L. (2009) *Field Identification of the 50 Most Common Plant Families in Temperate Region (Including Agricultural, Horticultural, and Wild Species).* New Brunswick, Rutgers, The State University of New Jersey.

Tengberg, M. and Kharanaghi H.A. (2016) Results of the Archaeobotanical study of Rahmatabad, Fars. In K. Roustaei and M. Mashkour (eds) *The Neolithic of the Iranian Plateau. Studies in Early Near Eastern Production, Subsistence and Environment 18*, 137–148. Berlin, Ex Oriente.

Wheeler, E., Baas, P., and Gasson, P. (1989) IAWA List of Microscopic Features for Hardwood Identification. *International Association of Wood Anatomists Journal* 10 (3), 219–332.

Zohary, D., Hop, M., and Weiss, E. (2012) *Domestication of Plants in the Old World.* Oxford, Oxford University Press.

Chapter 5 Prologue

Imperial land management strategies in Iran

After the fall of the Achaemenids to the forces of Alexander of Macedon and Alexander's death in 330 BCE, Iran became part of the Seleucid Empire, ruled by the Macedonian general Seleucus Nicator. While the capitals of the Seleucid Empire (323–64 BCE) were in the west, Iran and particularly the Persian Gulf were critical to its success (Messina 2023). Within a century of their rise to power, a rival to the Seleucids was gaining ground in northeastern Iran: a semi-nomadic group called the Parni, under the leadership of Arasces, that would become the powerful Parthian (Arascid) Empire (247 BCE–226 CE). The Parthians ruled over an enormous territory for more than 500 years, surviving threats from nomadic peoples in the north, and attempts by the Romans to annex them from the west (Hauser 2012, 1010). In the end, a minor Iranian noble from Fars – Ardashir – led a successful revolt and was crowned the first ruler of the Sasanian Empire.

Under the Sasanians' rule, the empire stimulated the foundation of many cities in various parts of its territory, other significant settlements, large-scale irrigation systems, and fortifications, defensive walls, and moats in the borderland areas. This was all part of the ambitious plan for the transformation of both its territory and population (Alizadeh *et al.* 2021; Ur and Alizadeh 2022). The clear increase of the number of cities and infrastructure during the later Sasanian era are good indicators of economic prosperity and political stability. In the following chapter, Zohreh Zehbari and her colleagues introduce the site of Dehqāed, one of the little-known urban centers in southern Iran near the Persian Gulf which reached its apogee during the Sasanian period.

The Sasanian Empire soon after its foundation by Ardashir I in 224 CE became one of the two great empires of Late Antiquity in southwestern Asia. The Sasanian era was probably one of the most transformative and consequential eras in the history of Iran. By uniting temple and state, the Sasanians developed a theocracy. The 5th century in particular witnessed major transformations, including the construction of infrastructural complexes and the rescaling of the Sasanian empire. The empire reached its height during the reign of Khusro I (531–579 CE), during which it was reorganized into a new feudal order with more centralized power and a reformed administration. The Sasanians expanded their dominance over much of western Asia before the Islamic conquest and are considered to be one of Iran's most important dynasties (Payne 2017).

The Sasanians controlled and managed highly variable economic and social landscapes, sometimes even creating such landscapes. Their strategy was to focus on resource-rich centers, or 'nodes', within their territory and control those centers across regions. Their territory was not singular and homogenous; rather, it was dynamic, and the investments were selective and strategic. In fact, territoriality and the management of resources by the Sasanian Empire might be better understood by applying the node-and-corridor model of landscape use (Smith 2005; Payne 2017, 192). The Sasanian investment in Dehqāed – surrounded by other large settlements within an agriculturally productive land between the coastal ports of the Persian Gulf and the heartland of the empire (Priestman 2022) – is a good example of a node that received enormous imperial support, and imperial policies in general. As Zehbari and her colleagues demonstrate in their article, Dehqāed was crucial for the sustenance and prosperity of coastal ports, particularly Bushehr (see also Priestman 2022, 169, 171).

Although the Sasanians engaged in the infrastructural projects from very early on and founded a few cities or *Šahrestān*, their ambitions with large scale projects took a new turn after the reforms of Qobad/Kavad in the beginning of the 6th century CE. Most of the newly founded cities were meant to serve the state ideological, administrative, and economic purposes. It is argued that the cities were often founded in 'the nodal points of heavily irrigated hinterlands on which the kings of kings wielded direct authority, likely forming components of the royal *dastgird*' (Payne 2017, 192).

In order to achieve their goals, such as building defensive walls and fortifications, digging irrigation canals, and founding cities, the Sasanian Empire needed a huge laboring population. The empire often transferred people from the borderland areas to heartlands and vice versa. Often times these people were war captives that the Sasanians settled within walled or fortified cities to serve economic functions (Alizadeh 2019). Overall, our knowledge about the Sasanian urbanism is very limited. We know that most of the Sasanian cities were rectilinear, fortified, and founded in an agriculturally productive land. Due to deportation and/or population transformation, the Sasanian cities were multicultural. As centers of revenue-generating industry, Sasanian cities were pivotal for the economy of the empire (Simpson 2017).

In addition to the agricultural surplus production, overland and maritime trade also had a significant place in the Sasanian imperial policies. As discussed by Zehbari and her colleagues in the following chapter and demonstrated by Seth Priestman (2022), the coastal ports of the Persian Gulf flourished during the Sasanian era. In the following article, Zehbari and her colleagues argue that urban centers such as Dehqāed played a significant role during the Sasanian era connecting inland Fars with the coastal ports. This finding is critical as it demonstrates the interrelatedness of production centers, markets, and coastal ports.

Bibliography

Alizadeh, K. (2019) Overlapping Social and Political Boundaries, Borders of the Sasanian Empire and the Muslim Caliphate in the Caucasus. In A. Asa Eger (ed.) *The Archaeology of Medieval Islamic Frontiers: From the Mediterranean to the Caspian Sea,* 139–167. Louisville, University Press of Colorado.

Alizadeh, K., Mohammadi, M.R., Maziar, S., and Feizkhah, M. (2021) The Islamic Conquest or Flooding? Sasanian Settlements and Irrigation Systems Collapse in Mughan, Iranian Azerbaijan. *Journal of Field Archaeology* 46 (5), 316–332.

Hauser, S.R. (2012) The Arsacid (Parthian) Empire. In D.T. Potts (ed.) *A Companion to the Archaeology of the Ancient Near East*, 1001–1020. London, Blackwell.

Messina, V. (2023) Seleucia-on-the-Tigris: Embedding Capitals in the Hellenizing Near East. In M. Canepa, T. Daryaee, and R. Rollinger (eds) *Iran and the Transformation of Ancient Near Eastern History: The Seleucids (ca. 312-150 BCE),* 101–124. Wiesbaden, Harrassowitz Verlag.

Payne, R.E. (2017) Territorializing Iran in Late Antiquity: Autocracy, Aristocracy, and the Infrastructure of Empire. In C. Ando and S. Richardson (eds) *Ancient States and Infrastructural Power: Europe, Asia, and America*, 179–217. Philadelphia, University of Pennsylvania Press.

Priestman, S.M.N. (2022) Bushehr, Dashtestan and Siraf: The Transformation of the Maritime Trade Network in the Middle Persian Gulf. In St. J. Simpson (ed.) *Sasanian Archaeology: Settlements, Environment and Material Culture*, 153–177. Oxford, Archaeopress.

Simpson, St. J. (2017) Sasanian Cities: Archaeological Perspectives on the Urban Economy and Built Environment of an Empire. In E.W. Sauer (ed.) *Sasanian Persia: Between Rome and the Steppes of Eurasia*, 21–50. Edinburgh, Edinburgh University Press.

Smith, M. L. (2005) Network, Territories, and the Cartography of Ancient States. *Annals of the Association of American Geographers* 95 (4), 832–849.

Ur, J.A., and Alizadeh, K. 2022. The Sasanian Colonisation of the Mughan Steppe, Ardebil Province, North-West Iran. In St. J. Simpson (ed.) *Sasanian Archaeology: Settlements, Environment and Material Culture*, 80–89. Oxford, Archaeopress.

Chapter 5

Dehqāed: A lesser-known Sasanian center in the Borāzjān Plain, Southern Iran

Zohreh Zehbari, Nasrollah Ebrahimi, and Mehrdad Parsaei Borazjani

Abstract

Our recent survey has revealed that the site of Dehqāed, situated in the Borāzjān plain, spans across 35 mounds within a 7 km area along the southern bank of the Dālaki River. Archaeological evidence from various sites suggests the existence of an urban environment not only during the Sasanian period but also dating back to the Achaemenid and Seleucid/Parthian periods. This complex likely served as a multifaceted urban center, housing military installations, industrial manufacturing facilities, and ceremonial areas. It played a crucial role in establishing a vital communication network that connected the Fārs highland with the Būshehr hinterland. This paper aims to explore the archaeological potential of the Dehqāed site, with a particular focus on the Sasanian period.

The landscape and strategic location of Dehqāed

Būshehr province, situated in the southern region of Iran, boasts over 600 km of coastline along the Persian Gulf. Prior to the Iranian revolution, Būshehr was part of Fārs province, and historically it is regarded as an extension of Fārs province, the homeland of the Achaemenid and Sasanian empires. Borāzjān, a town in the Būshehr province, is located approximately 65 km northeast of the Būshehr city (Plate 5.1).

The Borāzjān plain is located between the Zāgros mountain (the Gisakān and Siāh Mountains) and the hinterland of the Persian Gulf. The area, located in the Dashtestān county according to modern geographical divisions, experiences low rainfall and very warm, sultry weather. Dehqāed is situated within the Borāzjān flatland, and this region is characterized by the presence of two rivers, namely the Shāpūr (Shirin) and Dālaki (Shour). These rivers originate from the Gisakān Mountain and serve to irrigate the alluvial plain of Borāzjān. The point where these two rivers converge gives rise to the Hilleh river, which ultimately flows into the Persian Gulf. The alluvial deposit from the flooding of the Dālaki river created a great opportunity for farming, and for this reason, there are intensive settlements in Dehqāed. The expanse of the agricultural activities in the plain decreases towards the west and coastal area. Along the rivers, the Sasanian city of Bishāpūr was accessible to the Borāzjān flatland and then along the Hilleh river to the Persian Gulf. Dehqāed lies midway along this route, a clear indication of the importance of the area. The intermediating role of Borāzjān continued after the Sasanians; in the Qajar period, the official Moshir-al-molk built a bridge on the Kāzerūn–Borāzjān route and a caravanserai in the modern Borāzjān. Although Dehqāed played a strategic role in the Sasanian era, it was very likely important in communication with other Sasanian sites south of Dehqāed, in hinterland regions like Tol-e Jid, Khosh-Āb, Isāvandeh, Rishehr/Rev Ardashir and Shif island (see Carter *et al.* 2006, 96).

Historical texts dating back to the Achaemenid period appear to mention the Borāzjān plain. One notable toponym, 'Tamukkan (Taḫmâka or Taocê)', appears in three distinct sources, including late Babylonian records, the Persepolis Fortification Archive,[1] and some classical texts. This toponym strongly suggests a connection to the Achaemenid palatial structures located in the Borāzjān plain (Hallock 1959; Henkelman 2008, 306). Subsequently, in later sources, the name Tūz/Tūj/Tūzag surfaces as the 45th city among 60 Šahrestāns (Provincial Capitals) (Daryaee 2002, 20, 24) and is also associated with Ardašīr-Xwarrah during the Sasanian era (Istakhri 1961, 100; Schwarz 1969–1970, 66–67; Ibn Khordadbeh 1992, 37; Daryaee 2002, 20, 24). Transitioning into the Islamic period, the region was known as Tawwaj, and historical documents clearly indicate its strategic location along the route connecting Fārs to Būshehr. Furthermore, philological analysis reveals that Taocè/Tamukkan and Tūz/Tūj/Tawwag/Tawwaj are variations of the same place name, all referring to the same geographical area. On one hand, Tawwaj was located between Bishāpūr (Kāzerun) and Ganāveh port and on the other hand, on basis of Istakhri, Tawwaj was located at a distance of more than 70 km (12 *Farsangs*) from Ganāveh (Istakhri 1961, 114). Taken together, both archaeological and textual evidence corroborate the identification of this region as the Borāzjān plain which has two main Sasanian sites (each site includes several mounds): Dehqāed and Zirāh (Plate 5.1). Both areas are located in river environs and were dependent on the water.

The environmental and geographical potential of the Borāzjān plain have ensured the intensive settlement on the floodplain over centuries. Through limited fieldwork, also illegal excavations and accidental discoveries, we have learned that the plain was an important region with occupational evidence from multiple empires. For this reason, Borāzjān is a good place to study the transformation of institutional landscapes. The area was witness to the prehistoric, Achaemenid, Seleucid/Parthian, Sasanian and the Islamic eras. Our knowledge of the Achaemenid occupation in the area is limited to the Achaemenid palatial structures. However, the recent survey by the Iranian–British team showed the distribution of the Achaemenid sites in the Būshehr province, but these sites were all followed by Parthian ones, and one cannot easily disambiguate them (Carter *et al.* 2006).[2] However, the archaeological evidence shows that the Sasanian landscape is more robust than others in the plain and was followed by the Islamic eras.

History of the study

Before delving into the specific details about Dehqāed, it is essential to provide an overview of the research background and field activities associated with the site. While Dehqāed has been briefly mentioned in some field reports, it has not received a comprehensive description.

Siraf, a thriving city during the Islamic era, has long been a subject of interest for researchers. And while the Būshehr peninsula has consistently attracted attention due to their strategic coastal locations, proximity to Elamite and more significantly, Sasanian settlements, the area of Dehqāed remained largely unexplored for many years (see Williamson 1972; Whitehouse and Williamson 1973). It appears that the initial fieldwork conducted at Dehqāed was carried out by Whitcomb in 1973, focusing on a survey in the Borāzjān and Ahram areas (Whitcomb 1987, 320, fig. E). From this survey, he published a limited amount of ceramics data only from two mounds at Dehqāed (see below 'Ceramic Assemblage of Dehqāed').

Ali Asghar MirFattah conducted a brief visit or survey of Tol-e Khandagh at Dehqāed, although no formal report of this endeavor is available (Yaghmaee 2008, 60). The turning point for Dehqāed occurred with the accidental discovery of a Greek-style marble statue by local residents in 1368/1989, as depicted in Figure 5.1. Subsequently, Mehdi Rahbar examined the statue and initiated a five-day program at the site. Unfortunately, his efforts did not yield the desired results in terms of gaining a deeper understanding of the statue's context or obtaining further insights within the region. Rahbar did publish an article that concentrated on the identification of the statue and offered a comprehensive explanation (1999; for a later 3rd century CE date, see Callieri 2007, 105–109). While this publication has proven valuable, it falls short of providing a comprehensive understanding of the Dehqāed site as a whole.

Fig. 5.1: The Pan statue discovered in the vicinity of Tol-e Kheshti B, Dehqāed (Photo: © Regional Museum of the Persian Gulf, Būshehr).

Subsequently, Ismaeel (Ehsan) Yaghmaee, who had been actively involved in excavating Achaemenid palatial sites near Borāzjān, initiated some archaeological work in the Dehqāed region. His efforts focused on excavating two mounds, namely Tol-e Kheshti and Tol-e Gowd-Saeedi, in addition to establishing a site location boundary program at Tol-e Khandagh (Plate 5.2). This project spanned three different seasons, carried out in 1994, 2004, and 2010 (Yaghmaee 2008; 2015; 2018, 229 and 233–246). Yaghmaee's excavation work at Tol-e Kheshti, which began in the autumn of 1994 and lasted for two months, led to the discovery of a *chārtāqi* (Yaghmaee 2008). A decade later, he returned to Dehqāed, this time concentrating on Tol-e Kheshti again, along with the new excavation at Tol-e Gowd-Saeedi. The decision to excavate Tol-e Gowd-Saeedi arose from his concern about the threat of looters at the site, prompting him to take action to preserve the structures. Finally, in 2010, he revisited Dehqāed for a site location boundary program at both Tol-e Khandagh and Tol-e Kheshti.

Yaghmaee has authored two papers in the 'Bāstānpazhuhi' journal, written in Persian, which primarily delve into his excavations in the region. The focus is predominantly on Tol-e Kheshti (Yaghmaee 2008; 2015) with a brief two page mention of Tol-e Gowd-Saeedi (2008, 73–75). Furthermore, his book touches upon a few mounds at Dehqāed and others in the Borāzjān plain (2018, 196–246). He recently published two books on Tol-e Kheshti that include the data reported in his papers (Yaghmaee 2023a; 2023b). Notably, the published materials emphasize only a limited selection of ceramics, despite the pottery collection unearthed offering a valuable reference point for comprehending the Sasanian pottery culture in the southern region of Iran.

In addition to the excavations, Ali Akbar Sarfaraz, along with one of our co-authors, N. Ebrahimi, conducted a survey in Dashtestān county, covering the areas of Dehqāed and Sa'ad Abad in 2006. However, their survey was primarily focused on the Sa'ad Abad region. In the Dehqāed area, they gathered ceramic artifacts from various mounds, including Tol-e Gel-Mirou, Tol-e Bāgh-Mil, Tol-e Khandagh, Tol-e Sang-e-Āsiāb, Tol-e Ganji, Tol-e Bāghi, Tol-e Naqāreh-Khuneh, and Tol-e Gowd-Saeedi. In 2004, an Iranian–British expedition commenced a survey of Būshehr province. They documented 56 sites within an area measuring 90 km from southeast to northwest and 60 km from southwest to northeast. These sites spanned from the Chalcolithic to the Islamic periods in the province (Carter *et al.* 2006, 64, 68). Their primary objective was to investigate the historical connection between Mesopotamia and coastal Iran, particularly during the Chalcolithic, Ubaid, and Neolithic periods. Nevertheless, most of the sites they identified actually dated from the Achaemenid to Sasanian eras, including the site of Dehqāed (Carter *et al.* 2006, 63–64).

Lastly, in 2019, our team conducted a surface survey aimed at locating ceramics in the Borāzjān plain. This survey identified a total of 35 mounds spread across a 7 km area at Dehqāed (Plate 5.2). This paper provides an initial survey report while also revisiting and reevaluating past excavations carried out at the site.

Dehqāed site

As was briefly mentioned above, the significance of the Borāzjān plain and the Dehqāed site had been clearly underlined from the texts, and archaeological proof bears witness to its importance. The potential benefit of the Dehqāed site to our comprehension of Sasanian material culture and architecture has been reported (Carter *et al.* 2006, especially 67, 96, 97, 98 and fig. 14; Yaghmaee 2018, 232–246; Matin 2020, 341). Most of the reports of the field activities are, as yet, unpublished and generally, a coherent investigation of the site has not yet been conducted.

The Iranian–British survey team conducted the most systematic survey in the area to date. However, they emphasized that 'these results are provisional, and that any future fieldwork would probably refine the dating and reveal undiscovered occupation horizons. Work on the ceramics is at a very preliminary stage, and date ranges of the sites and ceramic classes will certainly be changed pending a full analysis' (Carter *et al.* 2006, 75). Initially, the survey team considered Dehqāed a relatively smaller site (only 15 mounds)[3] and did not identify several mounds, like DQ20, DQ21, DQ28, DQ29, DQ30, DQ31, DQ32, DQ33, located in the western section of the town (Plate 5.2).[4] As their investigation progressed, they realized that the town extended further southward, encompassing the curve of the Dālaki river. Importantly, they did not include BH45–BH46 (Tol-e Bāgh-Mil) as part of Dehqāed, a mound that will be explored in the present paper (Plate 5.2, DQ34). In our recent survey, we identified more than twice the number of mounds at the site (compare Plate 5.2 with Plate 5.3). Their report only published six catalogs out of the 3000 potsherds collected, without separating the ceramics based on their historical periods, such as Achaemenid and Parthian, discussing them as a single category. It is essential to note that their survey lasted only three weeks before it was halted. Subsequently, they compiled all the results of their fieldwork in southern Iran, including this survey, into a comprehensive book. In the book, they recognized the persistent challenge of distinguishing Achaemenid from Parthian ceramics (Priestman and Kennet 2023, 45).[5] However, the ceramics from Dehqāed have not undergone examination in the book. Nevertheless, they underscored the importance of Būshehr province, specifically the ancient town of Dehqāed, which they frequently referred to as 'the Achaemenid-to-Sasanian town' (Carter *et al.* 2006, 67, 72, table 2, 75, 89, 94, 95, fig. 14, 96, 97, 98; Priestman and Kennet 2023, 44). In fact, Yaghmaee had already made this observation (2015, 56–57).

Unfortunately, the site has been subjected to looting, agricultural activities, and road construction, and it is quite possible that some of the mounds have been leveled by farmers. The Borāzjān-Sa'ad Abad Road has divided at least two of the tepes, namely Tol-e Khandagh and DQ14. As depicted in Plate 5.2, the distribution of tepes at the site is not uniform, and south of the river curve, no tepe is discernible on the surface because the remnants of these mounds are buried beneath cultivated lands.

The ancient town of Dehqāed was a complex settlement with diverse functions and occupations. Based on the findings from the limited archaeological excavations available to us, it is evident that the town comprised ritual and industrial sectors, defensive structure(s), and residential areas for the aristocracy. Although it is a preliminary assessment, it might be possible to consider dividing the urban space into private and public zones. Notably, most of the mounds at Dehqāed exhibit surface ceramics from the Sasanian period, while several also contain ceramics from the

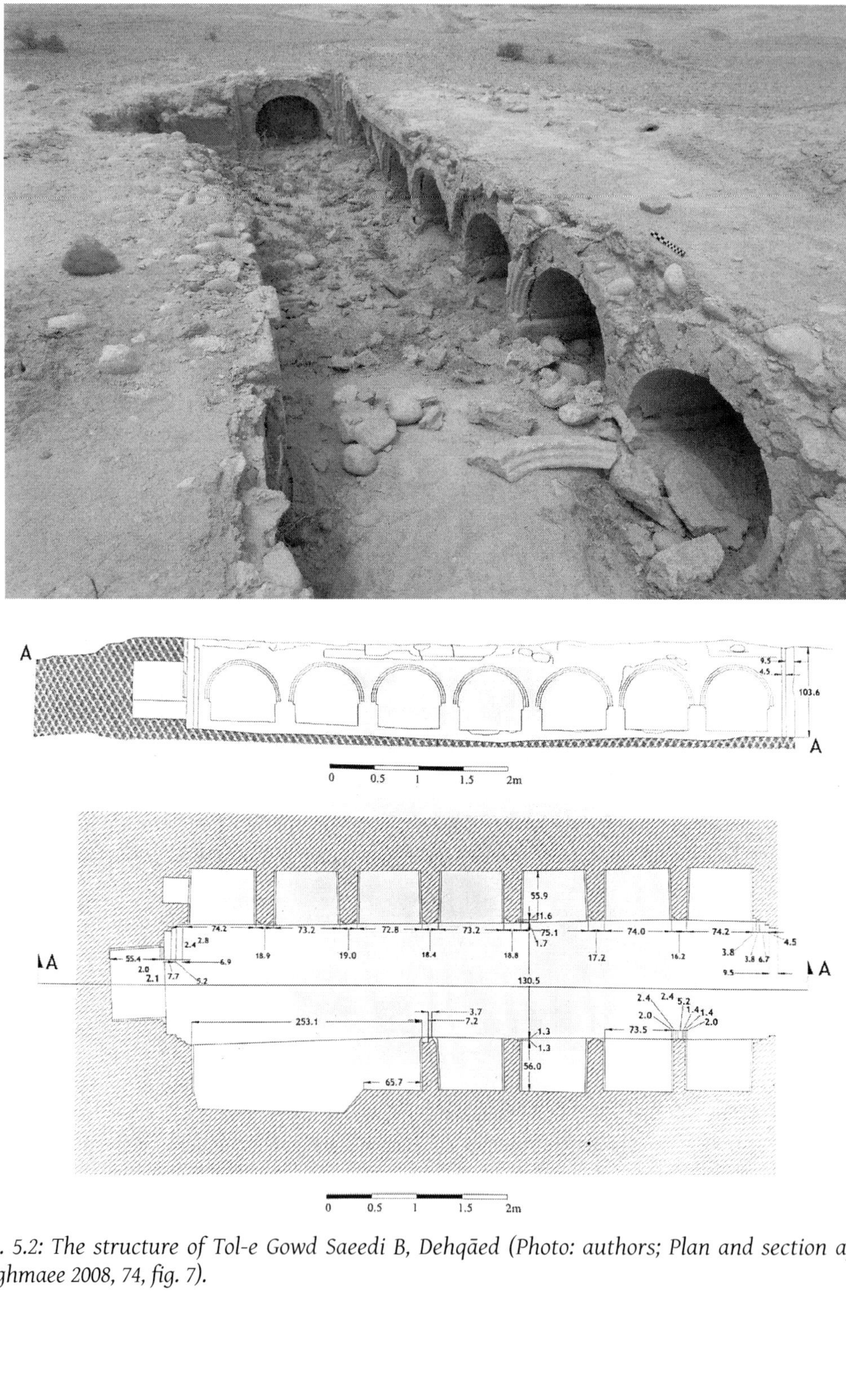

Fig. 5.2: The structure of Tol-e Gowd Saeedi B, Dehqāed (Photo: authors; Plan and section after Yaghmaee 2008, 74, fig. 7).

Achaemenid and Post-Achaemenid periods. Few of the mounds bear clear Sasanian architecture and materials which we know from previous, limited, excavations and illegal digging. In the town, a *chārtāqi* has already been discovered (see below Tol-e Kheshti). Additionally, a structure consisting of repeated arches has been discovered in several mounds at Dehqāed (Tol-e Kheshti, Tol-e Gowd-Saeedi and Tol-e Khandagh-Koochik, see Fig. 5.2). The function of the structure is discussed by the excavator as a temple of Mithras, which is a problematic debate (see below Tol-e Gowd-Saeedi).

In order to better understand the site, some of the tepes are described below (Plate 5.2).[6]

Tol-e Kheshti (DQ13)

This tepe, as the largest mound at the site, is situated 1.5 km north of Dehqāed village and 3 km west of Bārgāhi village. The name of this extensive mound has an interesting history: due to the abundance of brick fragments and architectural remains, local residents initially referred to it as Tol-e Kheshti, which translates to 'mound of mudbricks'. Later, as the remains of a chārtāqi (Zoroastrian ritual structure) and a stand of a type associated with fire temples became apparent, they began calling it Tol-e Ātashgāh or Tol-e Ātashkadeh, meaning 'tepe of the fire temple'. Refraining from making functional judgments about the structure, we refer to this section as 'Tol-e Kheshti A' (Fig. 5.3). The excavator, Yaghmaee, assigned different names to parts of this tepe based on the structures he unearthed there. He referred to the arched structure as 'mehrkadeh Mohammad-Abad' (Fig. 5.4 bottom), signifying the

Fig. 5.3: Tol-e Kheshti, the excavated structures: chartaqi *(Tol-e Kheshti A). So-called* 'mehrkadeh' *(Tol-e Kheshti B) (modified by the authors after Google Earth).*

Fig. 5.4: General view of architectural remains at Tol-e Kheshti. Top: Tol-e Kheshti A (Photo: authors; plan after Yaghmaee 2015, 52, fig. 2). Bottom: Tol-e Kheshti B (Photo: authors; plan after Yaghmaee 2008, 65, fig. 3).

Temple of Mithras of Mohammad-Abad, which we prefer to name as 'Tol-e Kheshti B'. Similarly, he separately named the chārtāqi structure 'Mohammad-Abad chārtāqi' (see Fig. 5.3 and Fig. 5.4 top), even though both structures are in close proximity on the same mound. In this paper, we determine to use the original name of the tepe, as known to the local people: Tol-e Kheshti.

As previously mentioned, a Greek-style marble statue was discovered at Dehqāed, with indications suggesting it originated from both Tol-e Khandagh (Rahbar 1999) and Tol-e Kheshti (Yaghmaee 2008, 60; 2015, 50). However, the correct findspot is Tol-e Kheshti B (Fig. 5.1). The latter tepe, Tol-e Kheshti, has been a point of interest for archaeologists and was the focus of two excavation seasons conducted by Yaghmaee in 1994 and 2004 (2008, 60; 2015, 50). This tepe spans approximately 7 ha in area and reaches a height of 8 m. Our knowledge of the architectural elements at Dehqāed primarily derives from Tol-e Kheshti and Tol-e Gowd-Saeedi. Within Tol-e Kheshti, there is a quadrilateral structure (chārtāqi) known as Tol-e Kheshti A, measuring approximately 11 m in size. It consists of four pillars, with each side averaging 270 cm in length (Fig. 5.4 top). Constructed using bricks and mortar, this structure features a base designed for a fire altar (Yaghmaee 2015, 53, figs 2, 3). On the plaster base, a trace of a fire altar measuring 63 cm in diameter is discernible. In terms of chronology, Yaghmaee attributed Tol-e Kheshti A to the Sasanian era.

The second section of the tepe that was excavated, known as Tol-e Kheshti B, is situated approximately 170 m southwest of Tol-e Kheshti A. This area contains a structure featuring vaulted niches, to which the excavator has assigned a Parthian-era date. However, this suggestion should be approached with caution. Yaghmaee proposed this chronological framework based on pottery findings at the site. Nevertheless, it remains unclear how he linked this pottery to the Parthian period, primarily because our knowledge of Parthian ceramics in the region is quite limited. This limitation arises from the absence of stratigraphic excavations that could offer insights into the sequence of ceramic layers in the area. While other methods, such as radiocarbon dating from excavations or comparing the pottery at Tol-e Kheshti with securely dated Parthian ceramics from southern Iran, have proven useful in similar studies, none of these approaches were utilized in Yaghmaee's excavation. It is important to note that in another part of his work, Yaghmaee suggests that the structure belonged to the Parthian–Sasanian periods (2015, 50). One clue in his paper suggests that Yaghmaee may have considered the structure as Parthian because of the discovery of a torpedo jar at Tol-e Kheshti (2015, 72). However, the torpedo jar, which has been found not only in various parts of Dehqāed but also in several coastal sites along the Persian Gulf, can be dated to the late Sasanian to Early Islamic periods (Priestman and Kennet 2023, 170).

Tol-e Kheshti B is composed of five rectangular rooms interconnected by small corridors and is constructed using mud bricks and gypsum mortar. Among these rooms, L:1001 (measuring 5.85 × 1.60 m) and L:1003 (measuring 5.80 × 2.30 m)[7] stand out as they feature vaulted niches (Yaghmaee 2008, 61). Another rectangular room is located to the northwest, intersecting with the first two rooms. Along the length of L:1001, there are two sets of six niches on each side, totaling 14 niches, with an additional two on the back wall. These niches have an average size of 65 × 75 cm (with heights ranging from 66 to 76 cm) and are characterized by round-arched roofs constructed from baked bricks, forming an archivolt (for details, see Yaghmaee 2008, 61–67; Callieri 2014, 101). In the case of L:1003, there is only one row of niches, comprising a total of six niches. It is worth noting that these niches are positioned only 2 cm above the floor.

To the north and northwest of Tol-e Kheshti, there are seven mounds (as shown in Plate 5.2: DQ03, 08, 09, 10, 11, 12, and 35) that also went unmentioned by the Iranian–British expedition. Again, this omission could be attributed to their relatively small size and the limited presence of surface ceramics. The most northern of these mounds, DQ03, is situated near the Dālaki River. Its alluvial plain may have been suitable for dryland farming, especially in the southern part of the mound due to its compatible slope. This mound stands at an approximate height of 2 m and exhibits architectural evidence primarily on the northern side. Mounds DQ09 and 10, on the other hand, measure between 5 to 6 m in height and feature a scattered architectural structure comprised of rubble flooring with plaster mortar.

Tol-e Gowd-Saeedi (DQ01)

In the northeastern sector of the Dehqāed site, there is a tepe known as Tol-e Gowd-Saeedi. As was the case for other sites, Yaghmaee referred to this tepe by different names. There was an initial misconception, as he mistakenly heard 'Gow-Saeedi' and thought it was a dialect variation of 'Gav-Saeedi,' with 'gav' meaning cow in Persian. However, the accurate name is 'Gowd-Saeedi,' where 'gowd' signifies deep. Additionally, Yaghmaee sometimes called this place 'Tepe Keshāvarz' because the landowner's surname is Keshavarz.[8] Neither of these names corresponds to the original name nor the appellation used by the local residents, who identify it as Tol-e Gowd-Saeedi.

Similar to Tol-e Kheshti, the location of this tepe, Tol-e Gowd-Saeedi, holds the potential for agricultural activities. Its close proximity to the Dālaki River offers access to water canals and qanāts, with alluvial soil conducive to farming. Remarkable architectural remnants measuring about 20 × 20 m can be observed in Gowd-Saeedi A (Fig. 5.5).[9] It appears that this structure had various entrances and was constructed using rubble stones and mortar. The presence of collapsed bricks (measuring 32 × 32 × 7 cm) indicates that the building featured a brick arch. Traces of plaster are still visible on the walls, and stucco fragments are scattered throughout the structure.

In the northwest, approximately 70 m from Gowd-Saeedi A, there is another structure, Gowd-Saeedi B. This structure is constructed using rubble stonework and plaster mortar, with a plaster coating and two rows of vaulted niches, each about 70 cm

Fig. 5.5: General view of the large building at Tol-e Gowd-Saeedi A, Dehqāed (Photo: authors).

in height, 55 cm in depth, and 70 cm in width (Fig. 5.2). These niches are characterized by round-arched roofs built from baked bricks and adorned with a modeled archivolt. As a preliminary hypothesis, it is conceivable that the vaulted niches may have served as benches within the spatial context, as previously suggested in other instances (Yaghmaee 2008, 70; Callieri 2014, 101). However, it is important to note that the arched mouth of the niches measures approximately 60–70 cm in height, while the overall height is roughly 1 m. This height poses challenges for comfortable seating on such an elevated surface, making it evident that accepting this as a functional seating arrangement may not be straightforward.

The limited excavation at Tol-e Gowd-Saeedi did not yield enough information to establish a more definitive connection between Gowd-Saeedi A and B or to delve into other architectural aspects of Gowd-Saeedi B. What we have realized about Gowd-Saeedi B at this stage is the existence of a room measuring less than 8 m in length. Within this room, there are 15 vaulted niches, all positioned at a height of 10 cm from the floor (Fig. 5.2).

The vaulted structures at Gowd-Saeedi B bear a resemblance to those observed at Tol-e Kheshti and Tol-e Khandagh-Koochik, all within a close 1 km distance. This similarity raises questions about the purpose of these structures, which remains a subject of debate. Yaghmaee suggests that they could be temples of Mithras (*mehrkadeh*) (2008). However, this identification is challenging to support due to their close proximity to a *chārtāqi* with a fire altar, confirming the ritual function of the *chārtāqi* structure. Considering the vaulted structure as a temple of Mithras prompts questions regarding the vicinity of these two structures dedicated to different religions, and raises the question of why there might be multiple temples to Mithras in such close proximity on a single site? Indeed, these structures differ significantly from the Mithraic structures known in Western contexts and the Near East, such as those found at Dura Europos. Unlike the latter, which typically consist of a single hall instead of several parallel rooms, the seating areas along the walls in these structures are solid and lack the distinctive niches found in the Iranian site (Callieri 2014, 101).

At Qale Dokhtar in Firuzabad, similar vaulted niches can be found in courtyard B, as well as in Room 18 (Fig. 5.6 top left and middle). The excavator, Dietrich Huff, initially interpreted these as storage niches within a depot room. Huff also suggested that these niches could potentially function as seating areas (Huff and Gignoux 1978, 133). Pierfrancesco Callieri proposes an alternative function for the Borāzjān niches, partially influenced by Huff's idea of a storage area and partially by the discovery of torpedo jars and bone fragments at Tol-e Kheshti B. Callieri posits that, given the absence of natural rock walls in the surrounding area which are commonly used for storing *ostodan*, or ossuaries, in the Fārs region, it is plausible that this complex might have served as a storage facility for ostodan. This hypothesis gains support from the presence of benches constructed along the walls of the corridor encircling another fire temple in Kermanshah, western Iran, presently known as Palang Gerd (Callieri 2014, 102).

Palang Gerd is a recently discovered Sasanian site situated in the village of the same name in Kermansheh. At this site, excavators uncovered a fire temple, which includes rectangular ossuaries formed from plaster slabs. One of these ossuaries measures 250 cm in length, 55–60 cm in width, and 50 cm in height, and features a decorative keyhole motif (Khosrovi and Rashnou 2014; Khosrovi *et al.* 2018, 57). Human remains have been found within the ossuary, indicating it served as a secondary burial site (Khosrovi *et al.* 2018, 59). It's important to note that the keyhole motif on this ossuary appears to have a purely decorative function and doesn't serve an architectural purpose, in contrast to the structures at Borāzjān and Qale Dokhtar.

As previously mentioned, Callieri's suggestion regarding the function of the Borāzjān structure as an ossuary is influenced by the discovery of torpedo sherds and bone fragments at Tol-e Kheshti B. However, the nature of these bone fragments, whether they are human or not, has not been studied (Yaghmaee 2008, 73). It is important to acknowledge that while the use of torpedo jars in burial practices was common,[10] they also had significant trade-related functions (Priestman 2013, 21–22, 91). In the context of burial practices, it is worth noting another burial method involving fragmented bones found in Naus of Dalverzintepa, Uzbekistan, during the early Kushan period (2nd–1st century BCE).[11] Of particular interest is the architectural character of Naus, which features a vaulted facade, although

Fig. 5.6: Structures niches-like from different sites: Top left: Room 18, Qale Dokhar in Firuzabad (Huff and Gignoux 1978, 131, abb. 15); Top middle: Courtyard B, Qale Dokhar in Firuzabad (Huff and Gignoux 1978, abb. 7). Top right: Naus of Dalverzintepa in Uzbekistan (Abdullaev 2018, 306, fig. 4). Bottom: Qalā Gūri, Ramāvand (Hasanpour 2021, fig. 1).

it resembles a chamber more than a niche (see Fig. 5.6 top right), making it less comparable to the Borāzjān case.

In the western region of Iran, near the Seymareh River, specifically around Kuhdahst in Luristan, a recently excavated Sasanian site called Qalā Gūri, Ramāvand, has come to light. Among the unearthed parts are buildings constructed with rubble masonry. One well-preserved section of the portico spans 900 × 390 cm and features two columns adorned with stucco ornamentation (Hasanpour and Hashemi 2014; Hasanpour 2021). Geomorphological investigations of the landscape suggest that this location experienced recurring inundation by the Seyemareh River and had been abandoned at some point, likely during the Early Islamic era (Hasanpour 2021). The building exhibits keyhole niches on various walls, positioned at a distance ranging from 30 to 50 cm above the floors (Hasanpour *et al.* 2016, 44, 46) (Fig. 5.6 bottom). The excavator's belief is that these niches were necessary for accommodating lighting devices such as candleholders and oil lamps (Hasanpour *et al.* 2016, 52). However, it is important to note that the function of these niches may differ from the case of Borāzjān due to the greater height of the Qalā Gūri niches.

Overall, it appears that the closest match to these niches is found at Qale Dokhtar, resembling those at Borāzjān in terms of their size, keyhole shape, and their distance from the floor. We believe that further information will lead to a more reasoned conclusion regarding the function of these vaulted niches. Additionally, the structure will provide insights into the urban character of the Dehqāed site, but the unresolved questions await answers from future excavations.

Tol-e Bāgh-Mil (DQ34)

One of the intriguing mounds within the Dehqāed site is Tol-e Bāgh-Mil. Unfortunately, this site faces significant threats due to unauthorized excavation, the creation of tracks on the mound, the digging of water canals, the expansion of palm groves, and general agricultural activities. If we were to draw a hypothetical line between two Achaemenid palatial structure, Sang-i Siāh and Charkhāb monuments, Bāgh-Mil would lie along that line. Situated to the south of the Sang-i Siāh palace, Bāgh-Mil consists of a primary mound, ranging in height from 1 to 3 m, and is encircled by a few smaller mounds. The site likely covers an area of approximately 1 ha. Ongoing looting activities have exposed various materials, including plaster, stone, and brick fragments, suggesting the presence of structures constructed from these materials. Notably, a distinctive stone element, measuring 120 × 120 cm, came to light following unauthorized work by villagers, resulting in some damage (Fig. 5.7). This element bears a resemblance to the lower part of fire altars, yet it is premature to conclusively determine its function. The material appears similar to the black stone used in the Borāzjān palaces, but definitively identifying it as Achaemenid or post-Achaemenid is challenging at this stage. In addition to the stone piece, there is a possibility of a pottery workshop, indicated by recent damage to the mound, revealing a kiln.

Fig. 5.7: The stone element (lower part of a fire altar?), discovered during illegal digging at Tol-e Bāgh-Mil (Photo: authors).

Tol-e Bāghi (DQ18)

This mound is referred to as Tol-e Bāghi by the local villagers, but it is also known as Tol-e Shishegari, signifying the 'tepe of glassmaking'. Despite the damage inflicted by agricultural activities, Tol-e Bāghi retains discernible remnants of structures characterized by rubble stonework and plaster mortar. Furthermore, the most noteworthy surface discoveries on the mound include glass slags, forge welding pieces, layers of ash, and a wealth of glass fragments (Fig. 5.8). Yaghmaee's report even notes the presence of kiln remains at this site (Yaghmaee 2018, 196).

Surface pottery findings point to a Sasanian-era chronology for Tol-e Bāghi. The mound is positioned between two other mounds: Tol-e Pes-e Tol (to the north) (Plate 5.2: DQ19) and Tol-e Sang-e-Āsiāb (to the south) (Plate 5.2: DQ17). Both of these neighboring mounds are being adversely impacted by farming and the cultivation of palm trees, and the ceramics uncovered from surface surveys also indicate a Sasanian timeframe.

Tol-e Khandagh (DQ25)

This prominent hill is situated along the road that links the villages of Dehqāed and Nazar Agha. It essentially separates a small section of the hill on its western side. The hill is referred to as 'Tol-e Khandagh' (Moat Hill), a name derived from its distinctive characteristics, notably the moat-like depression that is conspicuously visible on its eastern side at present. Covering an area of roughly 32,600 m^2, Tol-e Khandagh features a well-defined oval structure.

The elevated position of the mound allowed one to monitor this plain, with its various Sasanian sites, a fact that played a significant role in the strategic placement and construction of Tol-e Khandagh, which likely served as a military stronghold or fortification. Its existence alongside notable sites such as Tol-e Gowd Saeedi, Tol-e Kheshti, Tol-e Sang-e-Āsiāb, Tol-e Bāghi, Tol-e Pes-e-Tol, Tol-e Naqāreh-Khuneh, and Tol-e Bāgh-Mil, coupled with environmental factors like the continuous flow of the Dālaki River and the southern riverbank, contributes to the overall richness of the Sasanian-era settlement landscape. When these elements are combined, they paint a comprehensive picture of an extensive urban settlement deeply rooted in large-scale agriculture and small-scale industries, supported by geographical and historical records.

Tol-e Naqāreh-Khuneh (DQ04)

The ancient mound known as 'Naqāreh-Khuneh' is one of the more prominent mounds in the Dehqāed region. It is situated approximately 2.5 km north of Dehqāed village, on the southern bank of the Dālaki River. This mound rises about 6 m above the surrounding ground level covering an area of half a hectare. Around the mound, especially on its eastern and southern sides, remnants of several qanat channels,

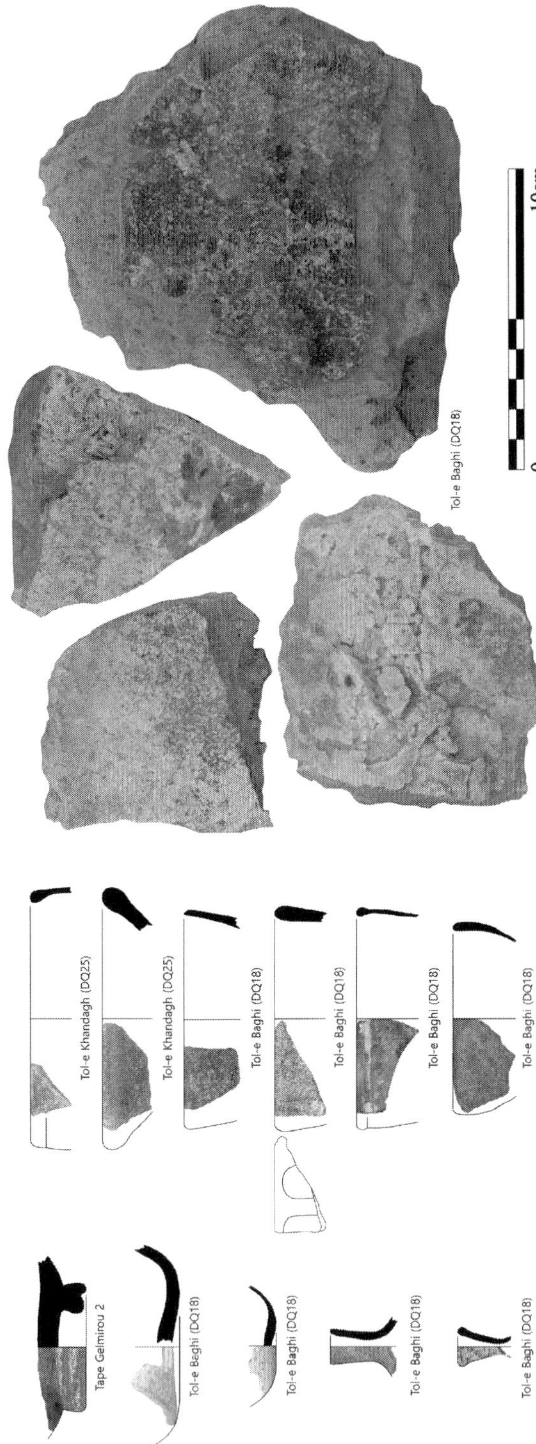

Fig. 5.8: Glass slags and vessels from the Dehqāed Site (Photos and drawings: authors).

which were used to transport water from the bed of the Dālaki River to the lower lands south of the mound, are visible. Archaeological evidence on the surface of Tol-e Naqāreh-Khuneh primarily consists of potsherds of the Sasanian period and the Early Islamic centuries. Additionally, in the central and northern parts of the mound, one can observe remnants of distinctive structures, the most prominent of which is the brick structure in the central part of the mound which featured remains of arches and large stone and mud-brick walls, some of which have been coated with bitumen and waterproofed.

Tol-e Sang-e-Āsiāb (DQ17)

Due to the presence of a large millstone on its slope, this mound is known as 'Tol-e Sang-e-Āsiāb' (Millstone mound). Its elevation is approximately 5 m, and it lies to the north of Tol-e Qaleh and southwest of Tol-e Kheshti, covering an irregular area of about 3 ha. Tol-e Sang-e-Āsiāb, like other ancient mounds in this region, is located in close proximity to the southern bank of the Dālaki River, which played an essential role in nourishing and fertilizing the lands of the area. Despite the risk of floods and river overflow during rainy months, this region has been conducive to agriculture and palm cultivation, attracting nomadic and settled communities during different periods. Particularly during the Sasanian period, the economic policies of the Sasanian Empire aimed at agricultural development led to the formation of numerous small and large ancient mounds in this area, with Tol-e Sang-e-Āsiāb and its neighboring mounds being examples of this phenomenon. Among the archaeological materials found on this mound, one can mention scattered architectural remains in the form of brick fragments and river pebbles along with gypsum mortar. Additionally, a collection of incised gray pottery fragments (SMAG, see below), which are indicative of Sasanian-era pottery types, can be observed.

Tol-e Sang-e-Shekasteh (DQ11)

Tol-e Sang-e-Shekasteh is a small and relatively elevated hill located within the Dehqāed region. It is situated approximately 1.9 km north of Dehqāed village and about 250 m northwest of the ancient mound, Tol-e Kheshti. The name of this mound derives from a large broken millstone at its eastern edge, which currently serves as a landmark bordering agricultural land. Tol-e Sang-e-Shekasteh has a relatively regular semi-circular shape, covering an area of approximately 1,200 m^2 and rising about 3 m above the surrounding terrain. Its structural and cultural layers, like other mounds in the Dehqāed region, have formed on alluvial deposits. The most notable cultural findings on the surface of the mound consist of scattered pottery fragments, primarily indicative of Sasanian-era pottery types and, samples that can be attributed, with some uncertainty, to the Early Islamic centuries. Additionally, faint traces of a floor-like structure with river pebble stones and gypsum mortar can be observed at the summit of the mound, similar to specimens found in other mounds within the vicinity.

Tol-e Pes-e-Tol (DQ19)

This tepe is composed of two interconnected mounds. Its name, 'Tol-e Pes-e-Tol', translates to 'a mound behind another mound', indicating its unique dual-mound composition. This mound is situated in close proximity to the southern edge of the Dālaki River, near a palm grove. Tol-e Pes-e-Tol rises to an elevation of approximately 2.5 to 3 m above the surrounding ground level and is considered one of the prominent mounds within the archaeological area of Dehqāed. A significant portion of the western mound has been leveled over the years for agricultural expansion by the landowner, causing its disappearance. Other areas around the mound have also suffered damage due to the development of palm groves and the creation of access routes to neighboring orchards and lands.

Ceramic assemblage of Dehqāed

Architectural remnants in the Dehqāed region have provided us with a schematic understanding, albeit through limited reports published by the excavator. However, what remains under-discussed in the literature are the ceramic attributes. The only reference to Dehqāed pottery is found in a book that is not primarily centered on Dehqāed itself. Yaghmaee included a handful of pottery illustrations from Dehqāed without providing any substantial discussions, comparisons, or classifications (see Yaghmaee 2018, 232–233, 243–246). Additionally, Donald S. Whitcomb, in the course of his research on the Angali canal, compiled a few ceramics from the Borāzjān region, among these, only one pertains to the Dehqāed area, encompassing Tol-e Khandagh (DQ25) and Tol-e Ghale (DQ20) (Whitcomb 1987, 320, fig. E.).

The research on ceramics in the Persian Gulf coastal regions, including Būshehr, has a distinct historical context. One notable collection is the Williamson Collection, which encompasses various ceramic types from the southern regions of Iran. This collection was curated by Andrew George Williamson during his doctoral studies at Pembroke College, Oxford, between 1968 and 1971. Unfortunately, his untimely death in Oman in 1975 prevented the thorough study and publication of this collection (Priestman 2005, 1). The Williamson Collection is currently housed at the Ashmolean Museum in Oxford and the National Museum of Iran.[12] Despite the importance of the ceramics from different regions in the south of Iran, only a few samples of surface pottery of Būshehr and Bandar Tāheri were collected, so pottery collections from the Borāzjān plain and other regions are not well represented in the Williamson Collection (Priestman 2003, 346, fig. 1; 2005, 364, table 15). The majority of the pottery from the Būshehr region in the Williamson collection dates from the 5th to the mid-7th century (Priestman 2013, 249). Subsequently, other British colleagues continued Williamson's research for several years, but their primary focus in the Būshehr province was on the Būshehr peninsula rather than the Borāzjān Plain (Priestman and Kennet 2023, 41–45 and 289–297).

Based on the pottery collected during our recent survey at Dehqaed, we have identified several Sasanian ceramic types. In this very brief and preliminary assessment, we have intentionally chosen a small set of ceramics from Dehqāed (Fig. 5.9) that display resemblances to other established Sasanian assemblages, especially those discovered in the southern regions of Iran near the Persian Gulf.

At this initial stage, it is evident to us that Dehqāed features several distinct SMAG types, as outlined in Table 5.1. SMAG stands for 'Small Gray Vessels', which encompasses four distinct groups denoted as A, B, C, and RC. These types predominantly consist of bowls and narrow-necked jars (Fig. 5.9, Nos. 1–4, 6–8, 10, and 16). Depending on the specific group, SMAG ceramics were prevalent during the 2nd to 9th centuries CE. Their origins appear to trace back to southern Iran, where they are found not only in coastal areas but also in the Fārs highlands, such as Tal-i Malyan, Qasr-i Abu Nasr, and Hājiābād. These ceramics typically exhibit a consistent fabric characterized by various shades of gray, often dark, occasionally dark reddish gray, and are primarily plain, mostly devoid of any decorative elements (see Kennet 2002, 157; 2004, 86; Priestman and Kennet 2023, 145–148).

The second type, known as TORP, served as a transport vessel with a function akin to Mediterranean amphorae (see Kennet 2002, 154–155). These vessels are recognized by their tall, torpedo shaped bodies with pointed bases, typically ranging in color from pale buff to orange (Fig. 5.9, No. 5 and 11). Often, they are waterproofed with bitumen on the inner surface of the vessel. TORP can be categorized into four groups based on their color and specific form details. They are predominantly associated with the late Sasanian to Early Islamic periods in the coastal regions of the Persian Gulf (Priestman and Kennet 2023, 170). However, they have also been found in contexts with varying dates, spanning from the mid-2nd to the 9th century CE, as observed in Sohar (Kervran 2004).[13] These vessels have been discovered at various sites along the Persian Gulf and the western Indian Ocean. On occasion, they are found in more distant locations, such as the Egyptian Red Sea coast at Berenike in the west and extending as far east as Thailand and Indonesia. Nonetheless, there is an ongoing debate concerning the precise origin of their manufacture (Tomber *et al.* 2022, 240).

TURQ, also known as 'Alkaline Glazed Ware', represents another pottery type characterized by its pale yellow, green, or turquoise glaze (Fig. 5.9, No. 9). This category typically includes bowls and large jars, with a monochrome glaze that is prone to weathering. Based on Kennet's classification, it is further divided into six classes, denoted as TURQ 1–5 and TURQ.RC. TURQ.1 dates to the Sasanian to Early Islamic period, extending up to the 10th century CE (see Priestman and Kennet 2023, 188–193).[14]

SLIP.R, or 'Red Slipped Ware', is another type of pottery found at Dehqāed. The identification of specific forms within this category is crucial for more precise dating.

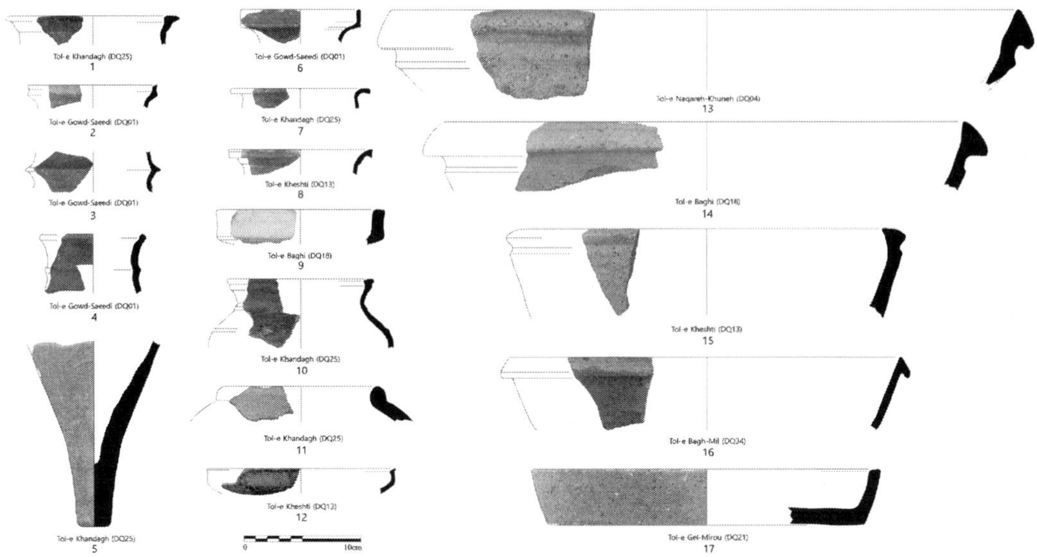

Fig. 5.9: Selected Sasanian ceramics from different tepes at the Dehqāed Site (Photos and drawings: authors).

Table 5.1: Descriptions and parallels of the selected ceramics in Figure 5.9.

No.	*Manufacture, Firing, Color (Int., Core, Ext.), Inclusions*	*Type/Dating*	*Parallel*
1	Wheel, Well Fired, Gray, Gray, Gray, Grit	SMAG. B/form 5 (3rd–6th CE)	Priestman and Kennet 2023, 354, fig. IV.1 m
2	Wheel, Well Fired, Pale gray, Pale gray, Pale gray, Sand	SMAG. A/form 2 (3rd–6th CE)	Priestman and Kennet 2023, 354, fig. IV.1 h
3	Wheel, Well Fired, Gray, Reddish Brown, Gray, Sand	SMAG. C/form 3 (2nd–3rd CE)[1]	Alden and Balcer 1978, 84, fig. 6, no. 6; Priestman and Kennet 2023, 359, fig. IV.6 m
4	Wheel, Well Fired, Gray, Gray, Gray, Grit	SMAG. B/form 5 (3rd–6th CE)	Whitcomb 1985, 153, fig. 57 u; Kennet 2002, 157, fig. 3; Priestman and Kennet 2023, 354, fig. IV.1 o
5	Wheel, Well Fired, Pale Buff, Pale Buff, Pale Buff, Sand	TORP.1 (late Sasanian–Early Islamic)	Kennet 1991, 111, fig. 6, no. 1021; Priestman and Kennet 2023, 399, fig. IV.46 b
6	Wheel, Well Fired, Gray, Gray, Gray, Sand	SMAG. B/form 7 (3rd–6th CE)	Priestman and Kennet 2023, 358, fig. IV.5 a
7	Wheel, Well Fired, Pale gray, Pale gray, Pale gray, Sand	SMAG. C/form 3 (2nd–3rd CE)	Priestman and Kennet 2023, 359, fig. IV.6 g
8	Wheel, Well Fired, Gray, Gray, Gray, Sand	SMAG. C/form 1 (2nd–3rd CE)	Whitcomb 1985, 153, fig. 57 u; Priestman and Kennet 2023, 359, fig. IV.6 d

(Continued)

Table 5.1: (Continued)

No.	Manufacture, Firing, Color (Int., Core, Ext.), Inclusions	Type/Dating	Parallel
9	Wheel, Well Fired, Pale Green glaze, buff, Pale Green glaze, Sand	TURQ.1/form 25 (Sasanian–Early Islamic up to the 10th CE)	Kennet 1991, 110, fig. 5, no. 1049; Kervran 2004, 281, fig. 2, no. 2; Priestman and Kennet 2023, 419, fig. IV.66 n
10	Wheel, Well Fired, Gray, Pale gray, Gray, Grit	SMAG. B/form 7 (3rd–6th CE)	Azarnoush 1994, 174e; Priestman and Kennet 2023, 358, fig. IV.5 d
11	Wheel, Well Fired, Pinkish Buff, Pinkish Buff, Pinkish Buff, Sand	TORP.1 (late Sasanian–Early Islamic)	Kennet 1991, 111, fig. 6, no. 1048; Priestman and Kennet 2023, 398, fig. IV.45 b
12	Wheel, Well Fired, Reddish brown, Red, Reddish brown, Sand	SLIP.R/form 9 (Parthian–Sasanian)	Azarnoush 1994, 171 f; Priestman and Kennet 2023, 411, fig. IV.58 n
13	Wheel, Well Fired, Buff, Buff, Buff, Grit	GRIT/form 2 (Sasanian)[2]	Potts *et al.* 2009, 693, fig. 6.25, MSP825; Priestman and Kennet 2023, 366, fig. IV.13 c
14	Wheel, Well Fired, Pale buff, Pale buff, Pale buff, Grit	GRIT/form 2 (Sasanian)	Potts *et al.* 2009, 693, fig. 6.25, MSP825; Priestman and Kennet 2023, 366, fig. IV.13 c
15	Wheel, Well Fired, Greenish buff, Greenish buff, Greenish buff, Grit	GRIT/form 2 (Partho-Sasanian)[3]	Lamberg-Karlovsky 1970, 9, fig. 3k; Priestman and Kennet 2023, 366, fig. IV.13 e
16	Wheel, Well Fired, Gray, Gray, Gray, Vegetal	SMAG. A/form 1 (4th–5th CE)	Azarnoush 1994, 204, fig. 182 a,b; Priestman and Kennet 2023, 356, fig. IV.3 i
17	Wheel, Well Fired, Buff, Buff, Buff, White particles	-	Whitcomb 1985, 141, fig. 52 e

1 SMAG. C/form 3 is ascribed to the 2nd–3rd century CE (Priestman and Kennet 2023, 147). Nevertheless, a similar type is discovered in grid square X-65 at the Tal-i Malyan site, which is dated to the early Sasanian period, approximately around 300 CE, through radiocarbon and thermoluminescence analysis (see Alden and Balcer 1978, 79).

2 The dating of this type remains uncertain, as noted by Priestman and Kennet in 2023, 150–151. However, during the survey and excavation of Mamasani, it has been regarded as Sasanian, see Potts *et al.* 2009, 693.

3 For the dating of the examples from the excavation of Tepe Yahya, which were categorized as Partho-Sasanian see Lamberg-Karlovsky 1970, 9.

Forms 1 to 7 closely resemble slipped wares from the Achaemenid period and the 3rd to 2nd century BCE. In contrast, forms 8 to 11, including form 9 (Fig. 5.9, No. 12), constitute a separate group dating from the Parthian to Sasanian periods, spanning from the 1st century BCE to the 6th century CE (Priestman and Kennet 2023, 173–174). Additionally, there are two potsherds (Fig. 5.9, Nos. 14–15) that resemble those classified under GRIT/form 2. This type, known as 'Coarse Grit-Tempered Ware,' consists of large, coarse vessels with grit inclusions. The precise dating of this type remains uncertain (Priestman and Kennet 2023, 150–151), although it was considered Sasanian during the survey and excavation of Mamasani (Potts *et al.* 2009, 693).

Conclusion

The Borāzjān region contains Sasanian sites that were inhabited prior to the Sasanian era. While Dehqāed can be identified as a Sasanian town in ancient times, its history and chronology beyond that period require further investigation. Surface pottery at the site spans from the Achaemenid to Sasanian eras, but the proportion of ceramics from different periods and their distribution varies. The exact period when Dehqāed evolved into a town remains unclear. Nonetheless, research on surface ceramics and limited excavations suggests that the Sasanian era marked the site's most thriving and active phase. The architectural evidence confirms an urban system in the town, a place that established different functionalities. Different functional aspects of the site become apparent through the architectural remains uncovered in official excavations and from unauthorized digging and looting.

It is essential to place Dehqāed and its Sasanian-era communication networks within a broader perspective. Dehqāed served as a pivotal point on the strategic route connecting inland Fārs with the coastal region, a role it played for centuries. It is important not to overlook its connections with other Sasanian sites in the Būshehr hinterland, such as Tol-e Jid, Khosh-Āb, Isāvandeh, Rishehr/Rev Ardashir, and Shif Island. An intriguing perspective lies in exploring the relationship between the Dehqāed site and its connections with Rishehr to the south and Bishāpūr and likely Tol-e Qale Seifābād to the north. In essence, by understanding the Borāzjān plain as the primary route from the highlands (Fārs) to the hinterlands (Būshehr), we gain insight into the control and administration of the Sasanian Empire spanning from the western part of the Zāgros to the Persian Gulf, a control that was inherited from the Achaemenids. Dehqāed possesses a significant repository of unexplored data, but without systematic research, including fieldwork, we cannot offer a precise interpretation. Future archaeological efforts could greatly enhance our understanding of various aspects. Several key questions remain to be answered, such as when the town's development occurred, what factors fueled its growth (environmental or institutional), and its status during the Parthian dynasty. Additionally, investigations into the communication links between Dehqāed and other prominent Parthian-era towns are warranted. Determining the timing of the town's decline is another critical aspect. Moreover, the site's status during the Achaemenid period and its relationship with neighboring palatial structures should be a priority for future research.

Acknowledgments

We would also like to express our appreciation to Kourosh Mohammadkhani, Naghmeh Rafiee, Yadollah Zekavatzadeh, Musa Bushehri, and Younes Yazdankhah for their generous support. In addition, we extend our special thanks to Ali Asadi and Alireza Khosrowzadeh for their insightful discussions. The current research was supported by the 'Deutschen Forschungsgemeinschaft (DFG, SPP 2176)' and we extend our sincere appreciation for their generous funding.

Notes

1 In Persepolis, two groups of tablets have been discovered: the Persepolis Fortification Archive (PFA) and the Persepolis Treasury Archive (PTA). These archives, closely linked with the reign of Darius I, stand as the principal written sources for the exploration of numerous facets of the Persian Empire. For a more comprehensive understanding of these archives see Azzoni *et al.* 2017.

2 On the Achaemenid structures in the Borāzjān area see Zehbari 2020 and Matin 2020.

3 The initial report cites BH29–BH44, amounting to 15 mounds (see Carter *et al.* 2006, 71). However, a subsequent report mentions 18 site components (Priestman and Kennet 2023, 45).

4 A few of the mounds bear local names like Tol-e Khandagh, Tol-e Kheshti, Tol-e Bāghi, Tol-e Gowd-Saeedi, Tol-e Bāgh-Mil, among others. However, some mounds do not have distinct names and are identified by numbers on our survey expedition maps, labeled as 'DQ'.

5 This challenge persists, and will until comprehensive stratigraphic excavations are undertaken, allowing us to differentiate and evaluate ceramics spanning from the Achaemenid to Parthian periods in the area.

6 We chose these mounds based on the available information, based in part on the discovery of architectural remains at Tol-e Kheshti and Tol-e Gowd-Saeedi.

7 It should be noted that the excavator reports the size, but this measurement is likely inaccurate. Even in the plan created by Yaghmaee's team, both rooms (L:1001 and L:1003) appear to be roughly the same size.

8 Yaghmaee has a tendency to alter site names, such as renaming 'Tol-e Khandagh-Koochik' to 'Tol-e Ajori' or changing 'Tol-e Bāghi' to 'Tol-e Shishegari'. The latter alteration was also adopted by Sarfaraz, perhaps originally initiated by him. In our efforts, we have opted for names currently in use among the local population, as this ensures that the names hold meaning for those residing in the area today, avoiding the use of names that may be unfamiliar to them.

9 The precise measurements of the building remain unknown due to the incomplete excavation. However, aerial photographs provide an estimate of the structure's approximate size.

10 As seen in the Sasanian Shoghāb cemetery in Būshehr, see Mir Fattah 1996. It is worth noting that at Palang Gerd, human bones were not found within torpedo jars (see Khosrovi *et al.* 2018, 58).

11 The dating of the Naus remains a subject of debate, see Abdullaev 2018, 307–308 for more details and research on fragmented bones suggesting that it is difficult to confirm the practice of exposing deceased bodies to further purify the bones from flesh.

12 For the samples at the Ashmolean Museum see Priestman and Kennet 2002; Priestman 2003; 2005; 2006. On the samples deposited at the National Museum of Iran see Khosheghbal 2019.

13 See also examples between the 3rd–5th centuries CE at Ras Hafun in Somalia, Smith and Wright 1988, fig. 9 a–h. For more information on Torpedo jars see Kennet 2002, 159–150; 2004, 85; Tomber *et al.* 2022; Priestman and Kennet 2023, 169–170.

14 For more useful information regarding the Alkaline Glazed Ware see Kennet 2002, 155; 2004, 35–39.

Bibliography

Abdullaev, K. (2018) Burials with Fractioned Bones in the Funerary Practice of Bactria in the Late Bronze and Early Iron Ages. In J. Lhuillier and N. Boroffka (eds) *A Millennium of History, The Iron Age in Southern Central Asia (2nd and 1st Millennia BC)*, 299–317. Berlin, Deutsches Archäologisches Institut, Dietrich Reimer Verlag.

Alden, J.R. and Balcer, J.M. (1978) Excavation at Tal-I Malyan: Part I: A Sasanian Kiln. *Iran* 16, 79–92.

Azarnoush, M. (1994) *The Sasanian Manor House at Hājiābād, Iran.* Monografie di Mesopotamia III. Firenze, Le Lettere.

Azzoni, A., Dusinberre, E.R.M., Garrison, M.B., Henkelman, W.F.M., Jones, C.E., and Stolper, M.W. (2017) Persepolis Administrative Archives. Encyclopædia Iranica, online edition, http://www.iranicaonline.org/articles/persepolis-admin-archive.

Callieri, P. (2007) *L'archéologie du Fārs à l'époque hellénistique.* Paris, De Boccard.

Callieri, P. (2014) *Architecture et représentations dans l'Iran sassanide.* Paris, Peeters.

Carter, R.A., Challis, K., Priestman, S.M.N. and Tofighian, H. (2006) The Bushehr Hinterland Results of the First Season of the Iranian-British Archaeological Survey of Bushehr Province, November–December 2004. *Iran* 44, 63–103.

Daryaee, T. (2002) *Šahrestānīhā ī Ērānšahr.* California, Mazda Publishers.

Hallock, R. (1959) The Elamite texts from Persepolis. In H. Franke (ed.) *Akten des vierundzwanzigsten internationalen Orientalisten-Kongresses München*, 177–179. Wiesbaden, Steiner.

Hasanpour, A. (2021) Ramāvand/Qalā Gūri. *The Archaeological Gazetteer of Iran, An Online Encyclopedia of Iranian Archaeological Sites.* https://irangazetteer.humspace.ucla.edu/catalogue/ramavand-qala-guri/.

Hasanpour, A. and Hashemi, Z. (2014) A Comparative Study of the New Sassanid Stuccos from Qela Gowri, Ramavand, Lorestan, Iran. In R. Stucky, O. Kaelin, and H.-P. Mathys (eds) *Proceedings of the 9th International Congress on the Archaeology of the Ancient Near East, 9–13 June 2014, Basel*, 1479–1490. Wiesbaden, Harrassowitz Verlag.

Hasanpour, A., Delfan, F., and Beyranvand E. (2016) Tahlili bar me'mari-ye makshufe az nakhustin fasl-e kavosh-e banaye Qalā Gūri, Ramāvand [An Analysis of the Unearthed Architecture from the First Season of Excavations at Qalā Gūri, Ramāvand]. *Asar* 74, 37–60. [in Persian]

Henkelman, W.F.M. (2008) From Gabae to Taoce: The Geography of the Central Administrative Province. In P. Briant, W.F.M. Henkelman, and M.W. Stolper (eds) *L'archive des Fortifications de Persépolis. État des questions et perspectives de recherches* (Persika 12), 303–316. Paris, Collège de France.

Huff, D. and Gignoux, Ph. (1978) Ausgrabungen auf Qal'a-ye Dukhtar bei Firuzabad, 1976. A. Vorläufiger Grabungsbericht. *Archaologische Mitteilungen aus Iran* 11, 117–150.

Ibn Khordadbeh (1992) *Kitāb al-Masālik wa l-Mamālik [book of roads and kingdoms]*, translated by Saeed Khakrand. Tehran, Miras Melal. [in Persian]

Istakhri, Abū Ishāq Ibrāhim (1961) *Masālik va Mamālik*, Anonymous Persian Translation from V/VI Century A.H., Iraj Afshar (ed.), Tehran, B.T.N.K. [in Persian]

Kennet, D. (1991) Excavations at the Site of Al- Qusūr, Failaka, Kuwait. *Proceedings of the Seminar for Arabian Studies* 21, 97–111.

Kennet, D. (2002) Sasanian Pottery in Southern Iran and Eastern Arabia. *Iran* 40, 153–162.

Kennet, D. (2004) *Sassanian and Islamic Pottery from Ras al-Khaimah, Classification, Chronology and Analysis of Trade in the Western Indian Ocean.* Oxford, BAR International Series 1248.

Kervran, M. (2004) Archaeological Research at Suhar (1980–1986). *The Journal of Oman Studies* 13, 263–381.

Khosheghbal, H. (2019) *Classification and Typology of the Potteries of Williamson Collection.* Unpublished MA thesis University of Tehran, Department of Archaeology. [in Persian]

Khosrovi, Sh. and Rashnou A. (2014) Kavosh-e ezterari-ye mohawate-ye Palang Gerd-e shahrestan-e Eslamabad, Kermanshah, [Rescue excavation of the Palang-Gerd site in the Eslamabad county, Kermanshah]. *Brief Articles 12th Annual Symposium on the Iranian Archaeology, 19–21 May 2014, ICAR*, Tehran, 177–179.

Khosrovi, Sh., Alibaigi S. and Rashnou A. (2018) The Ossuary of the Palang Gerd Fire Temple: New Evidence of Zoroastrian Funerary Practices during the Sasanian Period in Western Iran, Kermanshah. *Studia Iranica* 47, 1, 51–73. [in Persian]

Lamberg-Karlovsky, C.C. (1970) *Excavations at Tepe Yahya, Iran 1967–1969. Progress Report I*. American School of Prehistoric Research Bulletin, 27. Cambridge, Peabody Museum.

Matin, E. (2020) The Achaemenid Settlement of Dashtestan (Borāzjān): A View from Persepolis. *East and West* 60 (2), 333– 364.

Mir Fattah, A.A. (1996) Gourestan-e Shoghāb: arze dasht dar havaye azad va dafn be shive-ye ostokhandan [Shoghāb Cemetery: open body exposure and ossuary burials]. *Asar* 25, 41–61. [in Persian]

Potts, D.T., Roustaei, K., Petrie, C.A. and Weeks, L.R. (eds) (2009) *The Mamasani Archaeological Project Stage One*. Oxford, Archaeopress.

Priestman, S.M.N. (2003) The Williamson Collection Project: Sasanian and Islamic Survey Ceramics from Southern Iran, Current Research. *Iran* 41, 345.

Priestman, S.M.N. (2005) *Settlement & Ceramics in Southern Iran: An Analysis of the Sasanian & Islamic Periods in the Williamson Collection*. MA Thesis, Department of Archaeology, University of Durham.

Priestman, S.M.N. (2006) Conclusion of the Williamson Collection Project. *British Institute of Persian Studies Newsletter* 29 (November), 5–7.

Priestman, S.M.N. (2013) *A Quantitative Archaeological Analysis of Ceramic Exchange in the Persian Gulf and Western Indian Ocean, AD c.400–1275*. PhD Thesis, University of Southampton, Centre for Maritime Archaeology.

Priestman, S.M.N. and Kennet, D. (2002) The Williamson Collection Project: Sasanian and Islamic Pottery from Southern Iran. *Iran* 40, 265.

Priestman, S.M.N. and Kennet, D. (2023) *Sasanian and Islamic Settlement and Ceramics in Southern Iran (4th to 17th Century AD): the Williamson Collection Project*. Oxford, Oxbow Books.

Rahbar, M. (1999) Pazhuheshi darbareye yek mojasameh marmari yunani makshufeh az Borāzjān [A Study on a Marble Greek Sculpture from Borāzjān]. In A. Alizadeh, Y. Majidzadeh and S.M. Shahmirzadi (eds) *Bastanshenasi va honare Iran (bozorgdashte Ezatolla Negahban)*, 192–209. Tehran, Cultural Heritage Organization of Iran. [in Persian]

Schwarz, P. (1969–1970) *Iran im Mittelalter nach den arabischen Geographen*. Hildesheim, Olms Verlag.

Smith, M.C. and Wright, H.T. (1988) The Ceramics from Ras Hafun in Somalia: Notes on a Classical Maritime Site. *Azania: Archaeological Research in Africa* 23, 115–141.

Tomber, R., Spataro, M., and Priestman, S. (2022) Early Islamic Torpedo Jars from Siraf: Scientific Analyses of the Clay Fabric and Source of Indian Ocean Transport Containers. *Iran* 60, 240–263.

Whitcomb, D.S. (1985) *Before the Roses and Nightingales, Excavations at Qasr-i Abu Nasr, Old Shiraz*. New York, The Metropolitan Museum of Art

Whitcomb, D.S. (1987) Bushire and the Angali Canal. *Mesopotamia* 22, 311–336.

Whitehouse, D. and Williamson, A.G. (1973) Sasanian Maritime Trade. *Iran* 11, 29–49.

Williamson, A.G. (1972) Persian Gulf Commerce in the Sasanian Period and the First Two Centuries of Islam. *Bastan shenasi va Honar-e Iran* 9–10, 97–109 (Latin section), 142–151 (Persian section).

Yaghmaee, I. (2008) [2010] Kavosh-ha-ye bastanshenasi dar mehrkadeh Mohammad-Abad, Dashtestān (Būshehr) [Archaeological excavations in the Temples of Mithras of Mohammad-Abad Dashtestān (Būshehr)]. *Bastan-Pazhuhi (Persian Journal of Iranian Studies)* 6, 56–76. [in Persian with English abstract]

Yaghmaee, I. (2015) Chartaqi-ye Mohammad-Abad, Dashtestān/ Borāzjān. *Bastan-Pazhuhi (Persian Journal of Iranian Studies)* 9 (17), 50–58. [in Persian with English abstract]

Yaghmaee, I. (2018) *farzi'ye khastgah rastin Hakhamaneshian bar payeh kavosh'haye bastanshenasi kakh-e Bardak-e Siāh, Dashtestān, Borāzjān, Durodghah Village* [*=A hypothesis on the true origin of the Achaemenids based on Archaeological Excavations, Bardak Siāh Palace, Dashtestān, Borāzjān, Durodghah Village*]. Tehran, Research Institute of Cultural Heritage and Tourism publication. [in Persian with English abstract]

Yaghmaee, I. (2023a) niyayesh-e mehr dar Iran [Mithraism in Iran]. Tehran, Dadkin publisher. [in Persian]

Yaghmaee, I. (2023b) Sazeh-ha-ye viran-e Dashtestān [Ruined structures of Dashtestān]. Tehran, Karnamak publisher. [in Persian]

Zehbari, Z. (2020) The Borāzjān Monuments: A Synthesis of Past and Recent Works. *ARTA* 2020.002. http://www.achemenet.com/pdf/arta/ARTA_2020_002_Zehbari.pdf.

Chapter 6 Prologue

Filling in the gaps in Farsan County

Uneven archaeological research, both temporally and spatially, is one of the challenges in Iranian archaeology. Some areas, such as Khuzestan, Fars, Azerbaijan, and the entire western Iran, have been extensively explored, and then there are areas that we know almost nothing about archaeologically. The chapter by Alireza Khosrowzadeh and Hossein Habibi introduces us to the Farsan County of Chaharmahal va Bakhtiyari Province in southwestern Iran, an archaeologically understudied region in the Iranian Plateau, and one that was marginal to the ancient Iranian ruling dynasties such as the Parthians or the Sasanians. The authors' research on the Zāyandeh-rōd Lower Basin, an overlooked region, has yielded invaluable information about social developments from the Paleolithic through later Islamic periods. They provide us with detailed information about the environmental setting and then briefly introduce the type of sites and possible modes of subsistence of societies through time from the Paleolithic to the Islamic era, with a particular focus on the historic periods from the late Seleucid, Parthian, and Sasanian periods.

Most archaeological studies of the historical era focus either on art historical topics such as rock reliefs, seals and metalworks, architectural styles and techniques, settlement patterns, the foundation of cities, irrigation projects, and defensive mechanisms. This is particularly true to the studies of the Sasanian Empire. Scholars have also focused disproportionally on the heartlands and large plains such as southern Iraq and southwestern Iran where the empires have left lots of footprints (Alizadeh and Ur 2007). The past few decades have witnessed an increase in the diversity of research questions, and scholars are investigating regions previously overlooked (e.g. see Sauer 2017 and Simpson 2022). The article by Khosrowzadeh and Habibi participates in this shift.

The work of Khosrowzadeh and Habibi has revealed that the Sasanian Empire did not only invest in the agriculturally productive heartlands and vulnerable borderlands in the northwest and northeast of their empire, nor did they overlook intermountain valleys and small plains in between. This research shows a population boom in the Farsan area during the Parthian and the Sasanian periods, as well as a shift in settlement patterns, with sites increasingly appearing in the center of the plain. The plain itself was crossed by an important, interregional road connecting this region to important sites, like Susa, to the east. The increase of the number of settlements during this time possibly was supported by the intensification of agriculture, which is attested by the irrigation systems in the plain. The region also owed part of its population increase and economic prosperity to the administration by the autonomous state of Elymaea at the end of the Seleucid and the beginning of the Parthian periods.

Bibliography

Alizadeh, K. and Ur, J.A. (2007) Formation and Destruction of Pastoral and Irrigation Landscape on the Mughan Steppe, North-Western Iran. *Antiquity* 81 (311), 148–160.

Sauer, E.W. (ed.) (2017) *Sasanian Persia: Between Rome and the Steppes of Eurasia*. Edinburgh, Edinburgh University Press.

Simpson, St J. (ed.) (2022) *Sasanian Archaeology: Settlements, Environment and Material Culture*. Oxford, Archaeopress.

Chapter 6

Interregional developments in the Zāyandeh-rōd Lower Basin, based on the archaeological survey and excavations in Farsan County, Chaharmahal va Bakhtiyari, Iran

Alireza Khosrowzadeh and Hossein Habibi[1]

Abstract

Farsan County comprises topographically a valley system leading to a central plain with an elevation of just over 2000 m asl. Located in the heart of the Chaharmahal va Bakhtiyari Province to the south of the Central Zagros region, this archaeologically poorly known highland has historically been a main center for the Bakhtiyari nomads. However, recent archaeological fieldwork examined the spatial distribution patterns and morphology of sites from Middle Palaeolithic times to Late Antiquity and well beyond. Accordingly, sherd/flint-scattered sites in the piedmonts mainly provided evidence for the built environment of prehistoric Farsan. While the pastoralists of the region sustained the traditional economic strategies and settlement pattern, the cultural landscape of the plain changed in historical times. Appearing in Hellenistic sources, the Elymaeans of the region founded an important state in late Seleucid-Parthian times, dominating trade roads leading from the Zagros highlands and Iranian Plateau to the Susian and Babylonian lowlands and the Persian Gulf. Holding strategic roads, the population of Farsan increased in this era. The more noticeable development happened in the Sasanian period when the interregional administrative center of the canton of Rāwar-kust-ī-rōdbār was founded, and the spatial concentration of the sites shifted toward the central plain.

Although known in a general sense as a highland, mid-west Iran is a mosaic of microenvironments (Fig. 6.1). It is made up of the leeward and windward sides of ridges with intermontane valleys and plains of rather distinct topographic and geographical settings in terms of climatic factors and environmental resources (Alijani 2008; Azizi *et al.* 2010; Safarrad *et al.* 2013). Consequently, across the Central Zagros, various human groups have evolved different modes of subsistence adapted to the natural landscape and its accessible resources. These areas hold many important sites

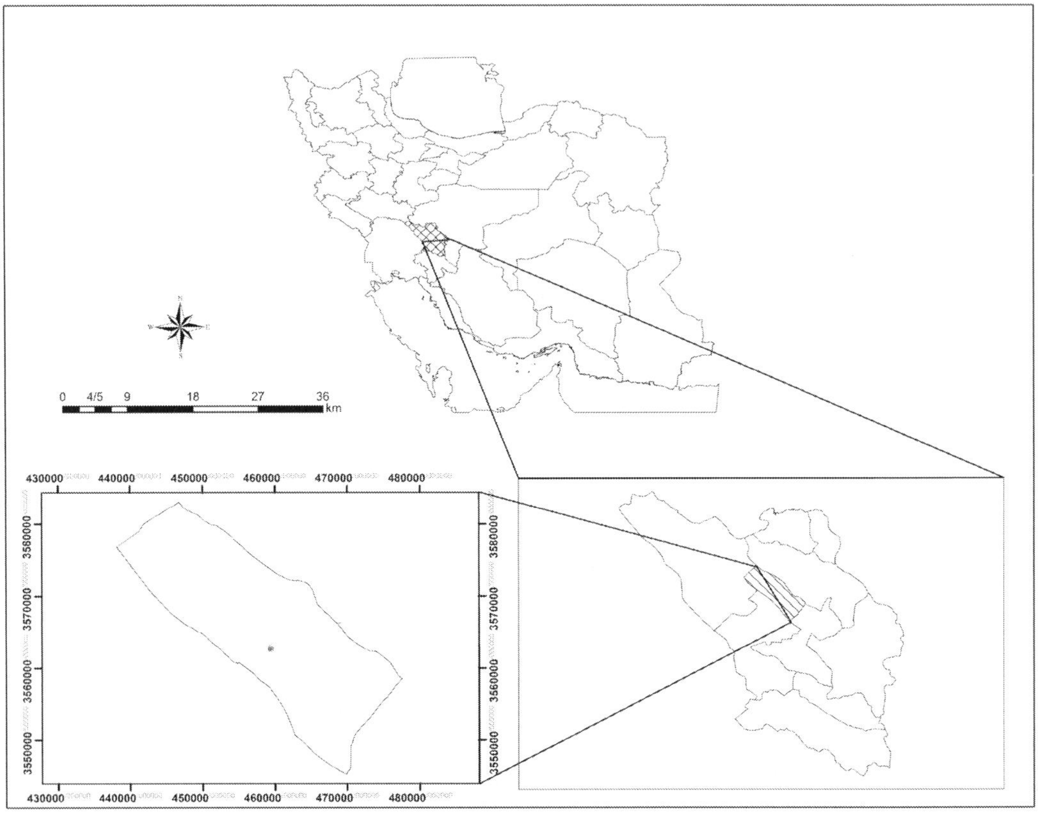

Fig. 6.1: Location of Farsan County, with the place of Tappe Bardnakōn marked, on the map of Chaharmahal va Bakhtiyari Province on Iran's map. Courtesy of Hossein Habibi.

of different eras, from caves, rock shelters, and open sites of the Palaeolithic and Epipalaeolithic periods to the relatively vast settlements, monuments, and nomadic campsites of historical times. The sites are related to different modes of subsistence: nomadic pastoralism with its long migrations between summer and winter quarters in two different environmental zones, agriculture-based economies of both dry and irrigation-based types, and transhumance and agro-pastoralism incorporating either animal husbandry or agriculture on different scales. The examination of the formation processes of these cultural landscapes is significant not only due to their distinct paths of cultural trends and historical development through history, compared with other zones, but also because of their long-term interwoven ties with the neighboring lowlands of southwestern Iran. Therefore, on the interregional scale, it is problematic to reconstruct the socio-political milieu of the adjacent alluvial plains of Khuzestan without taking into consideration the conditions in the Zagros highlands.

The mountainous areas to the east and northeast of Khuzestan in the province of Chaharmahal va Bakhtiyari have a strategic location between the different natural and cultural zones of the Central Iranian Plateau, Central Zagros, and Southern Zagros ranges and lowlands of southwestern Iran and Fars, via Kohgiluyeh va Boyer-Ahmad. Because of its intermediary area between distinct regions, the examination of the archaeological materials of Chaharmahal va Bakhtiyari Province may inform us better of the historical modes of subsistence and interactions of the groups inhabiting the region under study, along with parallel kinds of evidence such as literary data for cultural developments and political transformations in the adjacent areas. However, this region is largely overlooked archaeologically compared to neighboring areas. This is perhaps partly because of its overall topographic attributes and difficult terrains, alongside its marginality to the adjacent larger Khuzestan lowlands and Isfahan area. The results of the majority of the archaeological fieldwork done across the province for approximately the last two decades is yet to be published.

That being said, the recent intensive survey and excavations in Farsan County in the center of Chaharmahal va Bakhtiyari Province (Fig. 6.1) provided a rare case in the Zagros highlands where the long-term socio-economic transitions may be examined scientifically. Topographically, this county is made up of the central Farsan plain, measuring 20 × 6 km, and many small side valleys, eventually reaching the plain (Plate 6.2, b1, b2). The Farsan plain has an elevation of just over 2000 m asl and is particularly rich in the sense of its water resources and pastures. As a result, Farsan has been historically one of the main population centers of the summer quarters, *sardsīr*, of the Bakhtiyari nomadic tribes.

The multi-period Farsan Survey project in 2007 led to the identification of 216 sites from the Middle Palaeolithic to the Late Islamic periods, including different types of settlements, tepes, hilltop sites, nomadic campsites, cemeteries, buildings, caves, and rock shelters, while the most frequently found ones are nomadic in origin, usually in the form of sherd/flint scatters (Khosrowzadeh 2010, 318). The large settlement of Tepe Bardnakōn (Plate 6.1) was discovered in the course of this survey and subsequently excavated in two seasons in 2017 and 2018. This site is situated approximately 2.4 km southeast of Deh-cheshme village around the western edge of the central plain of Farsan and beside the Pireghar River (E 50°34′13.69″ N 32°12′42.17″). The excavations led to the discovery of huge architectural structures, a large corpus of 559 clay sealings, and assemblages of other kinds of artifacts including pottery sherds, fragments of glassware, metal and stone tools, and glass and metallurgical slags, alongside gems, tar pieces, oyster and cowrie shells, and a coin (Khosrowzadeh *et al.* 2020a). Most of the reverse surfaces of the sealings are concave or convex, and were probably used to seal documents, doorknobs, parcels, and merchandise. On these bullae are the impressions of stamp seals that are of different sizes, various kinds of administrative and non-administrative, and shapes such as domes, ellipsoids, conoids, and convex or concave bezels. The number of seals employed to seal each of the sealing artifacts varies too, from one to eight anepigraphic and/or epigraphic types (Khosrowzadeh *et al.* 2020a, 224–227, figs 9–12). Subsequently, and especially based on Rika Gyselen's epigraphic examination of the 22 administrative bullae among the sealings (Khosrowzadeh *et al.* 2020b; 2020c), this archaeological site was identified as a hitherto unknown interregional administrative center of the late Sasanian Empire.

Temporally, this article is mainly focused on the late Seleucid, Parthian, and Sasanian periods, encompassing the late 1st millennium BCE through the 7th century CE. However, as we are using a long-term approach, we will briefly reconstruct the long term cultural process and landscape transformations in Farsan County since prehistoric times according to the sets of archaeological material acquired from the field projects and the related historical evidence of literary sources available.

The earliest group of sites, encompassing nine caves, rock shelters, and open sites, are related to a span of time from the Middle Palaeolithic era through the Epipaleolithic period, according to the technology of their blades, bladelets, and bullet cores (Fig. 6.2). In the course of the following prehistoric eras, the number of sites increased until it reaches its peak in the Chalcolithic period (ca. 5000–3000 BCE) with 35 sites (Khosrowzadeh 2015). This is a trend already attested across the Bakhtiyari highlands (Zagarell 1982). After this period, and until around the last quarter of the 1st millennium BCE, the

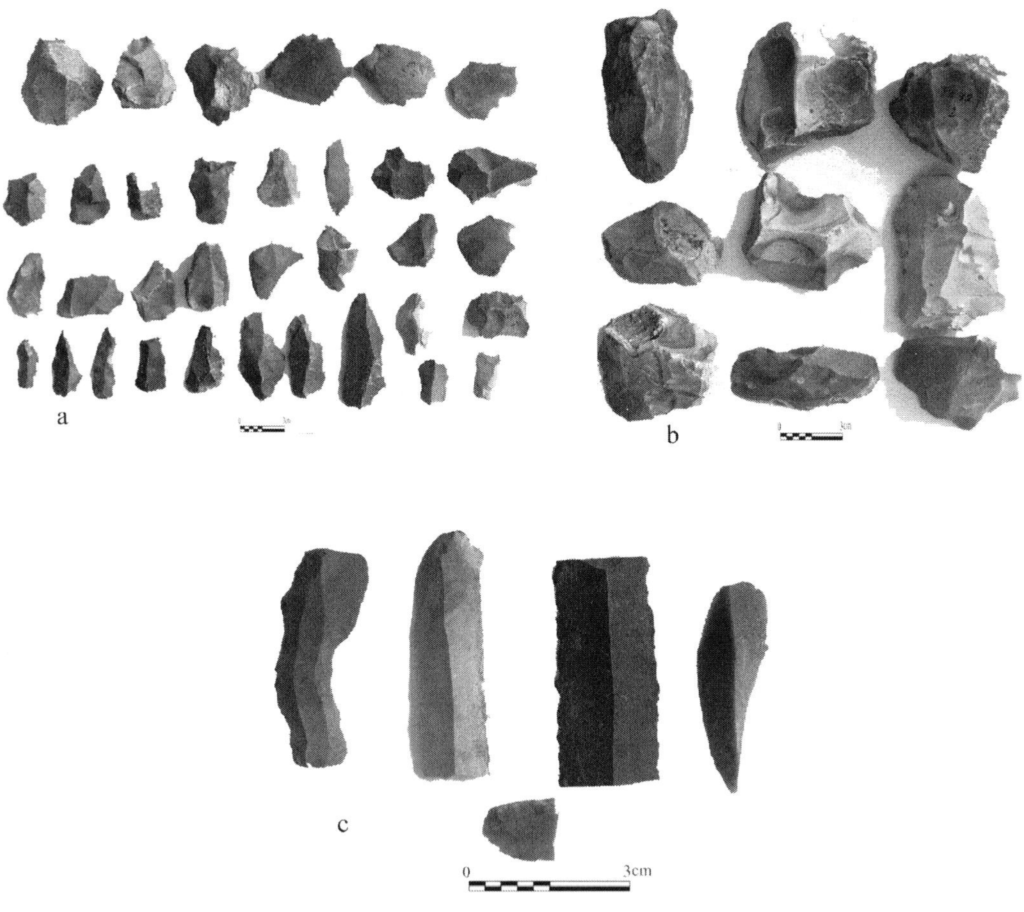

Fig. 6.2: Blades, bladelets, and bullet cores of the Middle Palaeolithic-Epipalaeolithic eras from the sites FS.035/Mārōn 1 (a), FS.032/Mey Zardāšti (b), and FS.001/Dar-škaft Cave (c). Photograph by Alireza Khosrowzadeh.

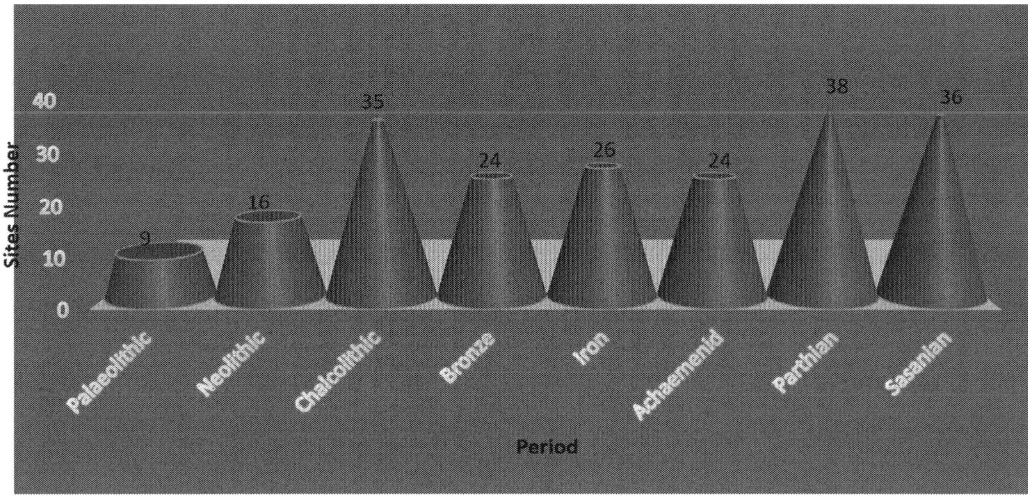

Fig. 6.3: Chart of the number of sites per period. Courtesy of Hossein Habibi.

number of sites remains relatively stable, averaging 25 per period (cf. Fig. 6.3). As early as the Neolithic era (ca. 8000–5000 BCE), the sites may be divided into two groups, permanent hill sites formed on the natural hills (Plate 6.2, a1 and a2), and temporary or nomadic sherd/flint scatters with no visible relief (Plate 6.2, b1 and b2). These two categories persisted as the main two types of sites through succeeding periods, as did the general distribution pattern of them and the key factors of site location until Late Antiquity. Avoiding the central plain, the sites are mainly located along the mild slopes of the mountains surrounding the Farsan plain and in the side valleys of the region where the springs are easily available.

It is noteworthy that some of the pottery wares related to the Late Bronze Age, early 2nd millennium BCE, are quite comparable with the contemporary collections in Khuzestan (Fig. 6.4; Table 6.1). These ceramic

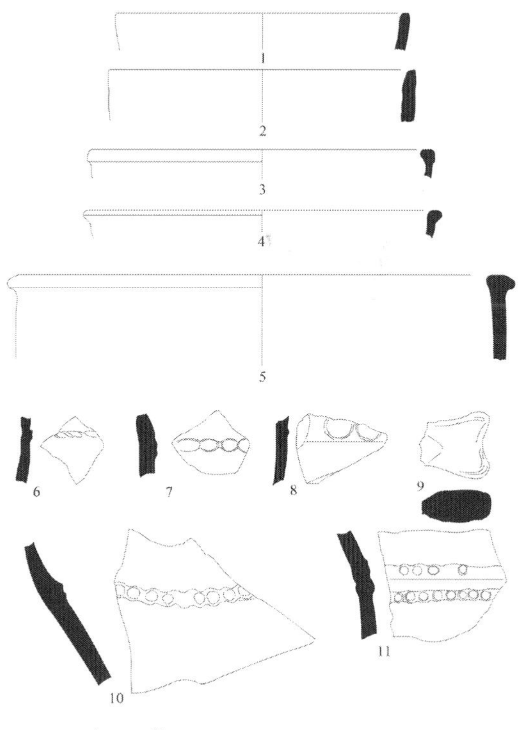

Fig. 6.4: Late Bronze Age ceramics acquired in the course of the Farsan Survey project. Courtesy of Alireza Khosrowzadeh.

Table 6.1: Description and comparison of the Late Bronze Age ceramics illustrated in Figure 6.4.

No.	*Site of discovery*	*Description**	*Comparanda*
1	FS.012	1. Bowl, 2. Wheel-made, 3. Enough, 4. Reddish buff, reddish buff, black, 5. Quartzite and grass or straw, 6. Medium, medium	Miroschedji 1981, fig. 11, 16
2	FS.105	1. Bowl, 2. Wheel-made, 3. Enough, 4. Brown, brown, brown, 5. Quartzite and grass or straw, 6. Medium, medium	
3	FS.075	1. Bowl, 2. Wheel-made, 3. Enough, 4. Orange brown, orange brown, orange brown, 5. Quartzite and grass or straw, 6. Medium, medium, 8. Light brown thick slip, 9. Light brown thick slip	
4	FS.162	1. Bowl, 2. Wheel-made, 3. Enough, 4. Orange, orange, gray, 5. Quartzite and grass or straw, 6. Medium, medium	Miroschedji 1981, fig. 11, 15
5	FS.075	1. Bowl, 2. Wheel-made, 3. Enough, 4. Brown, brown, orange, 5. Quartzite and grass or straw, 6. Medium, medium, 8. Cream thick slip	Miroschedji 1976, fig. 5, 11; 1981, fig. 11, 13
6	FS.105	1 ?, 2. Wheel-made, 3. Enough, 4. Orange, orange, black, 5. Quartzite and grass or straw, 6. Medium, medium, 7. Applied S-twist cordon, 8. Light brown slip	
7	FS.012	1. Jar, 2. Wheel-made, 3. Enough, 4. Orange red, orange red, reddish brown, 5. Quartzite and grass or straw, 6. Medium, medium, 7. Applied horizontally irregular finger-trailing rope pattern, 8. Dark brown thick slip	Zeidi *et al.* 2009, fig. 3127, TNP 2372
8	FS.001	1. Jar, 2. Wheel-made, 3. Enough, 4. Brown, brown, orange, 5. Quartzite and grass or straw, 6. Medium, medium, 7. Applied horizontally regular finger-trailing rope pattern,	
9	FS.105	1. ?, 2. Hand-made, 3. Enough, 4. Brown, brown, brown, 5. Fine sand, Medium, medium	
10	FS.012	1. Jar, 2. Wheel-made, 3. Short, 4. Light brown, light brown, gray, 5. Quartzite and grass or straw, 6. Medium, medium, 7. Applied horizontally irregular finger-trailing rope pattern	
11	FS.012	1. Jar, 2. Wheel-made, 3. Enough, 4. Brown, brown, orange, 5. Quartzite and grass or straw, 6. Medium, medium, 7. Two parallel applied horizontal decorations with irregular finger-trailing rope pattern impressions	Zeidi *et al.* 2009, fig. 3127, TNP 2372

* 1. Form, 2. Manufacturing technique, 3. Firing, 4. Fabric color (outer and inner margins and core), 5. Fabric inclusions, 6. Surface hardness (outer and inner), 7. Decoration (outer and inner surfaces), 8. Outer surface slip, 9. Inner surface slip

samples are particularly found in the central and southern areas of Farsan County, where most of the Late Bronze sites are found. The southern part of the county holds one of the most important passes of the region, Tang-e Darkesh-varkesh around 7.5 km to the south of Jōneqān city, connecting the Khuzestan lowlands to the plains of Shahrekord and Isfahan. Remains of historical roads through this mountainous area have been examined in the Darkesh-varkesh Pass (see the next section and n. 1). The main centers in southern Farsan whose material culture indicate clear association with Elamite culture in Khuzestan and Fars are the single-phase sites of FS.012, FS.075, FS.076, and FS.105. This phenomenon of the material culture may reflect the political conditions of this temporal horizon in west and southwest Iran when the mountainous areas of the Central Zagros, including the region under examination, were under the Šimaškian rule along with Susiana (Steinkeller 2014, 293; 2018, 195).

Transformation of the built environment of Elymaea: the late Seleucid-Parthian era

The Parthian era witnessed a major change in the number of sites and therefore the population density. The number of sites, 38, is the highest number of any period studied. Another significant change at this time was the unprecedented phenomenon in the settlement pattern when, apart from the traditional site location along the mountain foot slopes and in the small valleys, new sites were founded in the middle of the Farsan plain from scratch (Plate 6.3). Moreover, although the cemeteries and hilltop sites had become rather more frequent in the preceding Achaemenid period, stone-heaped cemeteries became the most commonly occurring type of sites in the Parthian era.

The demographic changes and settlement pattern transformations of this period were probably associated with the establishment of the powerful Elymaean state in this period. According to the allusions to it in the Hellenistic Greco-Roman sources (Nearchus apud Strabo *Geog.* XI. 13.6, XV. 2.8, XV. 2.14, XV. 3.12 & XVI. 1.17–18; Pliny *Nat.* VI. 29.116, VI. 31.131, 135), this region was part of Elymais, 'Ελυμαΐς, in the latter part of the Seleucid and Parthian period. The economy of this kingdom was based mainly on its control over international trade via significant interregional roads (Wenke 1981, 306; Alizadeh 1985, 184; Salaris and Basello 2019, 81) among which was the route linking Susiana and Gabae via the Bakhtiyari mountains and Chaharmahal area (Strabo *Geog.* XV. 2.8, XVI. 1.8; Arrian *Anab.* III. 19.2; Diodorus XIX. 34.7; Curtius V. 13.2; also see Ehlers 1988).[2] The Farsan plain owed its development during this period partly to its strategic location on this road. Moreover, the specimens of fine ceramics known as Clinky Ware, characteristic of the Central Zagros region, indicate the interactions of the Farsan region with these more northern areas during this time.

Settlement hierarchy and Sasanian administrative geography: Late Antiquity

In the Sasanian period, although the number of sites, 36, is not significantly different from the preceding era, the overall spatial distribution pattern of the settlements experienced a major change. Despite the continuity of the site locations along the mild slopes of the mountains around the plain and in the side valleys, the concentration of the sites shifted toward the central Farsan plain. This may indicate technological changes and investments leading to the transformation of settlement patterns and, hence, subsistence modes and economic development. The most important Sasanian settlements of Farsan, some of which are agriculturally based (see below), are located in the central plain. Moreover, the sites of this era are generally larger than the earlier ones. The change in the site location makes more sense in light of the fact that roughly half (49%), of the Sasanian sites were not in use during the previous period but were newly constructed (cf. Plates 6.3 and 6.4).

This shift was accompanied by the growth of the settlement hierarchy by the foundation of significant settlements such as FS 119 (1.5 ha) and FS 163 (4 ha) and the complex of the mounds of FS 208 and FS 209 (4 ha). The former, FS 119, is called Tepe Bardnakōn and, as mentioned above, appears to be an administrative center of the late Sasanian canton of Rāwar-kust-ī-rōdbār in the province of Gay in the region of Spahān. The administrative bullae uncovered at the site attest to its important interregional role in the political and administrative geography of the empire, lying between different provinces and regions, i.e., Gay in Spahān, Rām-Ohrmazd, Ohrmazd-Ardašīr, and Weh-Andiyok-Šābuhr in Hūzestān, and Īg in Pārs (Khosrowzadeh *et al.* 2020c, fig. 1). In this period, the increased hierarchy of the sites constituted networks of settlements where the top level (the above-mentioned sites) with their satellite sites (such as FS 87, FS 109, FS 110, FS 120, FS 121, FS 134, FS 158, FS 159, FS 160) were interconnected via middle range settlements (such as FS 117, FS 124, FS 170, FS 205) (Plate 6.4). It is not yet clear whether these transformations in the Sasanian canton of Rāwar-kust-ī-rōdbār, modern Farsan County were supported by the central state or the local authorities. In this regard, there is currently no primary source attestation or direct data, in terms of epigraphic and archaeological data, available. However, the settlement pattern shift toward the central plain and the unprecedented increase in settlement hierarchy and complexity probably could not have taken place without large scale investments in agriculture against the ancient pastoral backdrop of the region. This picture accords well with what is known about the late Sasanian administrative system, the landscape transformations, and economic and infrastructural developments attested in various territories under the Sasanian rule (e.g., Wenke 1975–1976; 1981; 1987; Alizadeh *et al.* 2015, 126, fig. 14, tab. 3; Lawrence and Wilkinson 2017; Habibi 2023).

Long-term processes of landscape transformation in a highland

As discussed, the archaeological fieldwork carried out in Farsan County provided valuable information about the region that had been previously unknown archaeologically. Based on these data, we can better understand the groups that inhabited Farsan, and their ways of life and built environment through history. As far as available data allow, the overall factors of site location in Farsan County followed a single pattern from prehistory until the Elymaeans' ascent to power. With some minor changes, such as the dimorphic temporary–permanent site typology (Plate 6.2) that emerged in the Neolithic era and the slight increase of the permanent hilltops in Achaemenid times, which reflect the socio-technological conditions in each period, the environmental settings of sites were stable over this very long span of time. Among the factors that indicate the considerable dependence of the economic structures on pastoralism, one may mention the position of the sites along the gentle slopes and inside the side valleys, mainly adjacent to the modern Bakhtiyari nomads' campsites, with access to the rich resources of water and pasture for which the region is renowned, their poor surface materials, morphology and form, as level as their surroundings (Plate 6.2, b1 and b2).

Notwithstanding its high elevation, Farsan County has attractive living conditions, as attested to by the considerable number of sites, ranging from Palaeolithic through historical and more recent Islamic times. Since the Chalcolithic period, this region held villages and among its inhabitants were also agriculturalist populations. According to the results of systematic surveys carried out across the province of Chaharmahal va Bakhtiyari, Farsan County, in contrast to its size, holds more historical sites related to the Achaemenid to Sasanian periods than any other county in this province. Its strategic location, with some of the (rare) passages through the arduous Zagros ranges, made possible the formation of a potent local state in Parthian times. In this period, the plain gradually attracted populations to establish some sites *ex nihilo*. Also noteworthy is that a demographic change could be possibly associated with the shift in the settlement pattern, itself related to the expansion of the agricultural economy.

However, it was not until the Sasanian period that longstanding patterns of site distribution in the region changed. The considerable growth of the number of agriculturally based settlements in the central plain in this period demonstrates more efficient exploitation of the natural resources, while the pastoral and nomadic sectors held on to the long-established economic traditions with their camps around the plain and inside the valleys of Farsan. Rāwar-kust-ī-rōdbār, modern Tepe Bardnakōn, in Farsan County participated in the administrative, military, and economic reforms of the late Sasanian state, from the 5th century CE onward, as an important administrative center in the Zagros highlands. This indicates that the location of the site between different administrative regions and cultural and natural zones – of Spahān, Hūzestān, and Pārs – was a factor as shown by the corpus of the administrative bullae of the Tappe. This unprecedented phenomenon, probably along with the investments of local authorities who were supervised by the central Sasanian state, had repercussions for the region under study in terms of the transformation of its landscape, and its socio-economic milieu in Late Antiquity. These issues will be examined more precisely through specifically designed, future excavation projects at the sites such as Tepe Bardnakōn in the near future.

Acknowledgments

The authors are very grateful to Megan Cifarelli and Karim Alizadeh for putting together this outstanding volume and giving us the opportunity to be a part of it. We also wish to thank the anonymous reviewers whose helpful recommendations surely enriched the final result.

Notes

1 Corresponding author.
2 This ancient road is accounted in the medieval Islamic literature as 'Atābaki', see Ibn Battuta 1371/1993, 241, and has also been partly examined in the course of the Farsan Survey project, see Khosrowzadeh and Habibi 2015.

Bibliography

Primary sources

Arrian (1967) *Anabasis Alexandri*, 2 Volumes, Vol. 1, trans. E.I. Robson. London, William Heinemann; Cambridge, Massachusetts, Harvard University Press.

Diodorus of Sicily (1947) *Diodorus of Sicily, Books 18 and 19 1–65* (Loeb Classical Library), 10 Volumes, Vol. 9, ed. and trans. R.M. Geer. London, William Heinemann; Cambridge, Massachusetts, Harvard University Press.

Ibn Battuta, Abu Abdallah (1371/1993) *The Travels of Ibn Battuta*, Persian trans. M. A. Movahhed. Tehran, Āgāh.

Pliny (1961) *Natural History* (Loeb Classical Library edition), 10 Volumes, Vol. 2, Books 3–7, trans. H. Rackham. Cambridge, Massachusetts, Harvard University Press; London, W. Heinemann.

Quintus Curtius Rufus (1854) *Life and Exploits of Alexander the Great*, ed. and trans. W.H. Crosby. New York, D. Appleton and Company.

Strabo (1930) *The Geography of Strabo* (Loeb Classical Library edition), 8 Volumes, Vol. 7, trans. H.L. Jones. London, W. Heinemann; New York, G.P. Putnam's Sons.

Strabo (1961) *The Geography of Strabo* (Loeb Classical Library edition), 8 Volumes, Vol. 5, trans. H.L. Jones. London, W. Heinemann; Cambridge, Massachusetts, Harvard University Press.

Secondary sources

Alijani, B. (2008) Effects of the Zagros Mountains on the Spatial Distribution of Precipitation. *Journal of Mountain Science* 5 (2), 18–31.

Alizadeh, A. (1985) Elymaean Occupation of Lower Khuzestan during the Seleucid and Parthian Periods: A Proposal. *Iranica Antiqua* 20, 175–195.

Alizadeh, A., Ahmadzadeh, L., and Omidfar, M. (2015) Reflections on the Long-term Socioeconomic and Political Development in the Rām Hormoz Plain, a Highland-Lowland Buffer Zone. *Archäologische Mitteilungen aus Iran und Turan* 45, 113–148.

Azizi, G., Sabokbar, H.A., Abaspour, R.A. and Safarrad, T. (2010) The Model of the Spatial Variability Precipitation in the Middle Zagros. *Physical Geography Research Quarterly* 72, 35–51.

Ehlers, E. (1988) Baḵtīārī Mountains. *Encyclopædia Iranica* 3 (5), 551–553.

Habibi, H. (2023) *Socioeconomic Transformation in the Sasanian Empire: Late Antique Central Zagros*. Edinburgh, Edinburgh University Press.

Khosrowzadeh, A. (2010) Preliminary Results of the 1st Season of Archaeological Survey of Farsan, Bakhtiari Region, Iran. In P. Matthiae, F. Pinnock, L. Nigro, and N. Marchetti (eds) *Proceedings of the 6th International Congress on the Archaeology of the Ancient Near East. May 5th–10th 2008, 'Sapienza' –*

Università di Roma. Volume 2, Excavations, Surveys and Restorations: Reports on Recent Field Archaeology in the Near East, 317–337. Wiesbaden, Harrassowitz Verlag.

Khosrowzadeh, A. (2015) The Chalcolithic Period in the Bakhtiari Highlands: Newly Found Sites of Farsan, Chaharmahal va Bakhtiari, Iran. *International Journal of the Society of Iranian Archaeologists* 1 (2), 32–53.

Khosrowzadeh, A. and Habibi, H. (2015) Study of the Sasanian Settlement Pattern in the Intermontane Plain of Farsan in Chaharmahal va Bakhtiari. *Pazhuhesh-ha-ye Bastanshenasi Iran* 8 (5), 99–118. [in Persian with an English abstract]

Khosrowzadeh, A., Norouzi, A., and Habibi, H. (2020a) A Newly-Discovered Administrative Center of the Late Sasanian Empire: Tappe Bardnakoon, Farsan, Iran. *Near Eastern Archaeology* 83 (4), 222–233.

Khosrowzadeh, A., Norouzi, A., Gyselen, R., and Habibi, H. (2020b) Administrative Seal Impressions on Bullae Discovered on Tappe Bardnakoon. In R. Gyselen (ed.) *Persia (552 BCE - 758 CE): Primary Sources, Old and New* (*Res Orientales* 28), 83–112. Bures-sur-Yvette, Groupe pour l'Étude de la Civilisation du Moyen-Orient.

Khosrowzadeh, A., Norouzi, A., Gyselen, R., and Habibi, H. (2020c) Administrative Bullae from Tappe Bardnakoon. A Newly Found Late Sasanian Administrative Centre. *Iranica Antiqua* 55, 165–220.

Lawrence, D. and Wilkinson, T.J. (2017) The Northern and Western Borderlands of the Sasanian Empire: Contextualizing the Roman/Byzantine and Sasanian Frontier. In E. Sauer (ed.) *Sasanian Persia: Between Rome and Steppes of Eurasia*, 1–27. Edinburgh, Edinburgh University Press.

Miroschedji, P. de (1976) Un four se potier de IVe Millenaire sur le Tel de l'Apadana a Suse. *Cahiers de la Délégation Archéologie Francaise en Iran* 6, 13–45.

Miroschedji, P. de (1981) Fouilles du chantier Ville Royal II a Suse (1975–1977): I. Neveaux Elamite. *Cahiers de la Délégation Archéologie Francaise en Iran* 12, 9–216.

Safarrad, T., Faraji Sabokbar, H., Azizi, G., and Abbaspour, R. (2013) Spatial Analysis of Precipitation Variations in Middle Zagros Using Geo-Statistical Methods (1995–2004). *Iranian Journal of Geography and Development* 31, 149–164.

Salaris, D. and Basello, G.P. (2019) ὀρεινὰ καὶ ληστρικὰ ἔθνη (Strabo XVI.1.17): Mountain Tribes of Elymais and State Powers, from Neo-Elamite Kingdom(s) to Alexander the Great. In L. Prandi (ed.) *EstOvest: Confini e conflitti fra Vicino Oriente e mondo Greco-Romano* (Monografie / Centro ricerche e documentazione sull'antichità classica; 46), 79–116. Roma, «L'ERMA» di Bretschneider.

Steinkeller, P. (2014) On the Dynasty of Simaški: Twenty Years (or so) After. In M. Kozuh, W.F.M. Henkel man, C.E. Jones, and C. Woods (eds) *Extraction and Control: Studies in Honor of Matthew W. Stolper* (Studies in Ancient Oriental Civilization 68), 287–296. Chicago, The Oriental Institute of the University of Chicago.

Steinkeller, P. (2018) The Birth of Elam in History. In J. Álvarez-Mon, G.P. Basello, and Y. Wicks (eds) *The Elamite World* (Routledge Worlds), 177–202. London, Routledge.

Wenke, R.J. (1975–1976) Imperial Investments and Agricultural Developments in Parthian and Sassanian Khuzestan: 150 BC to AD 640. *Mesopotamia* 10–11, 99–137.

Wenke, R.J. (1981) Elymaeans, Parthians, and the Evolution of Empires in Southwestern Iran. *Journal of the American Oriental Society* 101 (3), 303–315.

Wenke, R.J. (1987) Western Iran in the Partho-Sasanian Period: The Imperial Transformation. In F. Hole (ed.) *The Archaeology of Western Iran*, 251–282. Washington, DC, Smithsonian Institution Press.

Zagarell, A. (1982) *The Prehistory of the Northeast Bahtiyari Mountains, Iran: The Rise of a Highland Way of Life* (Tubinger Atlas des Vorderen Orients). Wiesbaden, Dr Ludwig Reichert.

Zeidi, M., McCall, B., and Khosrowzadeh, A. (2009) Survey of Dasht-e Rostam-e Yek and Dasht-e Rostam-e Do. In D.T. Potts, K. Roustaei, C.A. Petrie and L.R. Weeks (eds) *The Mamasani Archaeological Project Stage 1: A Report on the First Two Seasons of the ICAR-University of Sydney Expedition The 1st Season of Archaeological Survey of Farsan 3 to the Mamasani District, Fars Province, Iran*, 147–168. Oxford, Archaeopress.

Chapter 7 Prologue

Hydraulic management and human agency

Jaleh Kamalizad's work focuses on the hydraulic landscape of Iṣfahān, a major city in the center of the Iranian Plateau. Due to the arid and semi-arid environment in much of the Iranian Plateau, hydraulic systems providing water to the cities and irrigating agricultural land are life-saving innovations and the source of sustenance for human societies. As Tony Wilkinson (2003, 71) pointed out, irrigation is capable of shaping the structure of the landscape, and the case of Iṣfahān shows us, it has been the major source of life through its history. Iṣfahān is usually associated with the Safavids and its flourishing is attributed to their wise water management. Probing the historical records and indications, and also relying on the archaeological data produced by her own survey of the landscape of Iṣfahān, Kamalizad further argues that water management probably began far earlier than the Safavid period, with evidence for Sasanian period efforts to manage water. Her conclusions, it should be noted, correspond to the previous chapter by Khosrowzadeh and Habibi, who demonstrated significant Sasanian period investments in irrigation along the same river closer to its source in the Farsan County of Chaharmahal va Bakhtiyari Province, leading to a population boom and the intensification of agriculture.

In many cases, irrigation systems and other elements of infrastructure survived the Muslim conquest in the 7th century. Contrary to the popular notion that attributed the transformation of western Asia, particularly Iran, in the mid-7th century CE to warfare and the Islamic Arab conquest, recent studies in archaeology underscores some nuances and rejects the simplistic political explanations (see Avni 2014; Alizadeh *et al.* 2021). The analysis of some historical records indicated that the early Muslim rulers commissioned the repair and maintenance of irrigation canals in Khuzestan (Kervran 1985). The indication of continuity in the water management from the Sasanian through the Early Islamic era in Iṣfahān, discussed by Kamalizad, adds more to the body of research on this issue.

Another important takeaway from Kamalizad's article is that it reminds us of shortcomings of environmental deterministic approaches in past scholarship. The notion that environmental factors have shaped human societies was quite popular, and functionalists and early processualists in archaeology considered culture as an adaptive mechanism (Binford 1962) that enabled human societies to adapt to their environments. But the development and use of technologies for irrigation and water management by human societies in arid and semi-arid environments such as Iṣfahān reminds us of the significance of human agency. Humans were not passive receivers of environmental forces but rather they were active agents in their management. The initiation of the hydraulic systems at Iṣfahān led to the flourishing of the city and its hinterlands during the Safavid era in the Late Islamic period, as Kamalizad demonstrates using historical records and newly discovered archaeological remains of water management in the region of Iṣfahān.

Bibliography

Alizadeh, K., Mohammadi, M.R., Maziar, S., and Feizkhah, M. (2021) The Islamic Conquest or Flooding? Sasanian Settlements and Irrigation Systems Collapse in Mughan, Iranian Azerbaijan. *Journal of Field Archaeology* 46 (5), 316–332.

Avni, G. (2014) *The Byzantine-Islamic Transition in Palestine: An Archaeological Approach*. Oxford, Oxford University Press.

Binford, L.R. (1962) Archaeology as Anthropology. *American Antiquity* 28 (2), 217–225.

Kervran, M. (1985) Transformations de la ville de Suse et de son économie de l'époque sasanide à l'époque abbaside. *Paléorient* 11 (2), 91–100.

Wilkinson, T.J. (2003) *Archaeological Landscapes of the Near East*. Tucson, The University of Arizona Press.

Chapter 7

Iṣfahān Hydraulic Heritage Project: The history of Zāyandeh Rūd river water management and the resilience of Iṣfahān

Jaleh Kamalizad[1]

يا اصفهان الاحييت من بلد   يا زندروذ الاسقيت من واد

"الصاحب بن عباد، ولد سنه 362 ه.ق "

Abstract

Due to the arid and semi-arid climate of the Iranian plateau, throughout the history of Iranian civilization, the agricultural economy relied on artificial irrigation, especially underground qanats. However, agriculture in Iṣfahān was based on canal irrigation on the banks of the Zāyandeh Rūd River. Considering the extent and complexity of traditional water management along the Zāyandeh Rūd River, in 2021 a long-term project was defined entitled 'Iṣfahān Hydraulic Heritage' (IHH). The archaeological project aims to study the history of Zāyandeh Rūd water management and examine how this system had an effect on settlement patterns. The methods of landscape archaeology are applied to this large-scale irrigation system to uncover its significance. Preliminary results show not only how the administrative geographical divisions of Iṣfahān from the Sasanian period were affected by this integrated water management system, and that these geographical divisions were stable until the 20th century. In addition, the irrigation system had a notable impact on agricultural and hydraulic innovations, and in a wider perspective, on resilience and cultural continuity in the city and hinterlands of Iṣfahān after the Muslim conquest.

Introduction

From the past to the present, water scarcity has been a challenge in the Near East, and it is almost impossible to have any sustainable settlement and agriculture without a reliable irrigation system. In the Iranian plateau, while a great number of cities were formed with underground water canals or qanāt (Adle 2006), Iṣfahān is one of the ancient cities that developed with the benefits of the Zāyandeh Rūd river. Although the historic monuments of Iṣfahān have received scholarly attention, relatively little attention has been paid to its natural environment and the impact of the Zāyandeh Rūd river on the formation and development of the city and its suburban settlements.

At the beginning of the 11th century AH/17th century CE, when Iṣfahān was chosen as the capital of Safavid Dynasty (1502–1722 CE), regulation of the Zāyandeh Rūd river was written in detail in an edict or scroll attributed to 'Shaikh Bahā'ī'.[2] According to this edict, Zāyandeh Rūd water was distributed among the settlements of six districts of Iṣfahān, through a network of open-air artificial canals, known in Iṣfahān as '*mādī*'. These irrigation canals represent a specific hydraulic landscape in Iṣfahān and surrounding districts. With an awareness of the value of information in the Shaikh Bahā'ī scroll, Ann Lambton was one of the first people to publish an essay on the Zāyandeh Rūd water division and the implementation of the scroll regulations (Lambton 1938). Brian Spooner employed a more analytical view to study the impact of Zāyandeh Rūd water management on urbanization in Iṣfahān city during the Safavid period (Spooner 1974). Hosseini Abari as a geographer not only conducted fieldworks along the Zāyandeh Rūd, but also reviewed the edict's text and described the water shares of settlements located in the basin in detail (Hosseini Abari 2000). More recently, Mahmudian's work has focused on the political and economic aspects of this system in Iṣfahān during the Safavid period (Mahboudian and Qayyoomi 2017). Most of these researchers assumed that the irrigation system was created in the 17th century CE, focusing on the edict attributed to Shaikh Bahā'ī and particularly on the city of Iṣfahān during the Safavid period, while Iṣfahān is located in an arid and semi-arid region with 250 mm of annual rainfall and rain-fed agriculture was not possible. It is unreasonable to imagine that without a permanent water resource like Zāyandeh Rūd river and a water management system, the formation and survival of the city of Iṣfahān from antiquity to the 17th century CE. However, little attention has been paid to this problem.

In 2014, the author as her PhD thesis started research with a particular interest in cultural landscape archaeology in 'Lanjān', the first district of the Zāyandeh Rūd river basin. One of the findings was the enormous effect of the Zāyandeh Rūd water management on settlement patterns and agriculture in Lanjān during the Islamic period (Kamalizad 2016). Hence, she decided to continue this study while covering all six historic districts of Iṣfahān along the Zāyandeh Rūd basin, which in the current administrative divisions are located in the three counties of Lanjān, Felavarjan, and Iṣfahān. The research questions for this study are 'What was the impact of Zāyandeh Rūd water management in the development and duration of Iṣfahān over several centuries, despite different political and economic fluctuations, particularly those caused by the Muslim conquest or Mongol invasion?' and 'How would settlement patterns in Iṣfahān city and its hinterland be affected by the Zāyandeh Rūd?'

Considering the extensiveness and complexity of this large-scale integrated water management system across space and time, consistent and interdisciplinary research was required and as a result, in 2021, a long-term project entitled 'Iṣfahān Hydraulic Heritage' (IHH) was launched. The main objective of this project is to offer a new interpretation of the environmental-spatial-socio-economic dynamics of the Zāyandeh Rūd traditional irrigation system, in the long-term history of Iṣfahān city and its hinterland. This project aims to shed light on the water management system in Iṣfahān as a keystone resource for recognizing and understanding various aspects of a medieval society with irrigated agriculture. What distinguishes this research from the previous work, in addition to its archaeological approach, is the geographical and spatial extent which considers the system as a large-scale integrated irrigation system that aims to cover not only the city of Iṣfahān but also all six districts named '*Rūd Āb*', a term that means they received a special share of water from the Zāyandeh Rūd river. In the IHH project, landscape archeology and remote sensing are applied, techniques that have played a significant role in the recognition and study of ancient irrigation systems in the Middle East over the past 20 years (Wilkinson and Rayne 2010, 115).

In the 20th century and after using modern irrigation installations in Iran, there were attempts to increase the Zāyandeh Rūd water by merging the Kuh Rang river with the Zāyandeh Rūd's headstream and also erecting the Zāyandeh Rūd dam in 1971. These attempts completely changed the traditional water management system in Iṣfahān. Despite the increase in water resources of Zāyandeh Rūd, water scarcity has led to a continuing crisis in the basin during the past two decades and settlement patterns particularly in the downstream regions are facing the risk of destruction. The continuity of this crisis, even during years with normal or more than normal precipitation rates, reveals that this crisis is not caused by drought (Ziaei 2020). The unsustainable and rapid development of Iṣfahān city and its surrounding areas that today has led to the destruction and leveling of water canals and other traditional hydraulic structures makes it urgent to conduct archaeological surveys across the six historic districts of Iṣfahān. This article will try to take the first steps to investigating the questions above, and present a primary synthesis based on both written sources and recent survey data from the IHH project in 2021.

The history of the Zāyandeh Rūd river water management in Iṣfahān

The Zāyandeh Rūdriver basin covers 41,500 km^2 in the center of Iran. The river runs some 350 km roughly west–east from the Zagros Mountains to the Gavkhuni Swamp (Ziaei 2020) (Plate 7.1). Regarding the length of Zāyandeh Rūd river, its cultural zone consists of different landscapes: in the western parts the land is semi-mountainous in a narrow and steep valley, in the central parts, there are intermontane and flat plains such as Iṣfahān city, and the eastern parts include low plains that recently have become salt marsh and desert near Varzaneh (Hosseini Abari 2000, 10). Accordingly, the Zāyandeh Rūd river should be considered as one of the important environmental elements in Iṣfahān. This role is clear through the numerous mentions of the river in medieval written sources, which discuss the characteristics and importance of the river in the formation and development of Iṣfahān. Ibn Rusta, who was born in Iṣfahān,

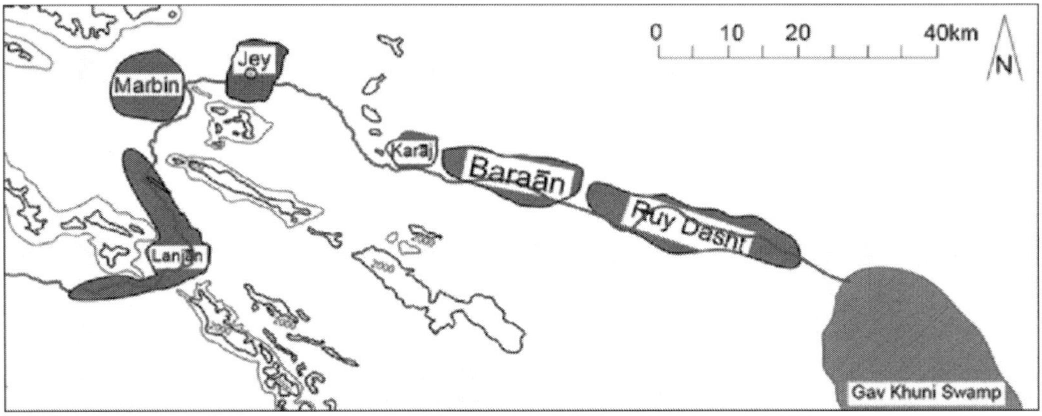

Fig. 7.1: The six historic districts, or rustāqs, of Iṣfahān along the Zāyandeh Rūd river (drawing: J: Kamalizad).

in 310 AH/922–923 CE stated the Sasanian founder, Ardashir I (r. 227–242 CE), not only chose the name of this river 'Zarin rud', but also ordered the establishment of a water distribution system in Iṣfahān with specific water shares and times for every village (Ibn Rusta 1892, 154–155). Ḥamza al-Iṣfahānī, a native historian in 4th century AH/10th century CE described comprehensive hydro-politic programs of Ardashir: 'He ordered to Mehr ibn Vardan to divide the water of Iṣfahān and Khūzestān' (Al-Iṣfahānī 1844). Archaeological data support that comprehensive programs of irrigation in Khuzestan were created by Sasanians and had no parallel in earlier periods (Adams 1962, 116).

Another document that proves that the division of Zāyandeh Rūd's water is rooted in antiquity and lasted after the Arab conquest, is a letter written by Ṣāḥib ibn ʿAbbād (b. 326 AH/938 CE–d. 385 AH/995 CE), the grand vizier of the Buyid government. He issued an edict for appointing the supervisor for Zāyandeh Rūd water management and in part of this edict stated: 'We chose you, due to your wisdom and experience in water division among the people of the villages and districts (Rostāqs) to receive their water share at the appointed time with justice and fairness. About water dividers and dams should be acted according to the ancient records and inherited traditions by using the help of trusted water inspectors (*Jū Baz*)' (Ebn ʿAbbād 1947, 54).

In the 4th century AH/10th century CE, Ibn Ḥawqal described the river's sources and its route in Iṣfahān: 'At its origin, the Zarin rūd is composed of two different rivers; the one comes from Janān, the other from Khankān ... This river joins the river of Janān near "Rūd bār" and its water used to be diverted towards Khān Lanjān town[3] and absorbed there. Some of this water flows out to the rural area of Māhrin rostaq.' He also reported that the water of 'Zāndah Rūd' was divided into many branches based on everyone's specific share and no water would be lost (Ibn Ḥawqal 1938, 365).

In the first half of the 5th century AH/11th century CE, when the Seljuq Toghril Beg besieged Iṣfahān, the irrigation system of Iṣfahān and the surrounding agricultural lands suffered, but Nasir Khusraw reported Toghril's efforts at restoring prosperity, by waiving taxes for three years and repairing the irrigation system, had been effective and agriculture was flourishing (Nasir-i Khusraw 2001, 125). Given the importance of Iṣfahān as the capital of the Great Seljuq state, al-Māfarrūḫī wrote a book extolling Iṣfahān, entitled 'Maḥāsin Iṣfahān'. At the end of one of the manuscripts of this book, some information stated about the division of Zāyandeh Rūd river from ancient times and also the need of Iṣfahān people to increase the river water resources during the reign of the Seljuq sultan Malekšāh (r. 465–485 AH/1073–1092 CE) (Eṣfahāni 1962, 97).

After the Mongol invasions, under the rule of the Il-Khanid dynasty in the middle of the 13th century CE, a relative political and economic stability was created. In this period, Ḥamd-Allāh Mustawfī considered the Zāyandeh Rūd river as promoting the fertility of Iṣfahān and irrigating farms and villages around Iṣfahān. He also stated that the river enters the city of Iṣfahān on the side of the qibla (south) and from this river, streams flowed through the city of Iṣfahān (Mustawfī 1993, 55).

During the Timurid dynasty, through a historical report, the existence of a water supply system in Iṣfahān was proved. In 809 AH/1407 CE, when the ruler of Fars province occupied Iṣfahān, he ordered a breach in a dam that served to regulate the water (Ḥasan Rūmlū 1971, 38, 39). This dam was located in Fīrūzān, one of the three top Ilkhanid cities in the Lanjān district (Mustawfi 1993, 57). Another notable example confirming that this irrigation system existed before the Safavid era is the story of a Timurid prince who died after attempting to leap across one of these irrigation canals (Quiring-Zoche 1980, 24).

In the early 11th century AH/16th century CE, Iran was united under the rule of the Safavid Dynasty, and this period is often considered as the beginning of modern Persian history. As mentioned above, one of the important primary sources dedicated to the division of Zāyandeh Rūd river is an edict attributed to Shaykh-i Bahā'ī. In the introduction of this edict was stated 'because of some disputes in the regulations and Zāyandeh Rūd river water use, this document is set'. In addition, the text of the scroll indicates that the Safavid version was modified and reorganized from an old document and that due to the recent construction of new settlements, monuments, and gardens in the new Safavid capital, there was a need to determine new watershares in the Zāyandeh Rūd irrigation system. According to Safavid edict, the Zāyandeh Rūd's water, under the supervision of '*Mirāb*' was divided into 33 shares and then distributed among the six districts of Iṣfahān located from upstream regions to the Gāv Khūni swamp (Hosseini Abari 2000, 67). Since people's livelihoods in Iṣfahān depended on agriculture, the water use described in this edict, with little alteration, was the basis for water management until the 20th century. In general, it is apparent that the management of the Zāyandeh Rūd water was a continuous and vital procedure for sustainable life in Iṣfahān and local rulers and elites during the various historical periods paid attention to it and made hydro-political decisions in its regulation (Table 7.1).

Table 7.1: The sequence and continuity of Zāyandeh Rūd water management in Iṣfahān before the Safavid period.

Historical periods	*Date (CE)*	*Source*
Sasanian Empire	224–651	Ibn Rusta (Ibn Rusta 1892)
Buyids Dynasty	945–1055	Ibn Ḥawqal (Ibn Ḥawqal 1938) Sahib Abād (Ebn ʿAbbād 1947)
Saljūq Dynasty	1081–1308	Nasir-i Khusraw (Nasir-i Khusraw 2001) Al-Māfarrūẖī (Eṣfahāni 1962)
Il-Khanid Dynasty	1256–1335	Ḥamd-Allāh Mustawfī (Mustawfi 1993)
Timurid Dynasty	1370–1507	Ḥasan Rūmlū (Ḥasan Rūmlū 1971)
Safavid Dynasty	1501–1736	Edict attributed to Shaikh Bahā'ī (923 AH?)

The integrated irrigation system and the resilience of Iṣfahān

According to the Sasanid administrative geographical divisions that were rooted in the late Avestan tradition, Ērānšahr (Land of the Iranians) included certain provinces (Ostan) and each province was subdivided into several Ḵorra. In the geographical units of Sasanian, Khoreh or Ḵorra was an administrative division smaller than the state that included several districts or 'Rostāq'. Rostāq was a rural district smaller than 'Ḵorra', which had been used in Isfahān until the Mongol period (Al-Hamawi 1397/1977; Kamalizad 2019). In this period, Iṣfahān Ḵorra had 30 Rustāqs, while Jay Rostāq played a central and military role (Abu No'aym 1410/1999, 33, 34). After the Muslim conquest, the Sasanian administrative divisions persisted but in some parts of Iṣfahān Ḵorra, the number of Rustāqs declined. An interesting point about the Rustāqs located along the Zāyandeh Rūd river is that according to the report by Ibn Rusta, the six Rustāqs of the 4th century AH/10th century CE completely correspond to the Sasanid divisions. These districts from the upstream to the downstream areas include Lanjān (Alanjān), Mārbin, Jey, Karāj, Baraān, and Rūydasht. He also stated that Alanjān Rostāq (the first district) had been chosen as a location for collecting and dividing the water of Zāyandeh Rūd (Ibn Rusta 1892, 154, 55) (Fig. 7.1). This text indicates not only that no change had occurred in the Sasanian administrative divisions along the river, but also implicitly demonstrates that the Sasanid water distribution procedure was still in effect during the Islamic period. Additionally, the continuity of irrigated agriculture in Iṣfahān is proved through a historical description from the capture of Iṣfahān by Muslim forces (Abu No'aym 1410/1999, 47).

The duration of names and locations of these six Rustāqs can be followed in Islamic written sources until the Mongol invasions (Ibn Ḥawqal 1938; Al-Hamawi 1397/1977). From the figures given by Ḥamd-Allāh Mustawfī (740 AH/1340 CE) after the Mongol invasions, we observe that major changes did not occur to the administrative divisions of the Zāyandeh Rūd valley in Iṣfahān, but the 'Rustāq' word was replaced by Nāhiat (Mustawfi 1993, 57). Finally, in the Safavid period, as mentioned before, the Zāyandeh

Rūd water regulations and their implementation in the six districts was reviewed and written in an edict attributed to Shaikh Bahā'ī. It should be noted that in this edict, the Zāyandeh Rūd water was assigned to each district according to population, the extent of agricultural lands, soil type as well as the level of access to water resources. For example, due to the importance and expansion of Lanjān district, 10 shares from 33 shares were allocated to this region while Jey district, which included the city of Iṣfahān, received six shares (Table 7.2). Then, these shares were further subdivided into irrigation canals and at a final level, between settlements and farmlands. These divisions were only enforced and supervised during the hottest 165 days (from June 5 until November 20) of every year, based on specific laws and regulations that were detailed in the scroll (Hosseini Abari 2000, 73). This evidence is useful for historical and archaeological research because it is a legal document that records accurately the division of the Zāyandeh Rūd water, the names and locations of all irrigation canals (about 100 canals) distributed across the historic six districts of Iṣfahān and their related settlements, as well as their watershares.

The regulations described in the edict attributed to Shaikh Bahā'ī were in use without interruption until the 20th century, when the Zāyandeh Rūd dam and a modern water system were established in Isfahān. As shown in Table 7.2, the scroll indicates that the traditional integrated water management system had a positive impact on the stability of geographical divisions of Iṣfahān and surrounding areas for more than a thousand years. It is worth mentioning that because this integrated irrigation system had an impact on all six districts, Iṣfahān must be considered as a whole with its surrounding districts. By applying this wider perspective, a better understanding and interpretation will be achieved of the cultural and economic dynamics of the medieval society of Iṣfahān. Moreover, from this point of view, the formation of main settlements and construction of distinguished monuments in Iṣfahān's hinterland, such as Jame Mosque of Barslān in the Baraān district during the Seljuq period or Pir-e Bakrān mausoleum in Lanjān district during the Ikhanid period, makes sense.

The effect of this water regulation system on the resilience of Iṣfahān also can be demonstrated after the devastation caused by the Mongol invasion of the 13th century CE when Iṣfahān suffered less than the other Iranian cities. Iṣfahān was spared because it was developed without a qanāt system, an advantage during the Mongol period when the qanāts were destroyed, whether deliberately or by neglect, a problem that proved extremely damaging to the survival

Table 7.2: Water divisions in the six districts of Iṣfahān based on Safavid scroll attributed to 'Shaikh Bahā'ī' (Hosseini Abari 2000).

		Zāyandeh Rūd	
	Iṣfahān districts	*Water divided into 33 watershares*	
1	Lanjān	10	Upper Lanjān (6) Lower Lanjān (4)
2	Mārbin		4
3	Jey (Iṣfahān city)		6
4	Karāj		3
5	Baraān		4
6	Rūydasht		6

of urban centers in Iran (Durand-Guédy 2018, 267). In addition, this traditional irrigation system helped to sustain the agricultural-based economy of Iṣfahān. For example, one century after the Mongol attacks, the comparatively high level of land tax from the country districts of Iṣfahān is a good indicator. Remarkably these taxes were nearly twice as high as they were at Tabriz, the capital of Ilkans (Mustawfi 1993, 57). In addition, pigeon towers, which have been built across all six historic districts particularly in Lanjān and Rūydasht, are also closely related to the agricultural economy of Iṣfahān and its traditional irrigation system (Beazley 1966). According to Iranian traditional agricultural texts, pigeon guano, compared with that of other birds, is the best and most beneficial fertilizer, especially for irrigated cultivation (Cassianus Bassus 2009, 45). Ibn Battuta, in his account of travel to Iṣfahān in the 8th century AH, noted the towers in the suburban farmlands (Ibn Battuta 1984, 42) (Fig. 7.2). This demonstrates the persistence of agricultural practices in Iṣfahān and surrounding settlements due to its integrated irrigation system even after the Mongols, despite the decline of numerous Iranian cities.

Fig. 7.2: Pigeon tower near the Zāyandeh Rūd river located in Rūydasht district (Kamalizad 2021).

Primary results of the first season of archaeological survey

In April 2021, within the framework of the IHH project, the first season of the archaeological survey was conducted according to a plan based on the six historic districts of Iṣfahān. In this one-month season, the three eastern districts (Rūydasht, Barāān, and Karāj) stretching from the lower reaches of the Zāyandeh Rūd river near the Gāv khūni swamp to the east of Iṣfahān city (around 120 km length) were surveyed (Fig. 7.3) These areas were chosen because they have almost common geographical and topographic characteristics. The remaining three districts (Jey, Mārbin, and Lanjān) will be studied in the future archaeological surveys.

Before the survey, to examine the role of 'anthropogenic agents' in the hydraulic landscape of Isfahān, a methodical study of documentary sources was conducted, including the Safavid edict, to understand the geographical location of irrigation

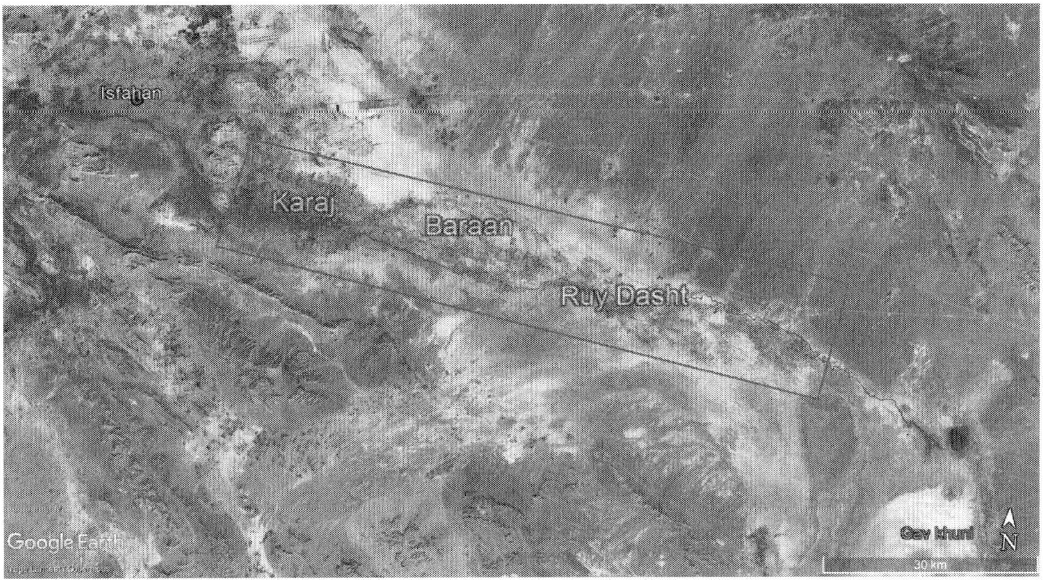

Fig. 7.3: The geographic location of areas under study in the east of the Zāyandeh Rūd basin (Google Earth 2021).

canals, water installations and their related settlements. In the next stage, remote sensing techniques, such as aerial photos of Iran National Cartographic Center taken in 1956, and satellite images, particularly Corona images taken in 1969, have been used. These images are particularly useful in this project because they were taken before the construction of the Zāyandeh Rūd dam in 1971 and the introduction of a modern irrigation system in Iṣfahān. This makes them more effective in the reconstruction of the traditional hydraulic landscape of Iṣfahān.

In our archaeological fieldwork, priority has been given to identifying and mapping irrigation canals. Canals show the pattern of settlements, and basically the objective of landscapes archaeology studies is to obtain a more comprehensive view of the relationship between the dynamics and structure of settlements and irrigation in time and space (Wilkinson 2003, 71, 89). On the other hand, due to the long period the Zāyandeh Rūd irrigation system was used and continuous reconstruction and dredging of canals made in soil, dating the canals is a fundamental difficulty. Therefore, relative chronology of settlements helps to provide an estimate of the history of this irrigation system.

In these three eastern districts, 18 irrigation canals and 13 dykes were identified. These dykes can be categorized into nine subsidiary and four main dykes or 'Band'. Subsidiary dikes were found in all three eastern districts, often constructed near watermills to control and restrain water, for example as in the Zovān (Plate 7.2). Main dikes including 'Marvān',[4] 'Goli' (Fig. 7.4), 'Jondij' or 'Allah Qoli,' and 'Shānzdah deh' had the primary role of carrying water to canals. They contributed to the creation

Fig. 7.4: East view of Goli dyke in Rūydasht rostaq (Kamalizad 2021).

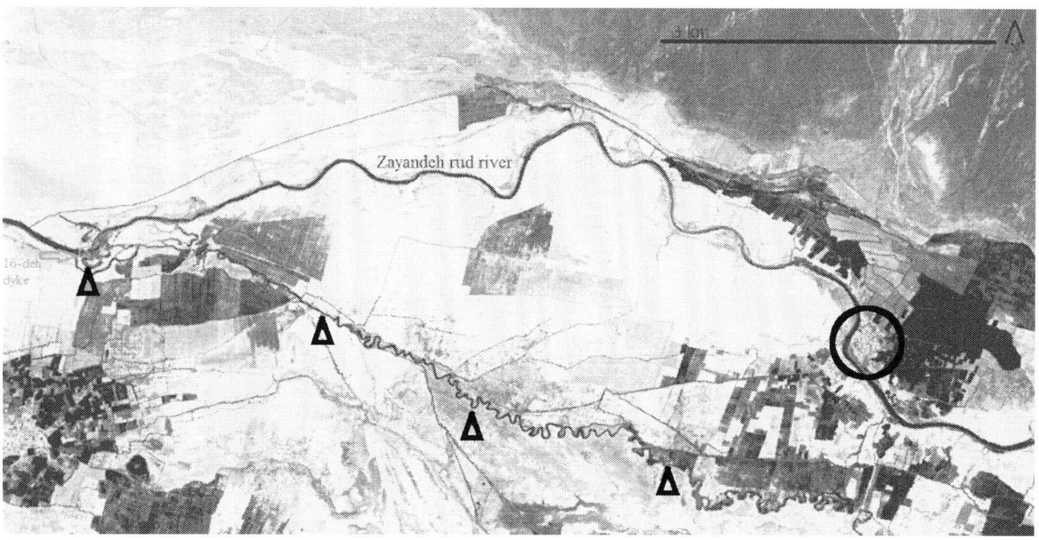

Fig. 7.5: The location of Shanzdah deh dyke, arrows indicate the 16 deh canal, the circle Qurtan Town (Corona Image, 1969).

of settlement patterns in the last district, Rūydasht, which was a low plain poor in groundwater and dependent on the waters from the Zāyandeh Rūd. Because of the geomorphological condition of Rūydasht, the main dikes were built to increase the water level of the river and direct it to irrigation canals (Hosseini Abari 2000). Without these small dams, the formation of settlements was basically impossible. The remains of old dykes in the riverbed around the Shānzdah deh dyke support this idea. This dyke is located in the north of Farfaan, a prominent Ilkanid city, and two irrigation canals branched off from both sides (recognizable in Corona image, Fig. 7.5). The southern wide canal, Shānzdah deh, flowed away to 16 settlements, including Varzaneh with a notable watershare from the Zāyandeh Rūd (Fig. 7.6) and another north irrigation canal was directed to 'Quratn', a fortified mud-brick town (Gerster 2009) (Fig. 7.7). Both Varzaneh and Qurtan settlements date at least from the 4th century AH/10th century CE (Ibn Ḥawqal 1938). Ceramic assemblages from the area also provide the same relative dating (Plate 7.3). In the future we hope to present a more precise relative chronology for the hydraulic structures by examining mortar samples. Other interesting archaeological finds include water dividers (Maqsam) built at the entrance of main irrigation canals to control the amount of incoming water, many of which have unfortunately been destroyed in recent years (Plate 7.5).

Fig. 7.6: The West view of Shanzdah deh irrigation canal in south of the Zāyandeh Rūd river (Kamalizad 2021).

Fig. 7.7: The fortified mud-brick town of Qurtan; Zāyandeh Rūd flowing on the north side of the town, probably in 1976–1978 (Photo: G. Gerster).

Conclusion

Concerning the semi-arid climate of Iṣfahān and the Zāyandeh Rūd river that passes through the province, the most significant factor in the formation of the Iṣfahān cultural landscape was the permanent access of residents to the river. Based on analysis and synthesis of the written sources, it seems that at least from the Sasanian period, there were specific regulations for water distribution in Iṣfahān and the surrounding regions. The areas located along the Zāyandeh Rūd river were divided into six districts or Rostāqs to ensure that all residents could benefit from fairly distributed and sufficient water. Accordingly, the administrative geographical divisions of the city of Iṣfahān and its hinterlands were affected by this irrigation system. After the Muslim conquest, due to the immense value of water in the agricultural economy of Iṣfahān and taxation, this efficient irrigation system was used continuously. As a result, we witness the duration in the administrative divisions of these six districts from the early Islamic period until the 20th century. In addition, the sustained agricultural activity that depended upon the water management of Zāyandeh Rūd helped the city of Iṣfahān and surrounding districts to stimulate the recovery of agricultural economy after the periods of destruction, particularly after Muslim and Mongol invasions, as demonstrated in the high rate of agricultural tax and socio-economic stability of Iṣfahān.

I have concluded from the above evidence that the history of the Zāyandeh Rūd water management system and related hydraulic structures definitely can be traced back to the pre-Safavid period and before the edict attributed to Shaikh Bahā'ī because in dry and semi-dry regions like Iṣfahān, there is always a meaningful relation between the formation of settlements and irrigation networks. Relative dating of some recognized settlements in our archaeological survey indicates that the creation of this irrigation system took place before the 17th century. This system, similar to other Middle East hydraulic systems, continuously and in accordance with political and economic conditions was reconstructed and reused. Archaeological surveys in the downstream areas also reveal a relationship between this traditional irrigation system and hydraulic innovations. Particularly in the relatively lower and drier Rūydasht district, the construction of the four main dikes are archaeological evidence for hydraulic innovations in this system that consequently resulted in more resilience in this part of the river basin and allowed the region to flourish.

Acknowledgments

Many thanks to Dr Zeinab Afzali, Mr Ebrahimi and Dr Maryam Dehqan for their cooperation in this archaeological survey. Also, I appreciate the warm hospitality and guidance of Mr Barqeri in Quratn village, Mr Dehqani in Barsian village and Mr Sadeqi in Karaj district.

Notes

1 Shahid Chamran University of Ahvaz, Ahvaz, j.kamalizad@scu.ac.ir.
2 BAHĀʾ-AL-DĪN ʿĀMELĪ, was an Imami scholar and author born in Lebonan 953 AH/1547 CE. He moved with his family to Iṣfahān and Shah ʿAbbās I (r. 996 AH/1588 CE–1038 AH/1629 CE), appointed him as šayḵ-al-eslām of Iṣfahān (see Encyclopedia Iranica 2012).
3 'Khān Lanjān' was a town with its mountainous fortification located about 30 km south of Iṣfahān city and in the center of 'Alanjān' or 'Lanjān' Rostāq. Stern, based on Ibn Ḥawqal's descriptions from the Zāyandeh Rūd river route, suggested that the possible location of Khān Lanjān town was around the current city of Felavarjān (Stern *et al.* 1971, 46) but I have argued elsewhere that he was mistaken, see Kamalizad 2021.
4 Near the Marven dike, around 80 pieces of prehistoric surface sherds were found which stylistically belong to the black on buff (BOB) painted fine pottery culture in Fars and in the chronological framework of this region, they are known as 'Bakun'. The Bakun period begins at around 5200 BCE and ends at 4350/3950 BCE (see Sardari *et al.* 2011).

Bibliography

Abu Noʿaym, Aḥmad b. ʿAbd-Allāh Eṣfahāni (1410/1999) *Ḏekr aḵbār Eṣbahān*. Beirut, Dar Al Kotob Al Ilmiyah. [in Arabic]

Adams, R.McC. (1962) Agriculture and Urban Life in Early Southwestern Iran. *Science* 136, 109–122.

Adle, C. (2006) Qanats of Bam: An Archaeological Perspective. In N. Honari, A. Salamat, J. Sutton, and J. Taniguchi (eds) *Qanats of Bam. A Multidisciplinary Approach*, 33–85. Tehran, UNESCO Tehran Cluster Office.

Al-Hamawi, Y. (1397/1977) *Muʿjam al-buldān*, 5 Vols. Beirut, Dār Ṣādir. [in Arabic]

Al-Iṣfahānī, Ḥ. (1844) *Sinī mulūk al-ʾarḍ wa-l-anbīyā*, 2 vols. Leipzig, Vogel.

Beazley, E. (1966) The Pigeon Towers of Isfahan. *Iran* 4, 105–109.

Cassianus Bassus, S. (2009) *Varznāmah*, ed. Ḥ. Ātifī, Teheran, markaz-e nashr-e daneshgahi. [in Persian]

Durand-Guédy, D. (2018) Iṣfahān During the Turko-Mongol Period (11th–15th Centuries). *Eurasian Studies* 16 (1–2), 253–312.

Ebn ʿAbbād (1947) *Rasāʾel*. ʿA. ʿAzzām and Š. Żayf (eds). Cairo, Dar Alfekr. [in Arabic]

Eṣfahāni, M.-M. (Arbāb) (1962) *Neṣf-e Jahān fi tʿarif al-Eṣfahān*. Tehran, Amir kabir. [in Persian]

Gerster, G. (2009) *Paradise Lost: Persia from Above*. London, Phaidon.

Ḥasan Rūmlū, Ḥ.B. (1971) *Aḥsan at-tawārīḫ*. Tehran, Bongah-e Tarjomeh va Nashr-e Ketab. [in Persian]

Hosseini Abari, H. (2000) *Zayandeh Rud, from the source to Swamp*. Iṣfahān, Golha Publisher. [in Persian]

Ibn Battuta, M. (1984) The Travels of Ibn-Battu¯ta (ed. S. Lee). London, Darf Publisher.

Ibn Ḥawqal, A. (1938) *Kitāb Ṣūrat al-arḍ*, ed. J.H. Kramers. Leiden, Brill.

Ibn Rusta, A. (1892) *Kitāb al-Aʿlaq al-nafisa*, ed. M.J. Goeje. Leiden, Brill.

Kamalizad, J. (2016) The Landscape Archaeology in Lanjān Plain of Iṣfahān, Iran, During the Islamic Period (650–1722 AD), *Archaeologies, Journal of the World Archaeological Congress* 12, 91–109.

Kamalizad, J. (2019) *Alanjān rostāq of Iṣfahān: An Introduction to the Environment and Subsistence Evolution in Lanjān Region During the Islamic Period*. Iṣfahān, Iṣfahān Studies Center's Publication. [in Persian]

Kamalizad, J. (2021) Khān Lanjān Town: Locating, Characteristics and its Place in Alanjān Rostaq of Iṣfahān from the Early Islamic Centuries to the Seventh Century A.H. *Iranian Archaeological Researches* 31, 219–240. [in Persian]

Kohlberg, E. (2012) BAHĀʾ-AL-DĪN ʿĀMELĪ. *Encyclopedia Iranica* III/4, 429–430.

Lambton, A.K.S. (1938) The Regulation of the Waters of the Zāyande Rūd. *Bulletin of the School of Oriental Studies* 9 (3), 663–673.

Mahmoudian, S. and Qayyoomi, M. (2017) The Norm of Madi: Managing Water in Safavid Iṣfahān. *Beiträge zur Islamischen Kunst und Archäologie Bd.5*, 57–69.
Mustawfī, Q.H. (1993) *Nuzhat al-qulub* (ed. G. Le Strange). Frankfurt Am Main, Institute for the History of Arabic-Islamic Science at the Johann Wolfgang Goethe University.
Nasir-i Khusraw (2001) Nasir-i Khusraw's Book of travels (Safarnamah) (ed. W. M. Thackston). California, Mazda.
Quiring-Zoche, R. (1980) *Iṣfahān im 15 und 16 Jahrhundert. Ein Beitrag zur persischen Stadtgeschichte.* Freiburg, Schwarz.
Sardari, A., Fazeli Nashli, H., Hejebri Nobari, A., Shahidi, H.K., and Rezaei, A. (2011) Northern Fars During the Bakun Period: Archaeological Evidence from the Eglyd District. *Journal of Archäologische Mitteilungen aus Iran und Turan* 43, 239–259.
Spooner, B. (1974) City and River in Iran: Urbanization and Irrigation of the Iranian Plateau. *Iranian Studies* 7 (3/4), 681–713.
Stern, S.M., Beazley, E., and Dobson, A. (1971) The Fortress of Khān Lanjān. *Iran* 9, 45–57.
Wilkinson, T.J. (2003) *Archaeological Landscapes of the Near East.* Tucson, University of Arizona Press.
Wilkinson, T.J. and Rayne, L. (2010) Hydraulic Landscapes and Imperial Power in the Near East. *Water History* 2, 115–144.
Ziaei, L. (2020) Zāyandeh Rūd River Basin: A Region of Economic and Social Relevance in the Central Plateau of Iran. In S. Mohajeri, L. Horlemann, A.A. Besalatpour, and W. Raber (eds) *Standing up to Climate Change.* Cham, Springer.

Plate 1.1: Central Alborz Mountains.

Plate 1.2: A: Raw material cobble on Wezwar surface. B. Concentration of lithic artifacts at Wezwar.

Plate 1.3: Shoupari Cave.

Plate 1.4: Alvat Mountain in Telar River Basin, Central Alborz. Note the escarpment where Liben is formed.

Plate 1.5: Liben Cave; A: view from inside, B: view to the historical structure close to the entrance, C: view to the Cave entrance and the slope in front of it.

Plate 1.6: Cave bear canine from Liben Cave (Ursus deningeri kudarensis)*.*

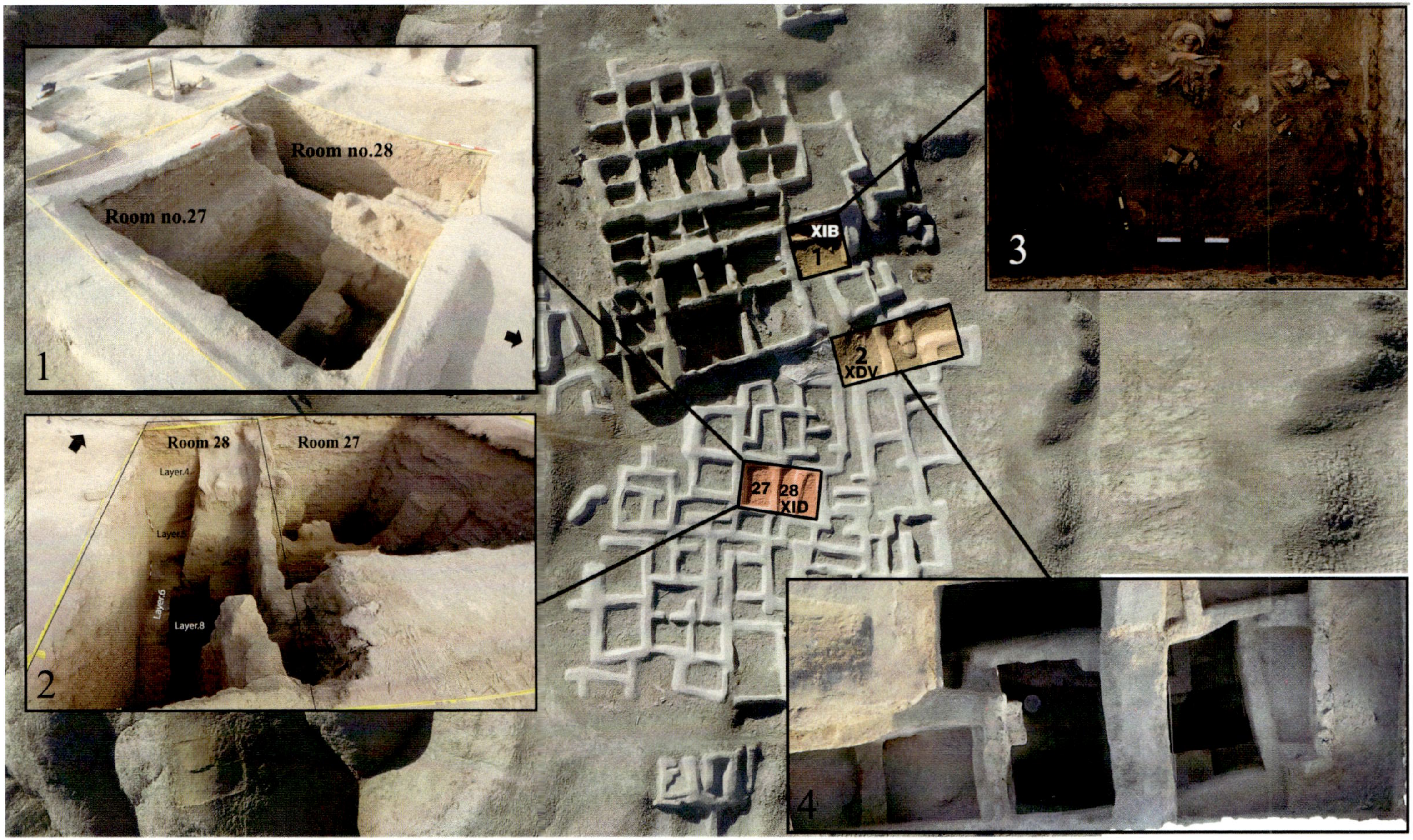

Plate 2.1: Aerial photo of ERA of Shahr-i Sokhta and the location of excavated rooms at ERA (1: Rooms 27–28, northeast view, 2: Rooms 27–28, southern view, 3: Room 88 in XIB and the large bones uncovered in Layer 3 of Proto-Elamite period, 4: Room 88a in XDV). All photographs by author unless otherwise noted.

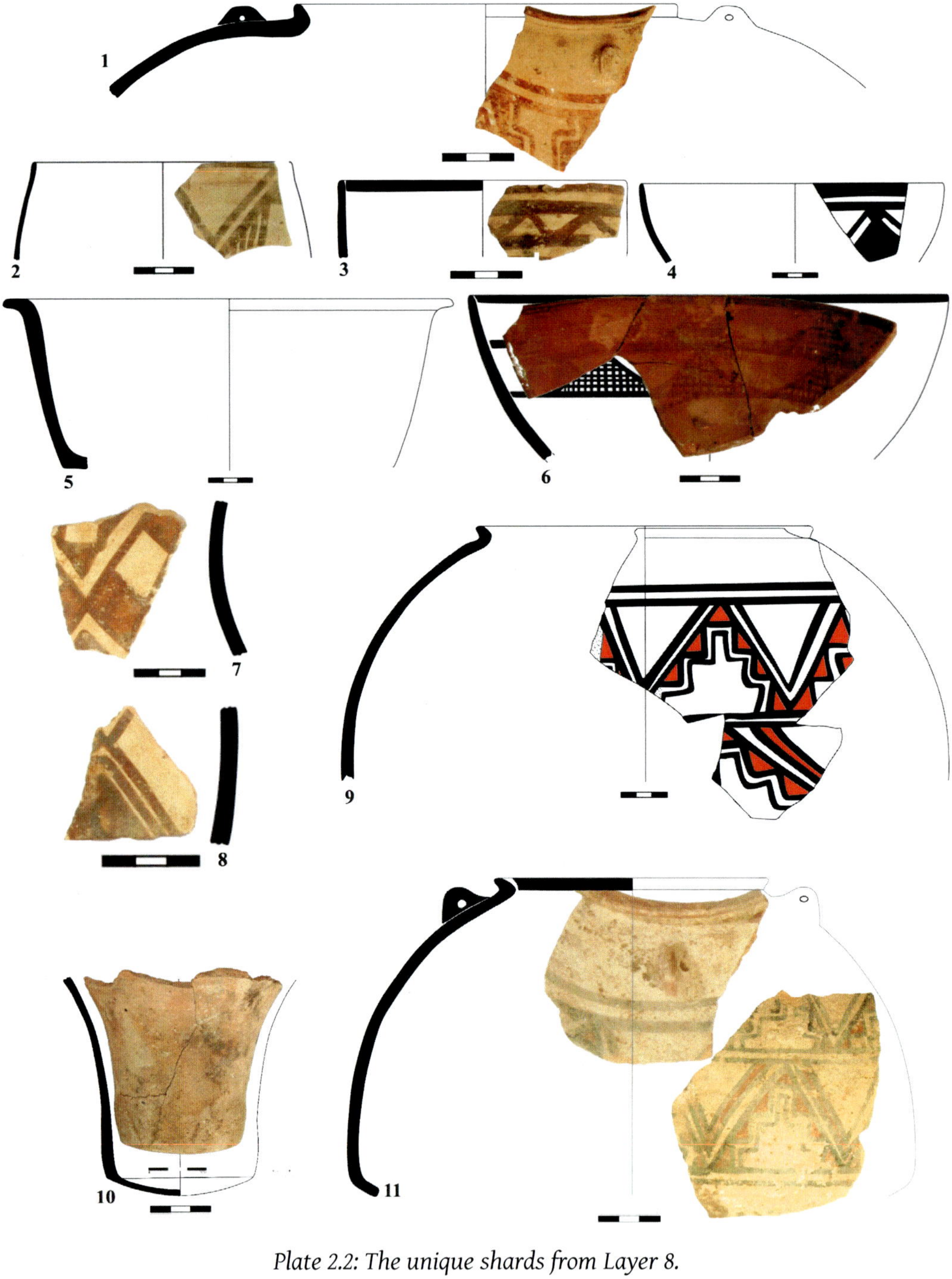

Plate 2.2: The unique shards from Layer 8.

Plate 2.3: Cultural materials found on the floor of Layer 8 (see Figure 2.9, 2.10).

Plate 2.4: Pottery and small finds from Layer 9.

Plate 3.1: General view of Tepe Naderi as seen from the east (Location of Trench 1 and 2 is marked).

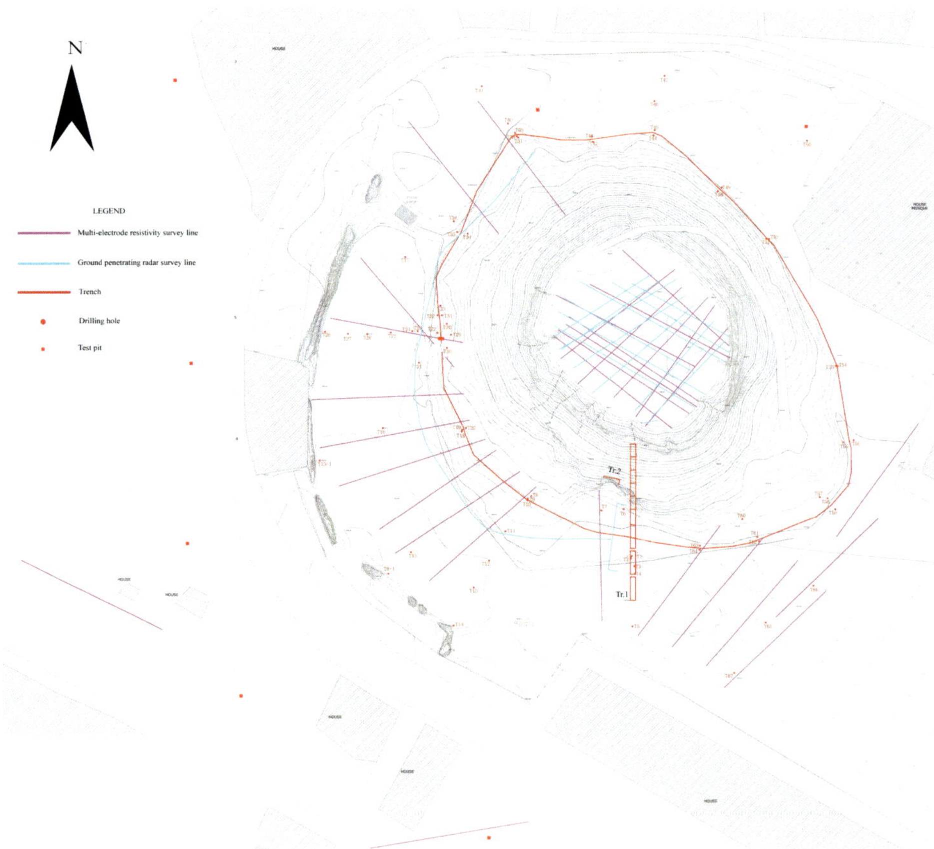

Plate 3.2: Contour map of Tepe Naderi showing location of Trench 1 and Trench 2 on the southern slope of the site.

Plate 3.3: Location and the arrangement of S1–11 in Trench 1.

Plate 3.4: Pottery from Trench 2, sub-layers 4-2 (1), 4–3 (2-3), 4-5 (4, 10), 5-2 (6-8), and F6 (5, 9).

Plate 3.5: Painted pottery from the ash deposits of S11: 1–3 (Layer 8), 4–10 (Layer 9).

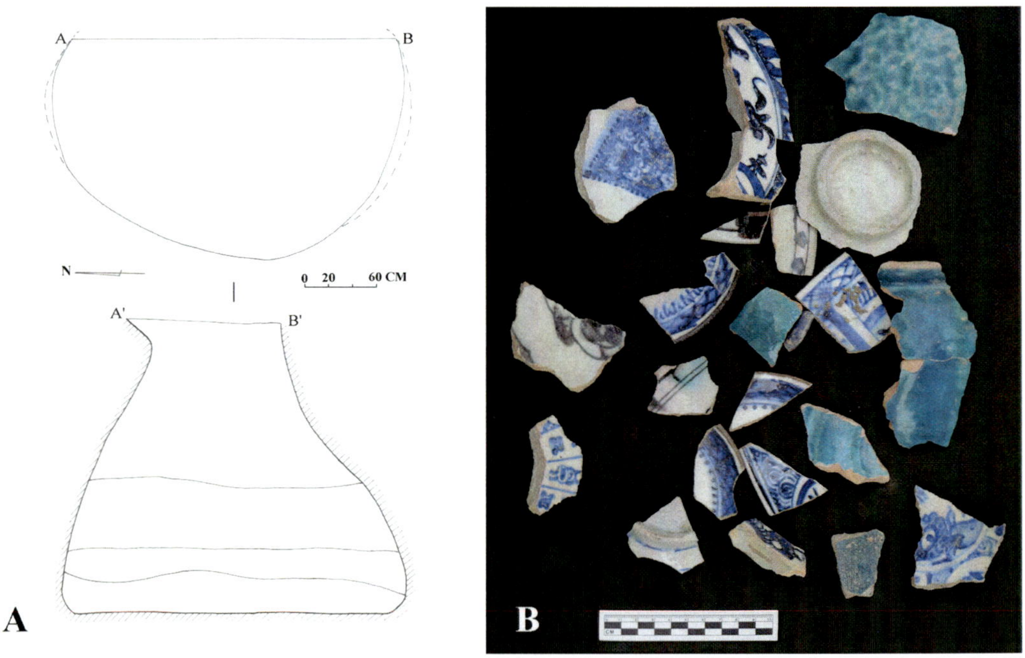

Plate 3.6: Plan of F5, Tr.1–S2 (A), and glazed pottery and blue-white stone-paste wares from F5 (B).

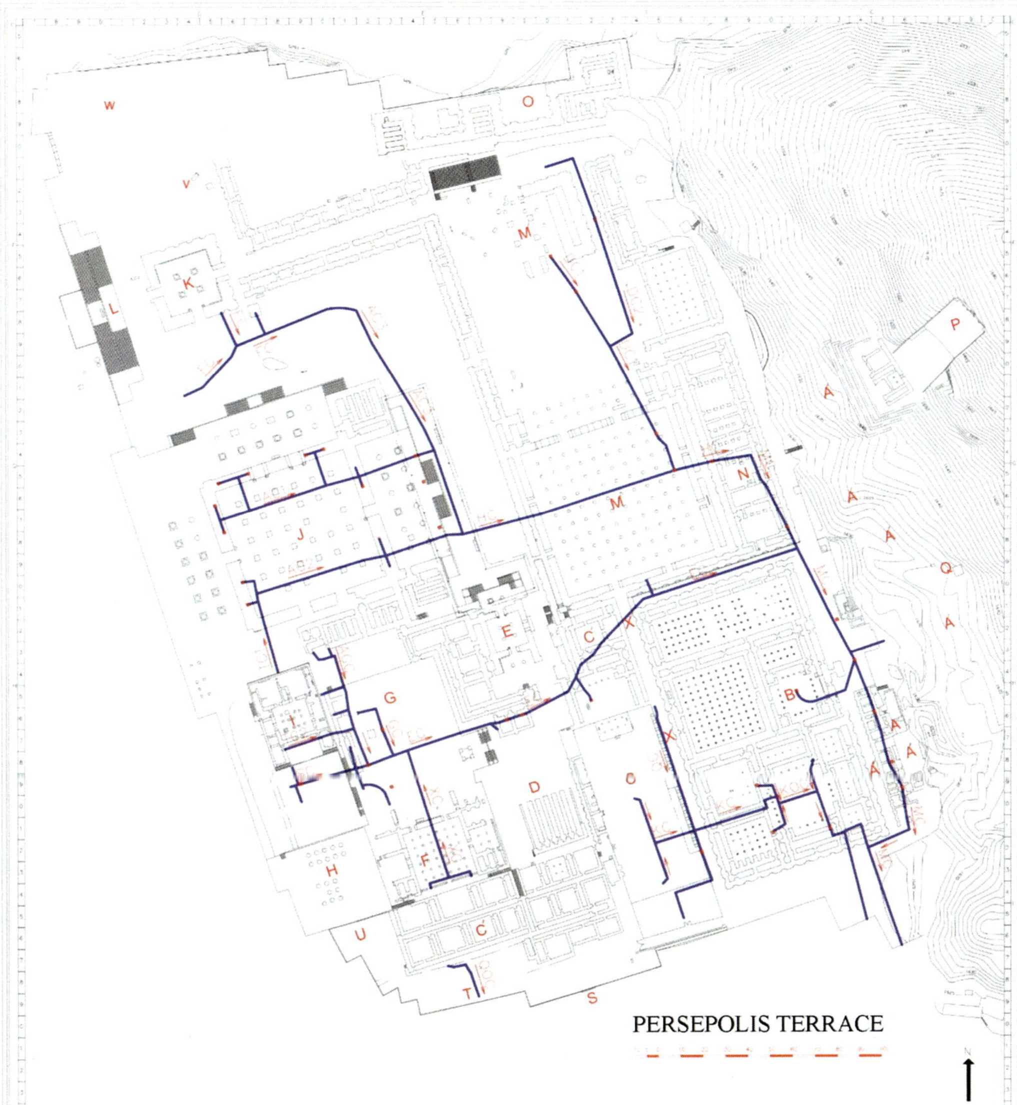

Plate 4.1: Persepolis terrace. Blue lines represent network of the channels (from Asadi 2021, 150).

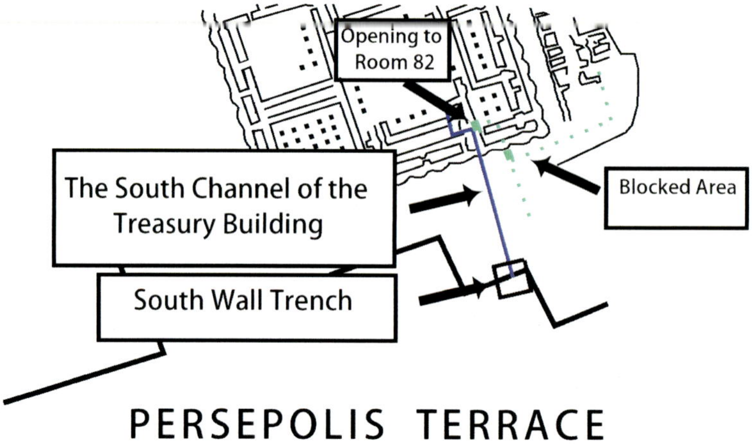

Plate 4.2: Plan of the southern channel of the Treasury building in the southeastern area of the Persepolis terrace (after Asadi 2021, 160).

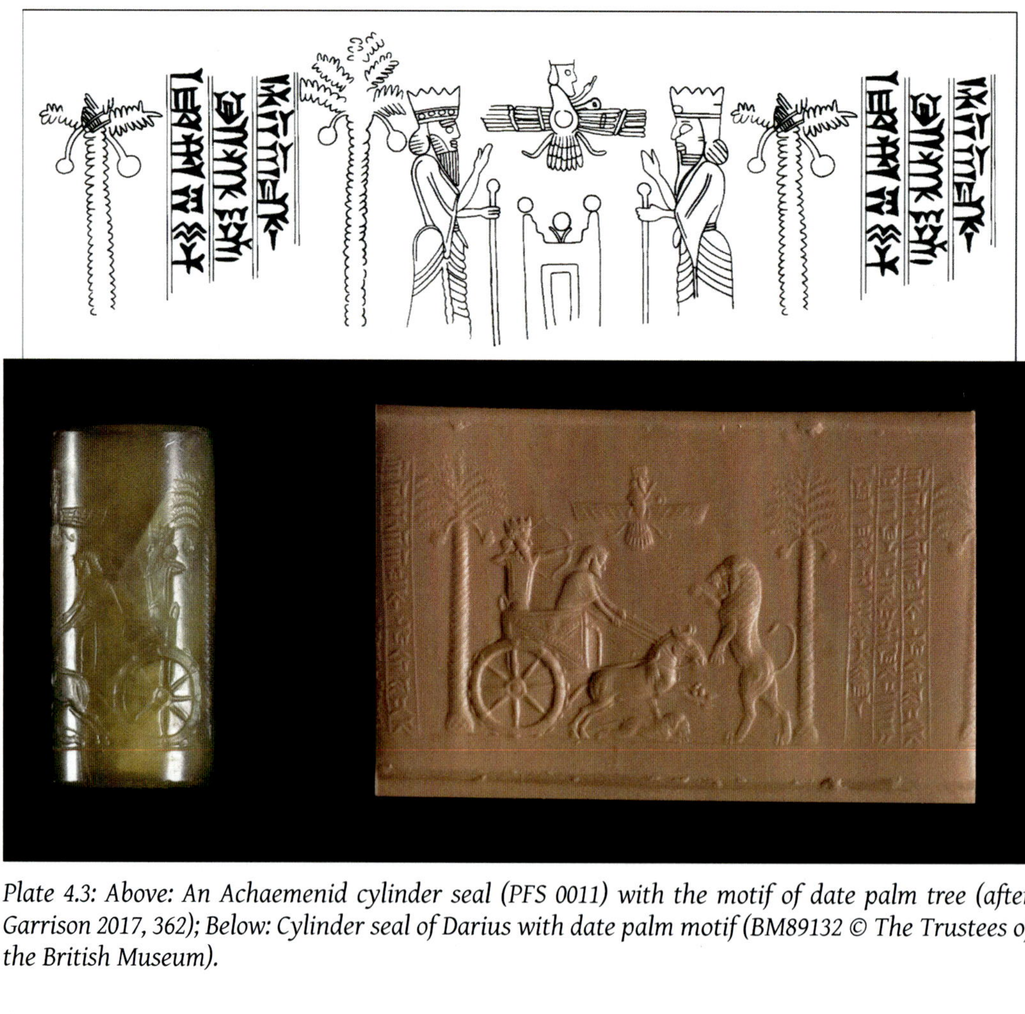

Plate 4.3: Above: An Achaemenid cylinder seal (PFS 0011) with the motif of date palm tree (after Garrison 2017, 362); Below: Cylinder seal of Darius with date palm motif (BM89132 © The Trustees of the British Museum).

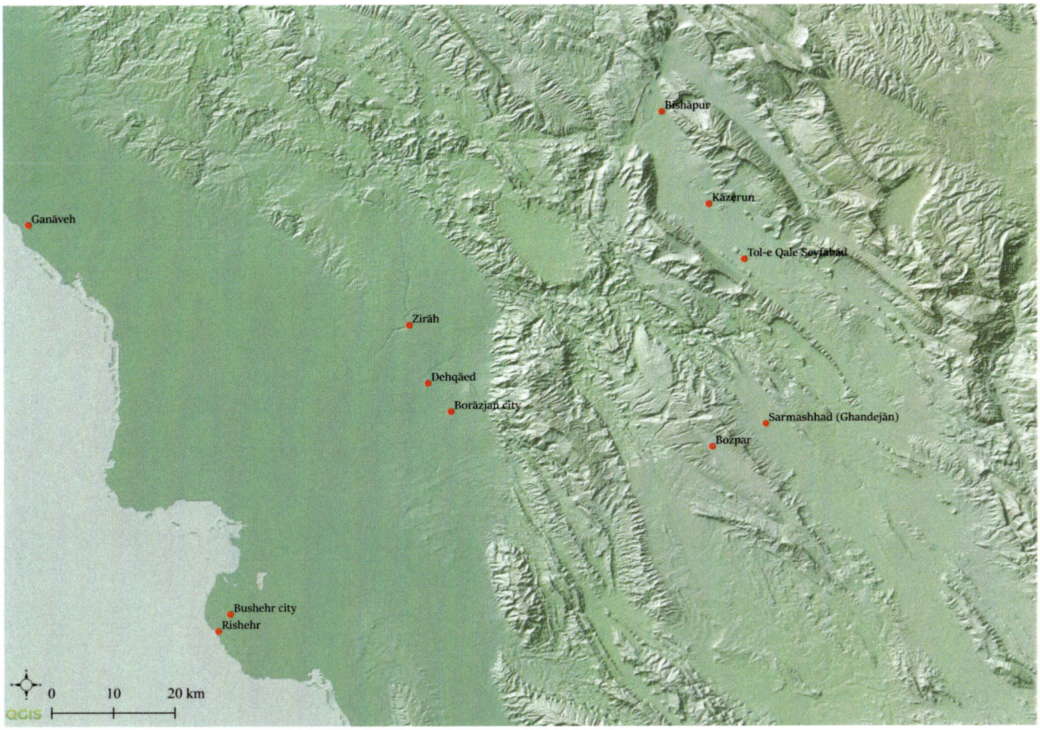

Plate 5.1: Location of Dehqāed, its connection with the mountain and the Persian Gulf and other mentioned regions in the paper.

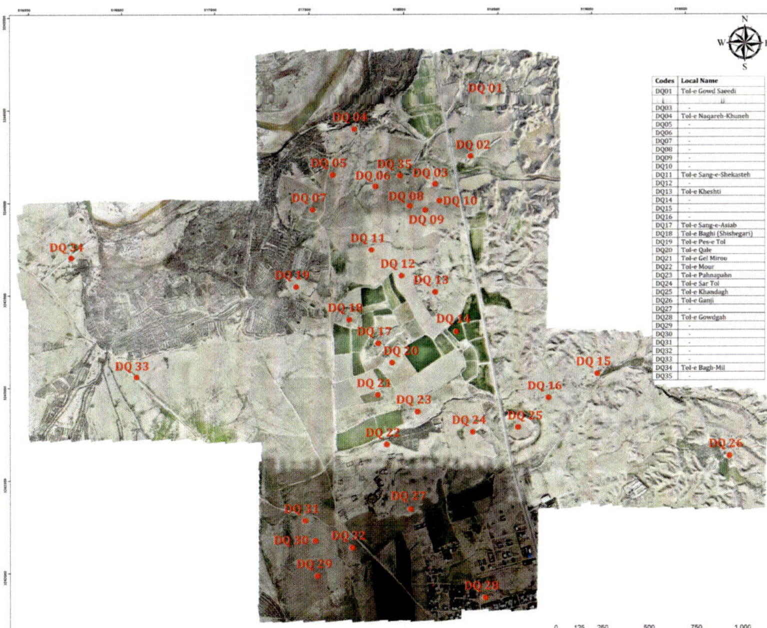

Plate 5.2: Different mounds identified during our survey at Dehqāed site.

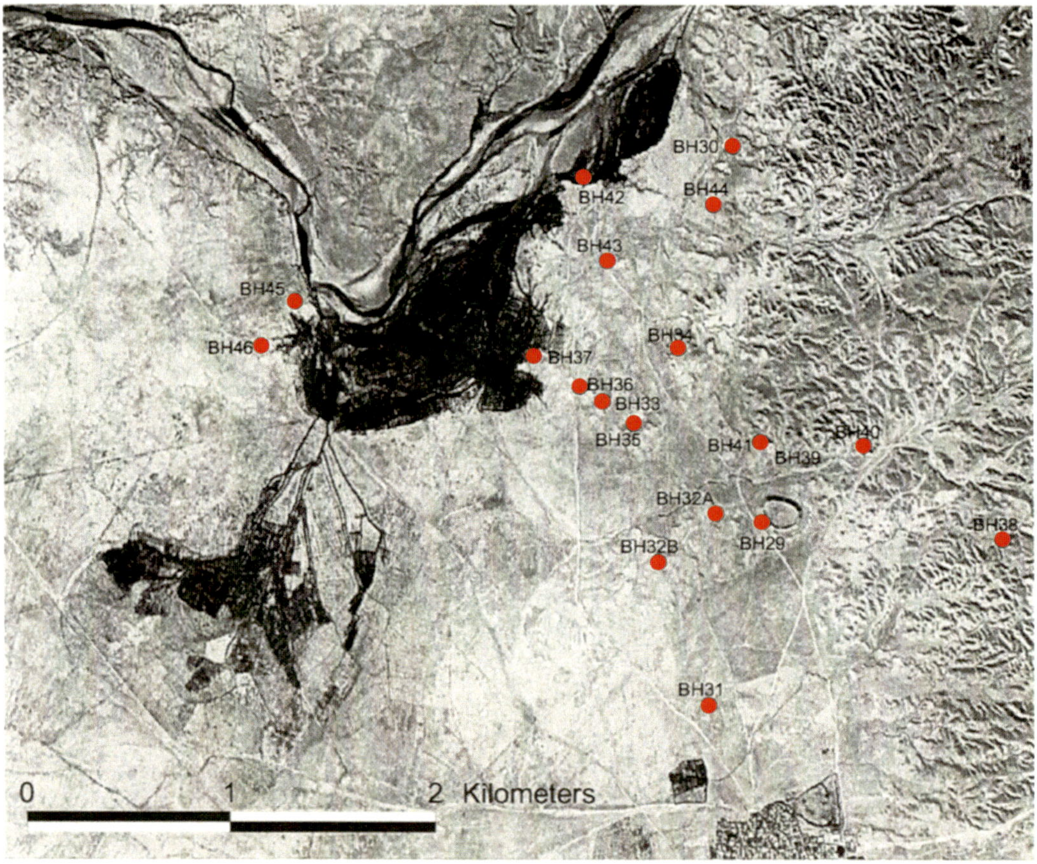

Plate 5.3: The arrangement of mounds in the Dehqāed site as observed in Carter's survey (after Carter et al. *2006, 95, fig. 14).*

Plate 6.1: Aerial view of Tappe Bardnakōn from the east showing the site before its excavations and several illegally dug ditches at its peak. Courtesy of Alireza Khosrowzadeh.

a1

a2

b1

b2

Plate 6.2: Examples of permanent sites (a1: FS.134, view from the west, a2: FS.183, view from the southeast) and temporary sherd/flint scattered sites (b1: FS.061 located on the edge of the central plain along the foot slope of Bar-āftāb Mount, view from the northeast, b2: FS.139 in the Hanā Valley, view from the south). Photograph by Alireza Khosrowzadeh.

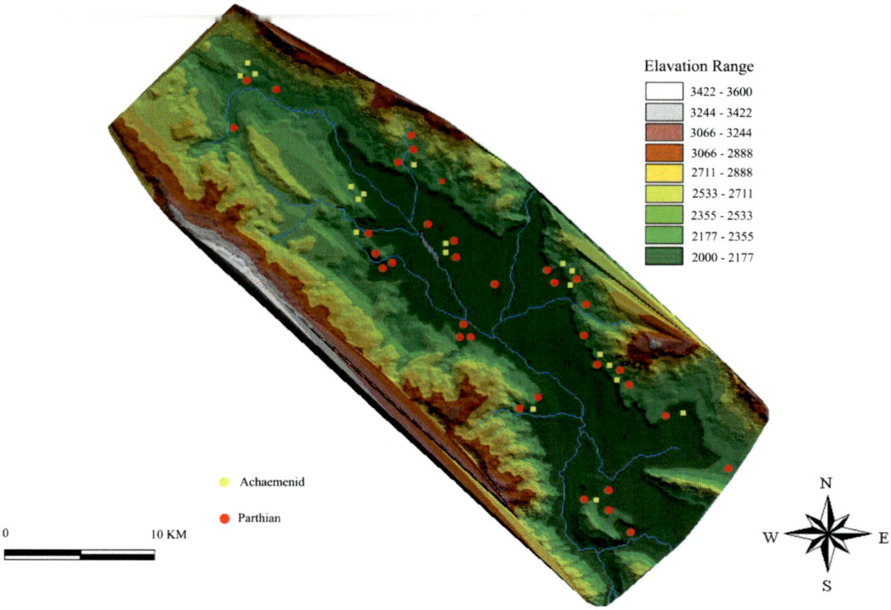

Plate 6.3: Spatial distribution map of Achaemenid and Parthian sites in Farsan County. Courtesy of Alireza Khosrowzadeh.

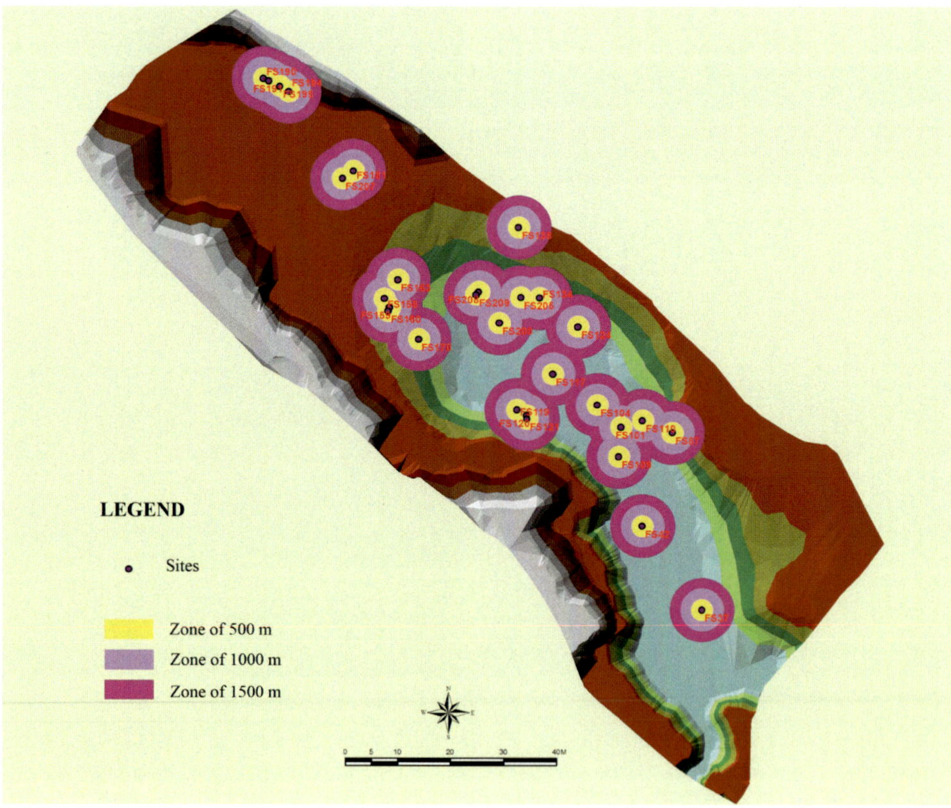

Plate 6.4: Spatial distribution map of Sasanian sites in Farsan County. Courtesy of Hossein Habibi.

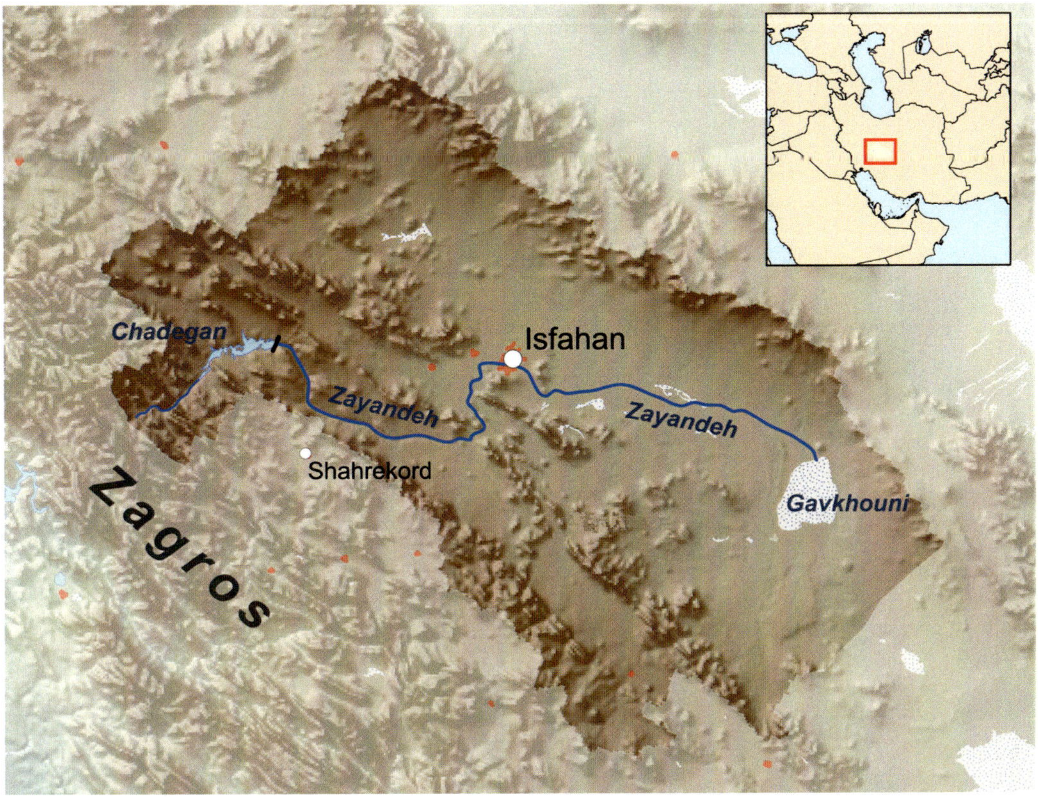

Plate 7.1: The location of Zayandeh Rud river basin in Isfahan province (Base map Wikimedia Commons 2021, additions by author).

Plate 7.2: Blue arrows showing Zovān dyke and its water mill in Karāj district (Kamalizad 2021).

Plate 7.3: Pottery sherd assemblage from Qurtan (Kamalizad 2021).

Plate 7.4: Water divider or Maqsam (Kamalizad 2021).